Language Two

Language Two

HEIDI DULAY

MARINA BURT

STEPHEN KRASHEN

New York   Oxford
OXFORD UNIVERSITY PRESS
1982

OXFORD UNIVERSITY PRESS

200 Madison Avenue, New York, NY 10016 USA

Walton Street, Oxford OX2 6DP England

OXFORD is a trademark of Oxford University Press.

Copyright © 1982 by Oxford University Press, Inc.

Library of Congress Cataloging in Publication Data
Dulay, Heidi
Language two.
Bibliography: p. 283
Includes index.
1. Language and languages—Study and teaching.
2. Language acquisition.   I. Burt, Marina
II. Krashen, Stephen   III. Title.
P53.D76   407   81-11229
ISBN 0-19-502552-0   AACR2
ISBN 0-19-502553-9 (pbk.)

Printing (last digit): 9 8 7 6 5

Printed in the United States of America.

To our mentors and friends

*Courtney Cazden, Noam Chomsky, Morris Halle,
and Alexander Lipson*

whose work inspired ours.

Acknowledgments

This book was begun six years ago. During that time many of our colleagues provided information, ideas, comments, and moral support for which we are most grateful. We have dedicated this book to the four to whom we owe the seminal ideas underlying the book. In addition, we would like to extend our deepest appreciation to James and Penelope Alatis, who gave much time to discussions of ideas and who facilitated our public presentation of many papers which have been incorporated into this book; Charles Ferguson, Mary Finocchiaro, and Robert Politzer, who provided valuable feedback on ideas and approaches new to the field; Morris Halle, Richard Light, Robin Scarcella, and Richard Tucker, who read and commented on early versions of the manuscript; Denise McKeon, who assisted in the error research and in formulating teaching implications; Roger Anderson, Lloyd Anderson, Nathalie Bailey, Eugene Briere, H. Douglas Brown, Annharriet Buck, Craig Chaudron, S. Pit Corder, Miriam Eisenstein, Ann Fathman, Sascha Felix, May Frith, Judith Olmsted-Gary, J. Hendrikson, Deborah Keller-Cohen, Carolyn Kessler, Diane Larsen-Freeman, John Macnamara, Betty Mace-Matluck, Joseph H. Matluck, Carolyn Madden, Jurgen Meisel, John Milon, John Oller, Jr., Christina B. Paulston, Jack Richards, Sandra Savignon, John Schumann, Catherine Snow, Irene Spilka, Peter Strevens, Elizabeth Traugott, Albert Valdman, H. G. Widdowson, and Henning Wode, who sent us valuable material, much of which had not yet been published; Maria Hyman and Marta E. Galindo, who produced the manuscript and trial version of the book with the aid only of a Lanier word processor; Mary Jean Haley, a freelance editor, who absorbed much technical material quickly and converted turgid prose into readable English; and our students in the 1979 Panama Canal Zone class of the University of Miami's course in ESL Methodology, who used the trial version of this book as their text and who gave us invaluable reactions to the material.

To all, many thanks again for your assistance and encouragement.

San Francisco   Heidi Dulay
August 28, 1981   Marina Burt
                                                                 Stephen Krashen

Contents

8 Acquisition Order   200

9 Special Constructions   232

10 Aspects of L_2 Research Methodology   244

11 From Research to Reality: Implications for the Teacher   261

List of Tables

List of Figures

Language Two

1

Overview

Learning a second language can be exciting and productive . . . or painful and useless. One's efforts can end in the acquisition of native-like fluency or a stumbling repertoire of sentences soon forgotten.

The difference often lies in how one goes about learning the new language and how a teacher goes about teaching it. To be successful, a learner need not have a special inborn talent for learning languages. Learners and teachers simply need to "do it right."

MAJOR FINDINGS IN SECOND LANGUAGE (L₂) RESEARCH[1]

During the last two decades, researchers have uncovered some critical ingredients of language learning. They have discovered, for example, that when children or adults are not forced to begin speaking the new language immediately, they typically go through a silent period, which lasts from a few weeks to several months. This comprehension period appears to accelerate learning to speak. Most second language courses, on the other hand, require students to produce and practice sentences in the new language from the first day of class. Apparently, it is better to wait awhile.

It also appears that the most beneficial language environment is one where language is used naturally for communication. While some aspects of language may need conscious study, the acquisi-

1. No bibliographical references are included in this section. The relevant studies are discussed and cited throughout the book.

tion of the basics of a language is best accomplished in contexts where the learner is focused on understanding or expressing an idea, message, or other thought in the new language. Concrete "here-and-now" topics are essential for language acquisition. Parroting activities, including most memorized dialogues and mechanical drills, appear to do little to encourage the development of fluent conversational skills.

Sometimes, however, even when teachers provide natural language environments and time for a silent period, some students still may not learn what is presented in a lesson. Other times, students may even correctly use structures the teacher did not teach. Researchers now hypothesize that several internal factors are responsible for these unexpected reactions.

When a student is exposed to a new language, the first internal hurdles are posed by the individual's emotional state and motivations. We have learned that language learners, consciously or unconsciously, select only certain types of people as models worth emulating. For example, a person who thinks American English is gauche will probably not learn as much English from Americans as a person who thinks American English is the best type of English to know in the modern world. Other filtering sources are the individual's anxiety levels, peer identification, and general motivation to learn the language. Together, they make up what we have called the "Affective Filter" or simply "Filter." The Filter acts to control entry to further mental processing.

Once incoming language has passed through the Filter, it reaches two other processors: the "Organizer" and the "Monitor." As the mind begins to take in some of the second language, it organizes it in a fashion which results in the common order in which grammatical structures are learned, in the systematic errors that are made, and in the interim constructions learners use. This organization does not necessarily reflect the organization of the teaching curriculum and it tends to be similar for most second language learners no matter what their first language is.

Monitoring, the third internal process, is a kind of self-editing in which persons who are very concerned about linguistic appearances use conscious rules to produce sentences. People who have a high desire to communicate and who are not embarrassed by making mistakes use the monitor less than those who are more self-conscious.

These three processors are affected by the learner's personality traits and age, which inhibit or enhance their activity. For example, a learner with an outgoing personality may filter out less language than one who is less confident, or an adult may organize more of the language at once than a young child.

Perhaps the most surprising finding in L_2 acquisition research concerns the errors second language learners make. For several decades, linguists and teachers assumed that most second language learners' errors resulted from differences between the first and second languages. This was the basis of the long-popular contrastive analysis theory. Now, researchers have learned that the first language has a far smaller effect on second language syntax than previously thought. Studies show, for example, that only 5% of the *grammatical* errors children make and at most 20% of the ones adults make can be traced to crossover from the first language. Learners' first languages are no longer believed to interfere with their attempts to acquire second language grammar, and language teachers no longer need to create special grammar lessons for students from each language background.[2]

Another surprising finding was that correcting students' grammatical errors seems to produce little improvement. Correction may, of course, serve other important purposes such as helping students and their parents feel that the teacher is earning her pay or providing the basis for a grade. Research suggests, however, that teachers need not bring every error to the attention of the learner for fear the error will become a habit.

As mentioned earlier, researchers have found that most people, whether their first language is Hindi or French, acquire a working knowledge of certain structures in English in a fairly set order. This natural learning order is observed regardless of the order in which the structures are presented in the language curriculum.

In addition to following a common order of acquisition for certain structures, both children and adults from numerous first language backgrounds generally learn complex structures such as English questions by progressing from such constructions as *Who that?* through *Who that is?* and finally to *Who's that?* Linguistic researchers have found that these and other transitional constructions are predictable and are produced by most L_2 learners no matter what their first language background.

One's perception of the order in which various elements of a language are acquired can be muddied by the fact that people who have to function in a foreign language frequently begin by mastering a few useful phrases that make life easier. These are things like *Pass the salt, please; What's that?; It's my turn.* Both children and

---

2. Pronunciation is more susceptible to first language crossover than grammar.

adults learn and use such phrases, called "patterns" and "routines."

In summary, there are several ingredients which are essential to understanding second language acquisition: the language environment, the learner's own controls over the learning process, and the language that learners produce. All are part of the learning and teaching process. The figure below illustrates how they work together.

BACKGROUND

What triggered the research that led to these discoveries? In the sixties, linguists experienced a theoretical revolution which began with Noam Chomsky's publication of *Syntactic Structures* in 1957. Chomsky upset the prevailing belief that language is learned by imitating, memorizing and being rewarded for saying the correct things (cf. Chomsky, 1957b; articles in Fodor and Katz, 1964; Fodor, Bever and Garrett, 1974). While these processes do have some role in language learning, Chomsky argued that the central force guiding language acquisition is a language-specific "mental structure" or "language acquisition device" (1965, pp. 47–59). According to Chomsky, the innate organizational principles of the language acquisition device govern all human languages, and determine what

FIGURE 1-A   Working Model for Creative Construction in L₂ Acquisition*

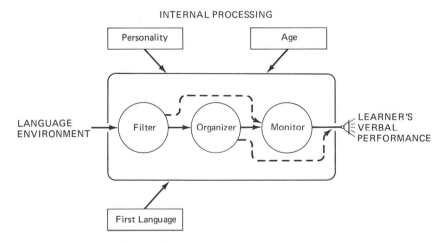

*An updated version of the chart on page 100, in *Viewpoints on English as a Second Language,* edited by Marina Burt, Heidi Dulay and Mary Finocchiaro. New York: Regents Publishing Co. Inc., 1977. Reprinted by permission.

possible form human language may take. This mechanism permits children to acquire the vastly complicated system that comprises a human language in a relatively short time. Exposure to a language triggers the language acquisition device and provides it with the details of the language to be acquired (cf. Chomsky, 1975, Ch. 1). Chomsky further stated that "uniformities in the output . . . must [be attributed] to the structure of the device if they cannot be shown to be the result of uniformities in the language the learner hears" (1965, p. 207).

This view of the language learning process inspired a great deal of psycholinguistic research. Roger Brown at Harvard and Dan Slobin at Berkeley, among others, undertook large-scale investigations of young children's behaviors as they learned first languages. These researchers were looking for evidence of Chomsky's "mental structure"—for uniformities in the verbal behavior of language learners. They followed two- and three-year-old children and their parents around for several years using tape recorders to catch natural exchanges in all kinds of situations. The psycholinguists found striking evidence that some learning behaviors are common to all children no matter what language they are learning. This was the beginning of what is now the well-established field of developmental psycholinguistics.

All over the world, children who are learning their first language during early childhood use similar kinds of verbal constructions and make the same kinds of grammatical mistakes. They learn the basic word-order rules of the language first and omit what are called "grammatical morphemes"—the little words like *the* in English or *el* in Spanish and *der* in German, or the markers like *-s* in *eats*. These markers contribute relatively little to communicating a message even though they are required for grammatical correctness.

R. Brown (1973) found that when children do learn grammatical morphemes, they learn them in the same order, and that order is not related to how often the children hear the structures nor to whether their parents reward them for producing correct structures. Slobin (1971) found that children learning Hungarian and Serbo-Croatian first learn grammatical markers that come after nouns and verbs, and then those that come before the nouns and verbs.

These and numerous other regularities that have been found in the developing speech of children have led psycholinguists to support Chomsky's thesis that the human brain is more than just a receptacle that parents and teachers fill with phrases and sentences. Its structure guides the way young children learn and internalize the language they hear around them. Language acquisition is now known to be an interaction between the child's innate mental structure and the language environment, a "creative construction" process.

These discoveries soon came to the attention of professors who were training second language teachers. Although well versed in teaching methods, some realized that they knew very little about characteristics of second language learners' speech and even less about the dynamics of the interaction between learner and environment. Second language researchers needed to catch up with first language research. Thus, in the late sixties, they began to turn on their tape recorders to catch the imperfect sentences their children or students were producing in a second language. They also analyzed written compositions. We now have a large body of information about the speech and writing of second language learners and about the environmental and mental factors that influence language learning.

PURPOSE

This book presents the exciting findings of the last decade in greater detail, together with their teaching implications. While the research continues, enough has been learned to suggest that the learner's contribution to the whole learning process has been highly underestimated, and that a knowledge of these contributions can help to improve current teaching practices.

Most second language teaching methodology has developed without the benefit of research on second language learning. Much of what we now know about the way people learn languages has been discovered only in the last twenty years, and many teaching methods are much older than that. Research is a slow and tedious process, and educators often lack the luxury of time to wait for its results. Students cannot be turned away when they want or need to learn a new language simply because researchers haven't caught up with classroom needs.

We hope that the information about natural learning processes that is presented in this book will help teachers devise effective lessons and develop materials that enhance natural developmental tendencies. Such knowledge should begin to help teachers understand why students perform well or badly, or in an unexpected manner, and it should provide an explanation to people who still cannot engage in a foreign language conversation after years in a language class. We hope it can help those who are trying to learn a new language on their own select activities and materials that will be most effective.

We would also like to alert college students, as well as general language scholars who have focused elsewhere, to the significance of second language acquisition research and to the contributions such research could make to theoretical and practical advancement in education, linguistics, and psychology.

IMPORTANCE OF KNOWING A SECOND LANGUAGE

Over a billion people in the world speak more than one language fluently. In the Philippines, for example, many people must speak three languages if they are to engage fully in their community's social affairs. They must speak the national language, Pilipino; one of the eighty-seven local vernaculars; and English or Spanish. In small countries, such as the Netherlands or Israel, most children are required to study at least one foreign language in school, and sometimes several. Most adults in the Netherlands speak German, French, and English in addition to Dutch. Even in the United States, whose inhabitants are notoriously unconcerned about languages other than English, about 10% of the residents usually speak at least one language in addition to English in the course of their daily lives (National Center for Education Statistics, 1978). Throughout much of the world, being able to speak at least two languages, and sometimes three or four, is necessary to function in society.

In business affairs, foreign language needs loom large. Economic futurists say that knowledge of a foreign language will be among the most sought after skills for business people from the 1980's on into the twenty-first century. A 1979 editorial by Grace Hechinger of *The New York Times* reminded American business people that most Japanese merchants bring fluent English to their transactions in the United States. Americans doing business in Japan, on the other hand, are often encumbered with the need for translators. This, according to Hechinger, may be one reason that Japanese companies are so often more successful in the United States than American companies are in Japan.

Despite the evident need for foreign language skills, a survey of the top U.S. corporation executives with responsibilities in export development and overseas manufacturing revealed that less than half of those who were born in the United States spoke a language other than English (Craighead, 1980). In contrast, 80% of the foreign-born executives spoke a language in addition to English, and 59% spoke three or more languages!

Survival language skills or business needs are not the only compelling reasons for learning a second language. Neurolinguistic research is beginning to suggest that people who know more than one language make use of more of the brain than monolinguals do (Albert and Obler, 1978). Though the evidence is scant, it appears that the part of the brain that is used in second language functioning remains underdeveloped in monolingual brains. Albert and Obler (1978) reviewed a series of post-mortem studies on polyglot brains—brains of people who spoke from three to twenty-six languages—and found that certain parts of these brains were especially well developed and markedly furrowed.

Psycholinguistic studies further indicate that people who control more than one language are verbally more skillful than monolinguals, and they mature earlier with respect to linguistic abstraction skills. Lerea and Laporta (1971) and Palmer (1972) report, for example, that bilinguals have better auditory memory than monolinguals[3], and Slobin (1968) found that bilinguals are better at intuiting meaning from unknown words. Feldman and Shen (1971) discovered that low-income bilingual children were better at learning new labels than low-income monolinguals, and Peale and Lambert (1962) concluded that ten-year-olds who spoke both French and English demonstrated higher skill in linguistic abstraction than their monolingual counterparts. Expanding mental abilities, therefore, may be reason enough to learn a second language.

DEFINITION OF TERMS

In this book we define **second language (L₂) acquisition** as the process of learning another language after the basics of the first have been acquired, starting at about five years of age and thereafter. Sometimes researchers refer to this process as **sequential language acquisition** to differentiate it from **simultaneous** or **bilingual acquisition,** which is the acquisition of two languages simultaneously from infancy. Apparently, when a young child learns two languages at the same time, the principles which govern monolingual first language acquisition apply to the acquisition of both languages. Leopold's prodigious four-volume analysis (1939–1949) of the German-English development of his daughter Hildegard, with comparisons to that of his second daughter, Karla, is the classic work in this area. (See also Burling, 1959; Padilla and Lindholm, 1976, for other studies of bilingual acquisition; and Padilla, 1980, for a review of the literature.)

Second language acquisition includes learning a new language in

---

3. Although Lerea and Laporta also report that their monolingual subjects learned *visual* stimuli in fewer trials.

a **foreign language** context (e.g. English in Mexico or German in the United States) as well as learning a new language in a **host language** environment (e.g. German in Germany). In this book, the term **second language** refers to both foreign and host languages, and the learning principles discussed apply to the acquisition of both. **Target language** refers to the language being learned or taught.

We use the words "learning" and "acquisition" interchangeably, although they are sometimes used in the L_2 literature to distinguish between **conscious** and **subconscious** language development. To express this important distinction, we use "conscious" and "subconscious," respectively.

The word **creative** is often used in the psycholinguistic literature to describe the process of language acquisition. To say that humans are creative with respect to language means that they do not simply imitate what they hear. In fact, they often use sentences they have never heard before. This central aspect of language acquisition is believed to be rooted in innate and universal structural properties of the mind.

In educational terminology, however, creativity has a different meaning. It often connotes an ability to produce solutions to problems and phrases that do not conform to what most people would be expected to produce. For example, using cooked rice as glue would be considered a creative use of rice. And someone who can imagine twenty uses of paper would be considered more creative than one who can imagine only five. In this sense of creativity, not everyone is creative.

Linguistic creativity, on the other hand, is not the privilege of a select few who might be poets; it is characteristic of all normal speakers of any language. In linguistics the essence of creativity is the use of linguistic rules which are accessible to every normal speaker. Speakers are said to be creative because they regularly produce and understand sentences they have never heard before. We have all internalized a system of rules that governs ordinary language use (Chomsky, 1965, p. 6). The sentence *Peter flew to Reno last night* is very ordinary, yet in the linguistic sense it is creative because it was generated from the speaker's own linguistic rule system rather than as a result of having imitated and memorized it.

Thus we use the term **creative construction** to refer to the subconscious process by which language learners gradually organize the language they hear, according to rules that they construct to generate sentences. The form of the rules is determined by mental mechanisms responsible for human language acquisition and use. These mechanisms appear to be innate. As the learner's language system develops, the learner's rules are gradually refined to incorporate more and more of the mature language system.

The creative construction model of second language acquisition was illustrated earlier in Figure 1A. It represents our view of the process of second language development. It also provides the basis for the organization of this book. Each aspect of the L_2 learning process is discussed in detail in the eight chapters that follow.

Two additional chapters dispense advice—one for teachers and one for researchers. For researchers we describe research methods and point out problem spots in the hopes that such efforts will prevent past errors from recurring and will enhance the amount and quality of L_2 research. The chapter on the application of research findings to teaching is an attempt to draw general implications for the second language classroom suggested by the research findings. To assist readers in digesting the information presented in this book, we have included summaries and study questions at the end of each chapter.

We believe that the ultimate goal of second language research is to increase second language learners' likelihood of success in acquiring a new language. We hope the following chapters contribute to that goal.

2

The Language Environment

The language environment encompasses everything the language learner hears and sees in the new language. It may include a wide variety of situations—exchanges in restaurants and stores, conversations with friends, watching television, reading street signs and newspapers, as well as classroom activities—or it may be very sparse, including only language classroom activities and a few books and records.

The quality of the language environment is of paramount importance to success in learning a new language. If students are exposed to a list of words and their translations, together with a few simple readings in the new language, they will perhaps be able to attain some degree of reading skill in language, but listening and speaking skills will remain fallow. As many high school and college students have learned, to their chagrin, if one is exposed only to classroom drills and dialogues, one may acquire substantial mastery of classroom communication skills but still remain at a loss in other areas of social discourse. And of course, with no exposure at all, no learning can take place.

In this chapter we have gathered together all the available research that indicates which environmental factors influence a learner's acquisition of a second language and under what conditions language learning is enhanced.[1] For example, it has been found that a "silent period" at the beginning of the learning process, dur-

---

1. We do not focus on research that describes the language environment without attempting to determine which features in the environment affect the learner.

ing which the learner simply listens to the new language and is not made to produce it, greatly enhances the speed and quality of learning. Natural communication (in which people care about the ideas being discussed rather than whether they are being expressed correctly) also seems critical to developing speaking fluency. But even natural communication is ineffective if it is about something abstract. Unless the learner can piece together the meaning of what is being said (with the help of concrete visual aids, for example), learning will proceed slowly.

Teaching a second language means creating for students a part or all of their new language environment. The entire responsibility for creating the language environment falls on the teacher who is teaching a language that is not used in the community. When teaching the language of the host community to immigrants or foreign students, however, the teacher has much outside help. In either case, environmental features that accelerate language learning can easily be incorporated into curriculum objectives, teaching techniques, and materials to increase the effectiveness of the language classroom.

MACRO-ENVIRONMENTAL FACTORS

Researchers have examined the effects of four **macro-environmental** features on the rate and quality of L_2 acquisition: (1) naturalness of the language heard; (2) the learner's role in communication; (3) the availability of concrete referents to clarify meaning; and (4) who the target language models are.

NATURALNESS

When the focus of the speaker is on the form of the language, the language environment is **formal;** when the focus is on the content of the communication, the language environment is **natural.**

An ordinary conversation between two people is natural, and so are verbal exchanges at a store, a bank, or a party. The participants in these exchanges care about giving and receiving information or opinions, and although they use language structures, they do so with virtually no conscious awareness of the structures used. On the other hand, an explanation of the rule for the formation of the past perfect subjunctive in Spanish is formal, as are the descriptions of any aspect of a language or the many drills and exercises that require conscious linguistic knowledge or manipulation of linguistic items. When we do such exercises, we don't really care that Mary has a white blouse, for example, or that John has a blue shirt. We care that the words "white" and "blue" are used correctly in the sentence pattern.

The distinction between natural and formal language is not new. It is usually made by language teachers who designate part of instructional time for formal activities (e.g. audio-lingual drills, structural explanations, translation, dictation, etc.), and part for natural communication activities such as free conversation, non-language games (e.g. indoor baseball), reading, or films.

Effects of Natural Exposure

A natural language environment appears to enhance the development of communication skills in a second language in both foreign and host environments. Apparently, natural exposure to the new language triggers the subconscious acquisition of communication skills in that language. The beneficial effects of exposure to natural communication in the target language have been demonstrated by three major empirical studies: two studies involved adults and one study involved children; all were acquiring a second language in foreign environments.

Carroll's (1967) survey of college language majors was one of the first studies to demonstrate the superiority of a natural over a formal language environment for L_2 acquisition. Carroll surveyed 2,784 college seniors who were majoring in French, German, Russian, and Spanish in American colleges and universities. All of them had taken the Modern Language Association *Foreign Language Proficiency Test* (Form A). Carroll found that foreign language majors performed rather poorly on the average: the median score on the MLA corresponded to a Foreign Service Institute rating of 2 plus (out of 5)— between "limited working proficiency" and "minimum professional proficiency." Not surprisingly, Carroll also found a strong relationship between time spent abroad in a host country environment and test performance: *those who reported a year's study abroad performed best; those who reported a summer abroad or a tour performed next best; and both of these groups outperformed those who had studied only in a foreign language environment* (in this case, the United States) in formally structured classroom situations.

Of course, one of the major distinguishing characteristics of an environment is the presence or absence of natural exposure opportunities. The host language environment permits learners to talk with native-speaking peers about issues relating to their lives in the new environment. The foreign language classroom situation, on the other hand, usually affords little opportunity to discuss matters of interest to the students. Instead, focus is typically on the formal aspects of the language being learned.

Similar findings are reported by Saegert, Scott, Perkins and Tucker (1974), who surveyed 114 students at the American University in Cairo, Egypt, and 71 at the American University in Beirut, Lebanon. Many of the students had attended schools in which academic subjects were taught in English. Saegert et al. gathered information regarding their subjects' English proficiency, the number of years of formal English language instruction, and whether they had had experience learning academic subjects in English or another foreign language.

The researchers did *not* find a steady improvement in English proficiency as the number of years of EFL study increased. The authors concluded that, "A better overall predictor of English proficiency was whether or not the subjects had experience with it as a medium of instruction." The students' exposure to English as a medium of instruction in biology, for example, showed a more systematic relationship to level of proficiency than the amount of time they had spent in the English language class.

Results from "immersion program" research also confirm the efficacy of the natural environment for language acquisition. Immersion programs were designed for students who speak a "majority language" (such as English in the United States) as their first language and who wish to learn the "minority language" (such as Spanish in the United States) as a second language. In these programs, the students' *second* language (e.g. Spanish for Anglo-Americans) is used as the medium of instruction in most classes. Such an environment is natural in that the second language is the medium, not the focus, of instruction. "Full immersion" refers to programs that begin in kindergarten and extend into the upper grades. "Partial immersion" programs also involve the use of the L_2 as a medium of instruction but may involve either some subjects in the L_2 and some in the L_1 ("early partial immersion"), or subject matter in the L_2 starting at upper elementary or high school, preceded by L_2 instruction for one year ("late partial immersion"). (See Swain, 1978b for full discussion.)

Full immersion programs using French as the medium of instruction have been in existence for at least the last decade for English-speaking children in Canada. More recently, full immersion programs, with Spanish as the language of instruction, have been in operation in Culver City, California. It has been demonstrated that children in these programs acquire impressive amounts of the second language, perform satisfactorily in subject matter taught in the second language and do not have significant problems in first language skills (Lambert and Tucker, 1972). Linguistic proficiency testing in the St. Lambert French immersion program in Montreal revealed that after seven years in the program, there were some gaps in the English speakers' control of French, but the "students [had] developed high levels of competence in a second language, reaching a stage that even the most optimistic second language teacher would not set for a student following the traditional FLES (Foreign Language in the Elementary School) program" (Bruck, Lambert, and Tucker, 1974, p. 203).

Limits on the Effects of Natural Exposure

Although natural exposure appears to be a necessary ingredient in the language experience of learners if they are to achieve fluency, other environmental conditions must be met. Several factors can limit the beneficial effects of natural exposure: a lack of peers who speak the target language natively, incomprehensibility of the communication, and lack of a silent period when one can absorb the new language but need not produce it.

Formal Environments

A formal language environment focuses on the conscious acquisition of rules and forms. It is severely limited in its potential to produce speakers who are able to communicate naturally and effectively. Although it has psychological value in that many adults like to have the satisfaction of seeing what they have learned (lists of words, structures, rules, etc.), its role in the development of communicative skills appears to be quite limited.

In **rule explanation,** learners are explicitly taught linguistic generalizations (or exceptions) about a target language. For example, in a formal Japanese class students might be told, or led to discover, how *wa* and *ga* are used; in a Spanish class, they might be told the difference between *ser* and *estar;* in a Hebrew class, they might learn how the definite article works. It is usually considered good pedagogy to introduce one such new concept at a time, and rules are usually presented in the order of their presumed linguistic complexity, simpler rules coming first.

Mechanical or **manipulative practice** in using or stating the rules may precede or follow the explanations provided by the instructor. When practice precedes the explanation, and when its goal is to help the student discover the form of the rule, it is called **inductive.**

When practice comes after the explanation and when its goal is to aid the student in practicing what was explained (to encourage "automatic" performance; see discussion below), it is called **deductive.**

The important characteristic of manipulative or mechanical practice, however, is not that it is inductive or deductive, but that it is conscious exercise in grammatical form. Such exercises are not intended to communicate ideas or transmit meaning. In fact, mechanical drills can be, and often are, done without understanding on the part of the learner. Consider, for example, the following common type of mechanical drill (a substitution drill from Paulston, 1972, tones omitted):

Example:

Pɔɔm:	nɑkriɑn	Pɔɔm
suuŋ:	nɑkriɑn	suuŋ
ꞌuɑn:	nɑkriɑn	ꞌuɑn

Continue the drill:
1. nɑɑw
2. rɔɔn

Correct response does not demand any knowledge of Thai:

nɑɑw: nɑkriɑn nɑɑw[2] etc.

Often, exercises may appear to be communicative, but in reality they are mechanical and focused on grammatical form. Consider the following exercise on the English reflexive:

John washes (himself, herself, itself).
Mary washes (himself, herself, itself).

While each sentence contains content words, no real message is intended. Instead, the drill focuses the student's attention on the form of the sentence rather than on its meaning, making it a formal manipulation exercise rather than a natural communication effort. (See Chapter 11, for further discussion of linguistic manipulation tasks versus natural communication tasks for research and testing purposes.)

Although various methods of foreign language teaching emphasize the formal environment, the most well known is the **grammar translation method.** In this method, the lesson typically begins with the statement of the new rule. This is to be consciously learned by

2. Phonetic drill, from C. B. Paulston (1972), "Structural Pattern Drills: A Classification." Reprinted with permission of *Foreign Language Annals 4,* 187–193.

the student. Next, there is a presentation of a bilingual list (a list of words in one language with their translation in the other), in which new vocabulary is introduced. This is followed by a reading selection which emphasizes the new vocabulary. Various manipulation exercises generally follow, including exercises of translation from the target language to the native language and vice versa. This method is almost entirely formal, focusing on the form of the language rather than on the meaning to be conveyed. Even the reading selection is often forced and too difficult for comfortable reading-for-meaning.

Other methods explicitly claim more naturalness, but close examination reveals that they also contain many formal language elements. The **cognitive-code method,** for example, like grammar translation, also typically begins with an explicit presentation of a rule. The exercises which follow are intended to help students learn the rule. The exercises are, in turn, followed by "communicative competence" activities, e.g. games, role playing, or dialogues. This approach is based on the presupposition that "competence must precede performance." (The cognitive-code use of these terms does not correspond to Chomsky's original use of them. According to Chomsky, 1965, competence represents tacit, or subconscious knowledge. Here it represents conscious knowledge.) Carroll (1967) asserts, "Once the student has a proper degree of cognitive control over the structures of a language, facility will develop automatically with the use of the language in meaningful situations." We shall see, however, that the notion that formal, explicit rule knowledge must precede natural use of the language is not supported by current research findings.

Benefits of Formal Exposure

Although research indicates that a formal language learning environment is not the best environment for learning language fluently, it does have certain benefits. First, speakers may modify their use of the new language through some of the low level rules they know. Thus, when rules are learned correctly, conscious rule application may contribute to increasing accuracy in some situations.

Another benefit of conscious linguistic knowledge is that it satisfies the curiosity that many adult learners have about language. For those who have an interest in the structures they are learning, formal environments are stimulating and useful. As most students of a foreign language already know, however, such knowledge does not necessarily make one a better language user in situations where the language is used for communication. In a sense, this is equivalent to a kinesiology course for an athlete. It may be useful to know which muscles are involved in certain activities, but this knowledge will not necessarily improve one's performance on a tennis court.

There are also language learners who apparently do not entirely trust their subconscious learning abilities and who feel more comfortable if they know the rules and structures consciously. In many cases, such conscious awareness increases the feeling of control one has over the learning situation. In fact, language teachers have reported that certain students are pleasantly surprised after consciously learning a rule that they have been unconsciously using correctly, commenting, "Oh yes, that's the way it works."

Limitations of Formal Exposure

Perhaps the greatest limitation of formal exposure to a language is the small role that the conscious knowledge of rules seems to play in either the acquisition or the conversational use of the language. For example, most normal children are successful language learners, whether they are learning a first or second language. Yet, we know that they do not typically have a conscious grasp of the rules they are acquiring. Similarly, adults normally use their first language fluently, though with varying degrees of sophistication, yet probably only the linguists or grammarians among them could state many of the rules they use when speaking or writing.

Unfortunately, being able to recite rules does not guarantee a proficient use of the language. Despite painstaking efforts on the part of both teacher and students to consciously focus on the structures, rules, and vocabulary of the target language, a minimum ability to communicate through the language still eludes most students who study foreign languages using traditional, formal methods.

THE LEARNER'S ROLE IN COMMUNICATION

We can distinguish three types of communication in which learners participate:

1. One-way,
2. Restricted two-way, and
3. Full two-way.

In **one-way communication,** the learner listens to or reads the target language but does not respond. The communication is one-way, towards the learner, not from the learner. Listening to speeches and radio programs, watching films and most television programs, and reading books and magazines are all examples of one-way communication.

In **restricted two-way communication,** the learner responds orally to someone, but the learner does not use the target language. The response may be in the learner's first language or some other non-target language and may include a nonverbal response such as nodding.

In **full two-way communication,** the learner speaks in the target language, acting as both recipient and sender of verbal messages.

This threefold distinction is important because each has its place in facilitating L_2 acquisition. Most of the available empirical research emphasizes the benefits of allowing one-way and restricted two-way communication during the early parts of the learning process and waiting until the student is ready to produce the target language before insisting on full two-way communication.

Language Learning among Vaupes River Indians   Information on language learning among Indians living in the Vaupes River area in South America (Sorenson, 1967) vividly illustrates the value of delaying full two-way communication. The Vaupes River Indians may well be the world's leading experts in practical language learning. Almost two-dozen mutually unintelligible languages are spoken in a small area populated by a group of about 10,000 people. Furthermore, it is the custom in this Indian culture to marry outside of one's language group—people must find mates who do not speak their language! As a consequence, children must learn at least three languages from the start: their mother's, their father's, and the lingua franca of the area (Tukano). More languages are typically acquired as the individual grows up, and this extraordinary language learning continues throughout adolescence, adulthood, and even into the later years.

While there is no empirical evidence demonstrating that the Vaupes River Indians are unusually successful in second language acquisition, such well-practiced language learners must certainly have something to show us about the ways of gaining some facility in new languages. Sorenson's description of how older learners go about accomplishing this is of great interest:

> The Indians do not practice speaking a language that they do not know well yet. Instead, they passively learn lists of words, forms, and phrases in it and familiarize themselves with the sound of its pronunciation

. . . They make an occasional attempt to speak a new language in an appropriate situation, but, *if it does not come easily, they will not force it.*

(Sorenson, 1967, p. 680, italics ours.)

The Silent Period for Child L₂ Learners

Children have almost always been observed to understand language before being able to produce it. In fact, there is also some rather extreme evidence from medical annals showing that some children may acquire comprehension abilities, but no productive skills at all, attesting to the independent and ordered development of these two types of skills.

Lenneberg (1962) studied a case of "understanding language without ability to speak." The subject was an eight-year-old boy who, because of congenital anarthria (a peripheral speech defect), had never spoken. Lenneberg reported that "from the patient's first visit to the clinic it has been obvious that he had a normal and adequate understanding of spoken language . . . At one time a short series of instructions were tape recorded and transmitted to the patient through earphones. He followed the instructions without being able to see the examiner." Thus, despite the lack of speaking ability, the child had acquired language well enough to understand it perfectly. Lenneberg notes that:

. . . a similar phenomenon in more attenuated form is extremely common. Understanding normally precedes speaking by several weeks or months. This discrepancy is regularly increased in literally all types of developmental speech disorders and is best illustrated in children who have structural deformities in the oral cavity or pharynx and who produce unintelligible speech for years, sometimes throughout life, without the slightest impairment of understanding. Congenitally deaf children also learn to comprehend language in the absence of vocal skills.

(Lenneberg, 1962, p. 231)

As first language learners, normal children begin by relying on one-way communication while they develop comprehension skills. Various L₂ researchers have also found this phenomenon in children who are learning a second language in natural settings. When adults do not force them to speak, children acquiring a second language typically exhibit a "silent period" for one to three months or so. During this period, the young second language learners, like the Indians in the Vaupes River area, concentrate on comprehension and opt for one-way or restricted two-way communication. Huang (1970) observed a five-year-old boy learning English as a second language at a play school in Southern California. The boy was reported to be an outgoing child, but he said absolutely nothing for the first two weeks in this environment, and he spoke only a few words during the second two weeks. Productive language did not emerge until ten weeks had gone by, although the boy was able to use some memorized phrases to communicate certain needs before this time.

A similar phenomenon was reported by Ervin-Tripp (1974), who described English-speaking children, aged four to nine, enrolled in Swiss schools where the language of instruction was French. She noted that the children did not volunteer anything in the new language for a prolonged period; some of the children said nothing for many months. Her own children did not begin to speak until six or eight weeks after they had been in the setting, and even then their speech was limited to greetings and other interactive phrases and routines.

A similar example is reported by Hakuta (1974), who studied a five-year-old girl learning English in eastern Massachusetts. He reports that he was unable to begin his study until some five months after the subject had been exposed to English because she produced almost no speech before that time. During the five months, Hakuta repeatedly tried to elicit language in natural play situations, but the little girl demonstrated only comprehension of the language.

It appears that one-way communication is a kind of self-imposed constraint which language learners, both first and second, seem to require in order for the acquisition process to unfold most naturally. This phenomenon has been noticed by curriculum developers and observant language teachers for both child and adult L_2 acquisition. Several recent, innovative teaching approaches which attempt to capitalize on the above observations about the language learning process have been developed. The success of these programs strongly suggests that adults also profit from having a silent period.

The Total Physical Response Method

Perhaps the most widely publicized of the newer approaches is Asher's "Total Physical Response" (TPR) method (Asher, 1965, 1966, 1969 a and b, 1972; Asher, Kusudo and de la Torre, 1974). During approximately the first ten hours of TPR, students remain silent but are required to obey teacher commands in the target language, beginning with simple imperatives (such as *Sit down*, or *Stand up*), to more complex sentences (such as *If Abner runs to the chalkboard, run after him and tap him with your pencil*).

Asher has conducted effectiveness studies comparing the TPR method with other approaches in which students are required to speak in the target language right away. In a study involving German as a foreign language in the United States, TPR students had significantly better listening comprehension scores after only 32 hours of instruction than students completing 150 hours of college German (Asher, 1972). Further, despite the fact that TPR students had little systematic training in reading and writing, they performed in those areas as well as the controls. These results have been replicated using Spanish as a foreign language (Asher et al., 1974) and German as a foreign language (Swaffer and Woodruff, 1978; see below).

The Natural Approach

Another foreign language teaching method which provides for initial restricted communication in the target language is called the "Natural Approach" (Terrell, 1977). In this method, the entire class period is devoted to communicative activities. Explanation and formal work are done outside the classroom as homework. Students are allowed to respond in the classroom in either their first language or in the target language, and early production of the target language is not required. Each student makes his or her own decision about when to begin to use the target language, much as Sorenson's Vaupes River Indians do. A student is likely to try to speak in the new language, Terrell states, "whenever he or she makes a decision to do so, i.e. whenever his or her self-image and ease in the classroom is such that a response in the second language will not produce anxiety."

Although no studies have been published comparing the results of the Natural Approach to those of other methods that do not include a restricted two-way communication period, Terrell's own experience suggests that the Natural Approach leads to rapid acquisition of listening comprehension as well as speaking skills.

Classroom Research on Delaying Oral Practice

Valerian Postovsky (1974, 1977) and Judith Gary (1975) conducted independent research studies on delaying oral practice in the classroom, furnishing the requisite hard data to support the benefits of a silent period. Postovsky's experiments focused on the effects of delayed speaking on second language achievement. Students studying Russian in an intensive six-hour-per-day course at the Defense Language Institute in Monterey, California were instructed not to respond orally, but to write their answers to classroom exercises. The students' success in learning Russian was compared to that of students who were given a great deal of oral practice from the beginning of the course. Postovsky found that those whose speaking was delayed during the first month of the intensive course outperformed control subjects "in both pronunciation and control of grammar" (Postovsky, 1977, p. 18).

Gary studied some fifty English-speaking children over a five-month period as they were learning Spanish in a southern California school. Gary divided the children into two groups: half of the children received a "regular" 22-week Spanish course in which oral responses in Spanish were required (full two-way). Her "experimental" subjects did not engage in any oral practice in Spanish for the first 14 weeks of the course (restricted two-way) and responded orally only for the first half of the lesson during the remaining 8 weeks. The children taught via the restricted communication method were required to indicate comprehension by nonverbal means, such as pointing or nodding their heads. At the end of the 22 weeks, both groups of children were tested for production *and* comprehension skills in Spanish. As might be expected, Gary found that the restricted group outperformed the full two-way group for listening comprehension. She also found, however, that even though the children in the restricted group had not practiced oral production for the first 14 weeks, when they began to speak, they did as well as the group which had been practicing speaking since the beginning of instruction.

Swaffer and Woodruff's 1978 study is also consistent with this conclusion. In their university-level German class, listening comprehension (Total Physical Response) and reading comprehension were emphasized, not spoken correctness. Students in such classes exceeded national norms and showed greater enthusiasm for the study of German than students in classes which emphasized spoken correctness.

These kinds of findings permit us to suggest that communication situations in which students are permitted to remain silent or respond in their first language may be the most effective approach for the early phases of language instruction. This approach approximates what language learners of all ages have been observed to do naturally, and it appears to be more effective than forcing full two-way communication from the very beginning of L₂ acquisition.

AVAILABILITY OF CONCRETE REFERENTS

The content of language that is directed at beginning learners must be such that learners can figure out the meaning to some extent. This raises a third macro-environmental feature that affects successful second language development: the presence or absence of extra-linguistic factors that can aid the learner in grasping the meaning of the strange sounds of the new language. A language environment may provide this type of support when it includes **concrete referents**—subjects and events that can be seen, heard, or felt while the language is being used.[3]

Since progress involves understanding or producing language which is slightly beyond one's present repertoire, the extra-linguistic context that accompanies such language must be relied upon as the context which will make the meaning of the new elements clear. Experienced second language teachers are, of course, already aware of the importance of providing contexts for the new language. They provide visual aids, motor activities and other "here and now" types of support to help make the meaning of the new language clear to beginning learners.

The clearest example of a language environment rich in concrete referents is one that mothers and other "caretakers" create when they talk to the young children around them. This kind of speech has been called "motherese." Mothers or other caretakers typically obey the **"here-and-now" principle.** They describe what the children do, or what has just happened: *Oh, you spilled your milk; That's a nice sandcastle!* Or they tell children what to do at a given moment: *Drink your juice! Stop that!* Or they ask questions about the children's ongoing activities: *Is that a doggie?; Where is your sock?*

Motherese speakers do not typically talk about activities that are displaced in time and space. They do not discuss what will happen next week, not to mention next year, what is going on down the block, or events in another country. As various researchers have pointed out, this focus on the here-and-now is not part of a conscious effort to teach language. Rather, it is a topical constraint on maternal speech (Newport, Gleitman, and Gleitman, 1977). The here-and-now principle derives from the fact that a limited set of topics

3. For discussion of the use of concrete referents in first language acquisition, see Bloom (1973) and Greenfield and Smith (1976).

are of mutual interest to both caretakers and young children. Newport et al. summarize it well: "Mothers want their children to drink their juice and clean up the playroom, so these are the things that are talked about."

Language environments for *child* second language learners are often concrete. Consider the following exchange witnessed by researchers studying a five-year-old learning English as a Second Language in California:

ADULT	PAUL
Is this your ball?	Yeah.
What color is your ball?	(no answer)
Is that your doggy?	Yeah.
Is that your doggy or Jim's doggy?	Jim's doggy.

(Wagner-Gough, 1975)

The adult is referring to objects that are visually available to the child, not to anything spatially or temporally distant. This adult is following the here-and-now principle, probably for the same reason parents do, discussing a limited number of topics of mutual interest.

Although the use of the here-and-now principle provides critical and necessary support for those faced with the first or second language learning task, it is much less frequently observed when the L_2 learners are adolescents or adults. Adults tend to talk to older learners about events and objects displaced in space and time, even though the students barely know English. The results are usually disastrous, as the following exchange shows.

Ricardo is a thirteen-year-old boy learning English in California, who had only been in the United States one month:

ADULT	RICARDO
What are you gonna do tonight?	Tonight? I don't know.
You don't know yet? Do you work at home, do the dishes or sweep the floor?	Water. (garbled)
You water?	Flowers.
Flowers.	Mud.
Oh, you wash the mud down and all that. What else do you do at home?	Home.

(Wagner-Gough, 1975)

Other questions asked Ricardo included:

What did he do yesterday?
What do we mean by "question mark"?
Did you ever have any trouble with your ears?

Although the questions and comments directed at this boy may not look difficult to a native English speaker, the fact that the language does not refer to a single concrete, here-and-now referent makes it impossible for the learner to figure out what the meaning is without knowing the meaning of all the words already.

Older learners, like younger ones, would benefit from adherence to the here-and-now principle, especially in the early stages of instruction. Of course, there is no doubt that older students are cognitively able to deal with abstractions, they just need concrete help when learning a new language. Rather than talking about "doggie" or "toys," however, one would select more appropriate objects and activities, such as money or food. Whatever the choice, the condition to be met is that the objects and activities chosen for use should have concrete referents so the learners can figure out the meaning of the language used.

Children themselves are aware of the importance of concrete environments for second language learners. In her study of five Spanish-speaking children in an American kindergarten, Fillmore (1976) noted that the native English-speaking children would automatically provide concrete environments for the children learning English by means of gesture, demonstrations, sound effects, and repetition. Yet when speaking to English-speaking adults they did not use the concrete approach. This is illustrated by the following exchange Fillmore observed in the classroom:

JESUS: (English learner): Hey, Matthew, wait!

MATTHEW: (Holds up his little car) Lookit, here's mine. Mine has got to go in here, and yours has got to go in there.

JESUS: Wha' happen? My God! (Shows Matthew a car which has the tires missing.)

MATTHEW: Wha' happen to this? Lookit. (His car is falling apart too.)

JESUS: My God!

MATTHEW: Where's another car for me?

JESUS: Four car.

MATTHEW: (To adult observer) Hey teacher, you've got a TV, right?

OBSERVER: Do I have a TV? Yes.

MATTHEW: Tell Jesus why he don't watch Channel 5. That program is going to on again.

JESUS: Channel 44!

OBSERVER: Why don't you tell him yourself?

MATTHEW: 'Cause he don't know what I'm saying.

(Fillmore, 1976, p. 696)

Fillmore notes that "Matthew had been playing and talking with Jesus for the entire hour in the playroom, but when he wanted to tell him something which could not be contextualized, he turned to the observer to translate for him."

The available evidence for both child and adult second language learners, in a host or foreign language environment, suggests that language environments rich in concrete referents appear to be a necessary environmental characteristic for beginning language learners.

TARGET LANGUAGE MODELS

In addition to the beneficial effects of a language environment in which natural language is the rule, in which learners are not forced to speak in the new language before they are ready, and in which the here-and-now principle is followed, there is a fourth significant macro-environmental factor: the source of the language the learners hear. There may be many speaker models available (anyone who speaks the target language is a potential model), but learners do not draw on them equally.

Although it is well known that learners do not learn everything to which they are exposed, it is perhaps not so well recognized that learners do not even attend to everything to which they are exposed. Unexpected learning outcomes may well be the result of selective attention to different speaker models rather than the result of some inherent learning problem.

Language learning research provides various examples of apparent preferences for certain speaker models over others under certain circumstances, preferences which seem to have obvious effects on the quality of the learner's speech. To date, evidence has been presented which demonstrates speaker model preferences of three sorts: peers over teachers, peers over parents, and own ethnic group members over non-members.

Peer Versus Teacher

When both a teacher and peers speak the target language, learners have been observed to prefer the latter as models for themselves. For example, a seven-year-old Japanese-speaking child who had immigrated to Hawaii acquired the Hawaiian Creole English of his agemates, rather than the Standard English of his teachers during his first school year. When the boy moved to a middle class neighborhood the following year, however, he quickly picked up the Standard English that his new friends spoke (Milon, 1975). In explaining this phenomenon, Milon states that "there is no question that the first dialect of English these young immigrant children learn is the dialect of their peers. If they learn productive control of the dialect of their teachers, it is not until later . . ." (p. 159).

Similar findings have been reported from studies of second language immersion programs in Canada and the United States. In immersion programs, the teacher is typically the only native speaker of the target language to whom the children are exposed during the school day. No native target-language speaking children are enrolled in the programs. The children are taught subject matter through the target language, but they speak their first language outside of the classroom.

In the case of the St. Lambert French immersion program in Montreal, the students who had entered the program at kindergarten and had continued in it for seven years still showed some gaps in their control of French and manifested non-native syntax and pronunciation (Bruck, Lambert and Tucker, 1975). Over the years, the type of oral French the students developed was qualitatively different from that of their teacher.

Similar results have been reported for a Spanish immersion program in Culver City, California, where Anglo-American native speakers of English were immersed in subject matter instruction through Spanish for the school day. (Again, no native Spanish speakers were in the program.) After four years in the program (having started in kindergarten), the children still made grammatical errors in Spanish which were characteristic of the younger learners in the beginning grades. These findings suggested the "lack of a definite trend in improvement across grades," at least in the development of the morphological agreement rules that were studied (Plann, 1977).

The development of such "immersion varieties" of target languages does not appear to be attributable to any learning problems of the children, nor to the quality of the target language spoken by the teachers during the school day. Instead, the outcome seems to be directly attributable to the preference these children have for their peers as speech models. In the case of the immersion programs, it happens that all the preferred models are themselves struggling with the new language.

Peer Versus Parent

In first language learning, it has been found that when the speech characteristics of peers and parents differ, the children will tend to acquire the speech characteristics of their peers.[4] For example, Stewart (1964; cited in Dale, 1976) reports that the black children he studied in Washington, D.C. acquired the dialect used by their peers (a dialect of Black English that is most different from Standard English), rather than the dialect used by their parents (a dialect of Black English closest to Washington, D.C. Standard English). Likewise, Labov (1972) found that both black and white children in a middle class area of northeastern New Jersey learned to pronounce the r's before consonants as their New Jersey friends did, rather than to drop the r's as their New York-raised parents did. These data, too, show "that children learn more language behavior from members of their own peer group than from their parents . . ." (Stewart, 1964; cited in Dale, 1976, p. 281).

Own Social Group Versus Other Social Group

Besides generally preferring peers over adults as language models, some children have been observed to tend towards the dialect or language spoken by members of their own ethnic group. For example, Benton (1964; cited in Richards, 1974), reports that Maori children learned the English dialect of their own ethnic group rather than standard New Zealand English spoken by other children. In some cases, this model preference is consciously articulated: One teacher reported that a Maori child had told her: "Maoris say, 'Who's your name?', so that's what I say." Maori English is often an important sign of group membership and a source of security for these children (p. 75). In this case, the learner simply stated that she wished to sound like the ethnic group with which she preferred to be associated.

As these examples have shown, the importance of language as an identification marker of the preferred social group cannot be under-

---

4. This observation is fundamental in accounting for language change over generations.

estimated in the second language classroom. The choice of peers over adults as speaker models, and among peers, the choice of members of one's preferred group over members of another social group, significantly affects the quality of the language produced. Needless to say, the differences in learner speech characteristics that result from model choice are due not to learning difficulties, but to preferred social group membership.[5]

The availability of different speaker models is a key macro-environmental factor operating in the classroom and elsewhere to affect the quality of the language that learners produce.

MICRO-ENVIRONMENTAL FACTORS

While macro-environmental factors are the broad overall characteristics of the language environment, **micro-environmental** factors are characteristics of specific structures of the language the learner hears. For example, one might ask how frequently *Yes/No* questions occur in a learner's environment, or whether teachers correct students when they make gender errors.

To date, three micro-factors of the language environment have been investigated from the perspective of their effect on the quality or rate of language acquisition:

1. Salience, the ease with which a structure is seen or heard
2. Feedback, the listener's or reader's response to the learner's speech or writing
3. Frequency, the number of times the learner hears or sees a given structure

The results of this research are often surprising. The micro-features do not seem to have the major effects on learning that were expected.

SALIENCE

Salience refers to the ease with which a structure is heard or seen. For example, most people can probably hear the English article *the*, which is a full syllable, more easily than the past tense *-ed*, which

---

5. The language program may, of course, choose to focus on teaching children another dialect or variety than the one of their preferred social group, providing the children with another option to use when necessary or appropriate. This goal should be clearly articulated, so that the learners understand the purpose of the instruction.

is simply a sound tacked on the last syllable of a verb, as in *talked* (pronounced taukt).

Psycholinguists have defined salience by referring to particular characteristics that seem to make an item more visually or auditorily prominent than another. Such characteristics include the amount of phonetic substance (whether the item is a syllable or not); or the stress levels of an item (the amount of emphasis placed on it), e.g., if a native speaker of English says *She doesn't want any*, *does* and *want* receive the most stress, *she* and *an* would be next, and *n't* and *-y* would receive the least. Position in the sentence has also been proposed as a variable affecting salience—some researchers have shown that children pay more attention to items in final position than in the middle of a sentence (Slobin, 1971; Ervin-Tripp, 1974).[6]

Of course, items which are not heard at all are unlikely to be learned, but there is no direct relationship between the degree of salience of items and the order in which those items are learned. Consider, for example, the subset of *-s* morphemes examined in many of the L_2 acquisition order studies (presented in Chapter 8). (A morpheme is the smallest meaningful unit in language. The word "*girls,*" for example, contains two morphemes: *girl* and *s.*) It has been repeatedly found that the contracted form of the singular verb *to be* (as in *He's fat*) and the short plural (as in *windows*) are learned relatively early. On the other hand, the short possessive (as in *the king's*) and the third person indicative (as in *sees*) are learned much later. Since the phonetic substance and stress levels of these *-s* morphemes are virtually the same, the salience of the items cannot be used to predict their differential acquisition order. The early acquisition of the contractible singular copula is especially interesting because its position in the middle of the sentence presumably makes it less salient than it would be at the end of the sentence. (Brown found that these *-s* morphemes were also acquired by first language learners at different points in time, although the order of the specific items was not quite the same as that found for L_2 learners.)

Another example of the indirect effects of salience on learning order is the late acquisition of the long plural morphemes, *-es*, relative to the short plural, *-s*. Even though the long plural is syllabic and the short one is not, the long plural is acquired much later than the short one (see Figure 2-A). The opposite learning order would be expected if salience influenced learning. Clearly, the effects of salience are tempered by other, as yet unknown, factors.

6. Salience in language acquisition research seems to be very similar to "stimulus intensity" in behaviorist learning theory.

FIGURE 2-A L₂ Acquisition Hierarchy for 13 English Grammatical Structures*

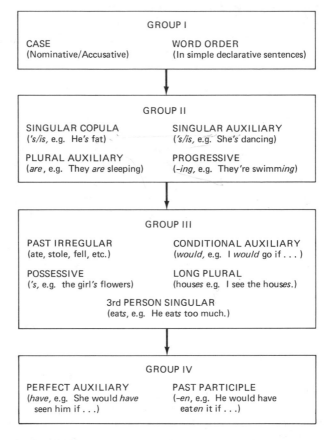

*Heidi C. Dulay and Marina K. Burt. 1975. A new approach to discovering universal strategies of child second language acquisition. In: *Georgetown University Round Table on Languages and Linguistics 1975*. Edited by Daniel P. Dato. Washington, D.C.: Georgetown University Press. Copyright © 1975 by Georgetown University, pp. 209–233.

FEEDBACK

In language acquisition research, feedback generally refers to the listener's or reader's response given to the learner's speech or writing. One type of feedback is correction, another is approval or "positive feedback," as some call it. Still another way to respond is to expand or otherwise modify the learner's speech without consciously calling attention to the modification. This type of response has been called "expansion." Correction and expansion have received the most research attention.

Correction

Research has produced a rather discouraging view of the effect correction has on learners' errors. Experienced language teachers have long known that correcting students' grammar or pronunciation can be immensely frustrating. Although students say that they want correction (Cathcart and Olson, 1976) and teachers try to provide as much as they can, it is all too obvious to both teachers and students that errors are often impervious to correction.[7] Several empirical studies have documented this point.

In a study designed to determine the effects of differential error correction on the compositions of adult ESL students, Hendrickson (1977) found that neither correction of all errors nor systematic selective correction made any significant differences in the students' written proficiency.[8] Hendrickson systematically corrected a total of 552 compositions over a six-week period: he corrected all the errors made by half of his twenty-four subjects, and corrected "global errors" for the other half. Global errors are those that affect overall sentence organization such as word order errors and errors involving sentence connectors. (See pp. 189–97 for discussion of global errors.) He found that "neither error correction treatment, regardless of level of communicative proficiency, made any statistically significant difference in students' written proficiency over the six-week treatment period" (p. 12). There appeared to be no relationship between the systematic corrective feedback of errors and their correct use by ESL students.

In another article, Plann (1977) reports that grammatical and morphological errors in the speech of children learning Spanish in an immersion program in the United States are not very amenable to correction. Plann writes:

> The third grade teacher has tried to call the children's attention to these
> errors by orally correcting them and having them repeat the correction;
> the fourth grade teacher has attempted to teach these grammar points

7. Our discussion refers to the corrections of language forms only, be it phonological, grammatical, or some other aspect of language form. Correction of content errors is a different matter altogether and is not taken up here.
8. Fanselow (1977) and Allwright (1975) have observed that teachers are not always clear and systematic when they correct students' linguistic errors. This observation was taken by many to mean that clear and systematic error correction might make a difference. Hendrickson found that it does not. See Long (1977) and Chaudron (1977) for research describing teachers' correction behavior.

more formally, giving the class explanations at the blackboard and then having the children do oral drills and written follow-up exercises. However, although the students seem to grasp the concepts, both teachers admit there has been little improvement in the children's speech.

(Plann, 1977, p. 222)

Similarly, Cohen and Robbins (1976) reported that correction of the written work of university ESL students did not influence the production of errors. Although Cohen and Robbins believe this lack of influence resulted from flaws in the quality and systematicity of the corrections, the above-mentioned studies give little reason to expect significantly different results with better or more systematic correction techniques.

Finally, a study by Holley and King (1971) suggests that students may improve their control over spoken language form without correction. In an experiment involving American university students who were learning German in the United States, one group of students were corrected for oral errors they made in the *content* of their responses only. They were not corrected for any errors of language *form.* The authors report that in over 50% of the instances they observed (and filmed), no correction was needed for the students to improve their language errors. Simply permitting the students more uninterrupted time to rephrase their responses resulted in improved performance.

While the studies described here involved different types of situations (ESL, FL, and immersion), different modalities (oral, written) and students of different ages, they all come to the conclusion that correction is not a very reliable tool in helping students overcome errors. These findings do not necessarily mean that correction plays no role in language learning. For example, future research may reveal that correcting wrong vocabulary may be helpful. Further research may also uncover specific situations in which error correction may be effective.

Expansion

Expansion involves the systematic modeling of either the correct or more complete version of the child's utterance without calling the child's attention to the activity. The effect of expansion on the development of child speech has been examined, so far, only in first language acquisition. For example, if a child says *Mommy eggnog,* the child's parents might say in response, *Mommy had her eggnog.* (Example from Brown and Bellugi, 1964, p. 13.) This practice is typical of parents when talking to their children.

The effects of expansions on language learning are not entirely clear. Cazden's 1965 experiment on the effect of expansions is the classic study in this area. Cazden hypothesized that systematic modeling of the grammatically correct versions of children's utterances might be a major force in acquisition progress. To almost everyone's surprise, she found that expansions, given for one hour per day over a three-month period, had almost no effect on the speech of the children she studied.

In a more recent study, Nelson et al. (1973) found that children who were systematically provided with sentence expansions over a 13-week period were somewhat more advanced linguistically on several language measures than controls who did not receive the treatment. (See also Cross, 1977, and Newport, Gleitman and Gleitman, 1977.) On the other hand, an experiment by Feldman (1971) comparing different expansion treatments versus none at all showed few differences between the groups at the end of the experiment. Thus, the precise effect of expansions, if any, on the language development of children is not yet clear.

FREQUENCY

In language acquisition research the frequency of occurrence of a structure refers to the number of times a learner hears a given structure. One might, for example, count how many times *wh*-questions occurred in the speech of a mother to her child during some discourse situations that might represent what the child hears overall. The count would be considered the frequency of *wh*-questions in the child's language environment.

Generally, it has been assumed that the more a learner hears a structure, the sooner it will be acquired. Although one research study supports this belief (Larsen-Freeman, 1976), other research investigations do not. In his four-year study of three unacquainted children learning English as a first language, Brown (1973) discovered that the children all learned fourteen grammatical structures in a certain order. He then looked at how frequently these structures were used by the parents of these children during parent-child conversation, thinking that the frequency of the structures might be responsible for the order in which they were learned. To the contrary, he found that the structures learned early were not also the ones used most by the parents. He states, "no relation has been demonstrated to exist between parental frequencies and child's order of acquisition" (R. Brown, 1973, p. 362).[9]

In their observations of a child learning English as a Second Language, Wagner-Gough and Hatch (1975) reported data with similar implications. Although two types of questions occurred with equal frequency in their subject's language environment, only one type of question was produced correctly and not the other. The *wh*-questions *What's x?* and *Where's x?* were produced correctly, whereas the question which required copula inversion (*Is this x?*) was not.

Learners' systematic use of certain structures that they do not usually hear or never hear at all is another curious fact relevant here. A seven-year-old child we studied, for example, would say *They looking at their chother* or *They love their chother* instead of *They're looking at each other* and *They love each other*. Obviously he had made up *their chother*, since none of the English-speaking adults or children around him used that phrase. Examples of structures L_2 learners create and use regularly while they are learning the new language abound in the literature (see Chapters 6 and 7). The use of such structures cannot possibly be attributed to their frequent occurrence in the environment since many never occur at all.

Finally, consider the well-known fact that specific English grammatical items that contribute little or nothing to meaning, such as articles (*a, the*), or tense and plural markers, occur more frequently than specific major content words (nouns like *tree, table*; verbs like *laugh, love*); and yet, "the early absence and long delayed acquisition of those more frequent forms has always thrown up a challenge to the notion that frequency is a major variable in language learning" (R. Brown, 1973, p. 362).

Some Effects of Very High Frequency

Although relative frequency of occurrence may not be directly related to the learning order of structures in the language, it appears that extremely high frequency may have unexpected effects on the learning and use of some aspects of language. When language patterns are used very frequently within the learner's earshot, the learner will tend to memorize them. Such memorization may cause some patterns to be excluded from normal analysis, delaying their

---

9. The Spearman rank order correlation (*rho*) between the children's rank order of acquisition and the rank order of frequency (average across the pairs of parents) was +.26 and was not statistically significant (R. Brown, 1973). See Appendix A for an explanation of how to compute rank order correlation.

incorporation into the new language system. For example, when the parents of Brown's three research children produced certain *wh*-questions (e.g. *What's that?*) at a very high rate during a period when the children did not yet know the structure of *wh*-questions, the children learned to produce the two most frequently repeated ones on "roughly appropriate occasions" (*What's that?* and *What are you doing?*). When, much later, "the children began to produce all manner of *wh*-questions in the preposed form (such as *What he wants?*), it was interesting to note that *What's that?* and *What are you doing?* were not at first reconstructed in terms of the new analysis . . . In terms of [the children's] new rules, they ought to have said *What that is?* and *What you are doing?* but instead, they at first persisted with the old forms" (Brown and Hanlon, 1970, p. 51).

Thus, one effect of very frequently occurring forms is that at least some of them will somehow be represented in the child's performance even if its structure is far beyond him or her. The child will render a version of it and will form a notion of the circumstances in which it is used. Such constructions will, in Brown and Hanlon's words, "become lodged in his [or her] speech as an unassimilated fragment" (p. 51). Furthermore, they suggest that extensive use of such unanalyzed or mistakenly analyzed fragments probably protects them, for a time, from re-analysis. Here, then, especially high frequency seems to interfere with the learners' productive integration of certain structures into their grammatical system. (See Chapter 9 for further discussion.)

Dulay and Burt (1977) noticed a similar type of phenomenon in second language acquisition in the development of embedded *wh*-questions for Keres- (Pueblo Indian) and Spanish-speaking children learning English. They found that although the children had learned to say *What's that?* long before they learned *What are those?*, later, when the children were producing sentences like *She doesn't care what they are,* they were still saying *I don't know what's that.*

The effects of frequency on the acquisition of syntactic and morphological structures seem to be far from clear or simple. We have seen some cases where certain structures are produced, while others that are heard with equal frequency are not. In other cases, structures are produced that were not heard at all, and in still others, some very high-frequency phrases are memorized before the learner knows their internal structure, apparently causing a temporary setback in acquiring their internal structure.

These findings are not entirely mysterious if one assumes that language learning is a two-way street where learners are affected by their environments, but at the same time contribute something to the learning process. The learner comes to language acquisition with a mental apparatus designed to gradually organize the initially foreign items of a new language into a system. Since the acquisition process is not instantaneous, the learner is ready to learn different structures at different times—when his or her emerging new language system is at the right point in development. No matter how often learners hear a structure that is far beyond their developing language system, they will not be able to integrate it and use it to produce sentences. Memorizing specific sentences containing the structure is as far as they can go.

The concept of readiness is common in education. Most children in American public schools are given reading readiness activities designed to bring them to the point where they can start decoding the written word. The same concept works here. Second language learners have to be ready to incorporate structures into their developing systems before exposure will make a difference. Thus, frequency serves primarily to increase the probability that learners will hear structures which they are ready to process, increasing the chances that they will be able to attend to and process them.[10]

ROLE OF MICRO-ENVIRONMENTAL FACTORS

A clear and important example of the specific type of interaction between the operation of internal factors, micro-environmental factors and the acquisition of new knowledge is found in the series of investigations conducted by Inhelder, Sinclair, and Bovet (1974), psychologists working in the tradition of the famous developmental psychologist Jean Piaget. Although these studies did not investigate language development per se, their assumptions, procedures and findings should be extremely useful to language acquisition researchers who are interested in the effects of factors in the language environment.

Inhelder et al. studied the effects of certain training procedures on children's progress in cognitive development. They conducted a series of learning experiments on the acquisition of the process of conservation and class inclusion. Before a certain point in cognitive development, children think that the height of a liquid in a container is the indicator of quantity. If a young child who had not yet acquired the principle of conservation was shown a fat squat glass

---

10. It is important to distinguish at least two different ways in which a language learner might use a structure in speech: 1) as a productive rule that has been integrated into the learner's target language grammar; and 2) as an unanalyzed fragment.

and a tall slim glass with the same amount of water in both, the child would think that the tall slim glass had more water, even if the water was poured from one glass to the other in front of the child, to make the quantity of the water obvious. Likewise, such children think that there are more items in a group that is spread out than in one that is crowded together, even if both groups include the same number of items.

Thirty-four children aged five years, one month to seven years old from the Genevan State nursery and primary schools were selected on the basis of cognitive developmental levels, ranging from those who never made a conservation judgment (Level I) to those who made such judgments most of the time (Level IV). The experimenters then provided various types of training sessions to see what their effect on the children's learning would be.

The training sessions "resembled the kind of situation in which [cognitive developmental] progress takes place outside an experimental set-up," that is, where children interact naturally with features of the environment provided by the experimenters, observing the characteristics of objects and making judgments about them. "Experimental situations that might almost automatically elicit the correct answers were avoided" (Inhelder et al., 1974, p. 24).

Interestingly enough, the training sessions, which were the same for all the children, had virtually no effect on the fifteen children at the non-conservation level. Only two of those children improved substantially, while most of the nineteen *intermediate* level children showed substantial progress. The authors take pains to point out that all the children noticed all the relevant observable features presented to them; however, only the more advanced children were able to use the information for solving the problem at hand. The beginners simply did not know how to use the observations they had made (p. 53). The provision of appropriate information, therefore, accelerates cognitive development *only when the learner has reached a cognitive level that permits the formulation of certain kinds of judgments.*

Although the findings of Inhelder et al. do not deal specifically with second language acquisition, they illustrate the importance of specifying principles of interaction between external factors and mental factors in the explanation of learning. This approach makes it possible to predict when a certain type of environment, in this case a type of training procedure, will significantly affect learning and when it will not.

SUMMARY

The language that learners hear and see around them is of paramount importance to the acquisition process. In this chapter, we have focused on aspects of the learner's language environment which research has shown are directly related to successful second language acquisition. We have also discussed aspects of the environment which are only indirectly related to acquisition, although they have been commonly thought to have a more direct role.

Four broad overall features of the environment (**macro-environmental** features) appear to directly affect the rate and quality of second language acquisition:

1. *Naturalness of the environment,* or the degree to which the focus of communication is on its content rather than on its linguistic form. Studies show that students who are exposed to natural language, where the focus is on communication, perform better than those in a formal environment, where focus is on the conscious acquisition of linguistic rules or the manipulation of linguistic forms. Some exposure to formal environments may be beneficial, however, especially to adults. It may satisfy their curiosity about the new language as well as their need to be consciously aware of what they are learning. Formal exposure may also, for some, increase accuracy in a few simple structures of the new language while the subconscious system is being acquired.

2. *The learner's role in communication.* Communicative exchanges may be defined according to the manner in which the learner participates in them. In one-way communication, the learner listens (or reads) but does not respond verbally. In restricted two-way communication, the learner listens and responds but the response is either nonverbal or not in the target language. In full two-way communication, the learner responds in the target language.

Studies conducted to date indicate that one-way and restricted two-way communication during the early part of second language acquisition have been found to benefit learning significantly. Delaying oral practice or observing a "silent period" until learners are ready to speak in the new language are beneficial classroom practices.

3. *Availability of concrete referents*—subjects and events that can be seen, heard, or felt while they are being talked about. Communication about the "here-and-now" ensures that the learner understands most of what is being said in the new language, and thereby becomes a critical aid to progress in acquiring new structures and vocabulary.

4. *Target language models.* The learner's choice of model significantly affects the quality of speech produced. Reasearch studies indicate the following preferences: peers over teachers, peers over parents, and members of one's own ethnic group over non-members.

Micro-environmental features are characteristics of specific structures of the language the learner hears. Three micro-features that have been investigated to date do not seem to have the major effects on learning that were expected.

Salience, the degree of visual or auditory prominence of an item, is not in itself a reliable predictor of when that item will be learned; neither is *frequency,* the number of times a learner is exposed to a particular item or structure. Very high frequency of a phrase or sentence, however, may result in a learner's memorizing it and using it in approximately appropriate contexts. *Correction,* whether it is systematic or random, does not seem to be effective in enhancing the acquisition of the corrected structure. However, correction may be used for other purposes, such as to satisfy certain adult needs and to give grades.

Micro-environmental factors may affect second language learning only when learners have reached certain points in their L_2 development such that they are "ready" to internalize a given structure. Once a learner is ready to learn a structure, the high salience or frequency of the structure may increase the probability that the learner will notice the structure and acquire it. Much more research is necessary before we can specify the conditions under which micro-environmental factors affect language acquisition.

STUDY QUESTIONS

1. Would it be easier to teach Spanish as a second language in Washington, D.C., or in Mexico City? Explain.

2. It is the second week of a 22-week course for high school students in the United States who are just beginning to learn ESL. The teacher is planning to show a movie about a high school football player.
   a. Discuss briefly at least three factors in this language environment that makes it an effective ESL lesson.
   b. Discuss briefly at least one factor that may be lacking to make the language learning situation ideal.
   c. After the movie, should the teacher have the students discuss the movie? Explain.
   d. Describe at least one follow-up activity you would consider doing after the movie.

3. Categorize the following activities according to: (1) whether they are essential; (2) not essential but useful; or (3) unnecessary and not helpful to second language acquisition:
   a. Mechanical or manipulative practice
   b. Full two-way communication
   c. The silent period or delaying oral practice
   d. Providing a Total Physical Response

   e. Teaching grammar rules
   f. Providing concrete referents
   g. Providing opportunities for child learners to play with children who are native speakers of the language.

4. Give the arguments you would use to convince a friend, who is planning to learn a foreign language, of your opinions in *question 3* above.

3

Internal Processing

In the last analysis, the precise manner in which human beings learn languages remains invisible. It takes place inside the mind of the language learner, where researchers can follow in only the most rudimentary manner. What we can do, of course, is observe what the language learner hears and then produces in the way of language learned. Probing researchers have long noted significant discrepancies between the two, and they have assembled an impressive pool of evidence showing that the discrepancies are systematic and characteristic of all sorts of L_2 learners. They are like imprints of the mind on learners' behavior.

This chapter represents our best inferences about the mental processes involved in second language acquisition, inferences based on numerous analyses of the data available on verbal performance and the effects of the language environment. Our intention is not to reduce the complex and intricate workings of the human mind to a series of mechanistic generalizations, but to bring certain factors in the language learning process to the attention of researchers and teachers.

The data suggest that three internal factors operate as people learn a second language. Two are subconscious processors, which we call the "filter" and the "organizer," and one is a conscious processor called the "monitor" (see Figure 3-A).

Language learners do not take in everything they hear. Their motives, needs, attitudes and emotional states filter what they hear and therefore affect the rate and quality of language learning. We

FIGURE 3-A   Internal Processors

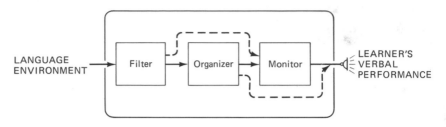

use the term *filter* to refer to these "affective" factors that screen out certain parts of learners' language environments.

The *organizer* is that part of a language learner's mind which works subconsciously to organize the new language system. It gradually builds up the rule system of the new language in specific ways and is used by the learner to generate sentences not learned through memorization.

The *monitor* is that part of the learner's internal system that consciously processes information. When the learner memorizes grammar rules and tries to apply them consciously during conversation, for example, we say the person is relying on the monitor.

THE FILTER[1]

The filter is that part of the internal processing system that subconsciously screens incoming language based on what psychologists call "affect": the learner's motives, needs, attitudes, and emotional states. The filter appears to be the first main hurdle that incoming language data must encounter before it is processed further. It determines (1) which target language models the learner will select; (2) which parts of the language will be attended to first; (3) when language acquisition efforts should cease; and (4) how fast a learner can acquire the language.

Learners, for instance, will select certain types of phrases or vocabulary items to learn and use over others; children, for example, tend to first learn phrases and sentences that are essential for social participation. Some learners will apparently stop acquiring the target language at a point before they reach native-like proficiency, but after they have acquired enough to communicate. These kinds of behavior may be attributed to the affective filtering which significantly reduces the data that are accessible to the other processors.

1. In previous writings, we used the terms "socio-affective filter" and "affective filter" instead of just "filter."

Social circumstances influence filtering. For example, the existence of a foreign language requirement in school gives shape to a student's motivation to learn a new language. Likewise, the characteristics of a community that speaks a particular language, along with the functions of that language in the learner's own life, influence the attitudes that a learner develops towards that language. Specific motives, needs and attitudes underlying second language acquisition take their shape from the niche in society that the individual occupies or wishes to occupy and the social activities in which the learner engages or wishes to engage.

Motivation

Motivation in L_2 acquisition may be thought of as the incentive, the need, or the desire that the learner feels to learn the second language. The research literature shows that three kinds of motivation affect language acquisition: (1) integrative motivation; (2) instrumental motivation; and (3) social group identification.

Integrative and Instrumental Motivation   Gardner and Lambert (1959) first made the distinction between integrative and instrumental motivation in L_2 acquisition. **Integrative motivation** may be defined as the desire to achieve proficiency in a new language in order to participate in the life of the community that speaks the language. It "reflects a sincere and personal interest in the people and culture represented by the other group" (Gardner and Lambert, 1972, p. 132). **Instrumental motivation,** on the other hand, may be defined as the desire to achieve proficiency in a new language for utilitarian reasons, such as getting a job. It "reflects the practical value and advantages of learning a new language" (Gardner and Lambert, 1972, p. 132). These two types of motivation are illustrated in the direct questionnaires Gardner and Lambert (1959) used in their investigations. They asked students to rank the following four possible reasons for studying French. Knowing French would:

1. Be useful in obtaining a job;
2. Be helpful in understanding the French-Canadian people and their way of life;
3. Permit meeting and conversing with more and varied people; and
4. Make one a better educated person.

Gardner and Lambert considered reasons (1) and (4) instrumental, while (2) and (3) were considered integrative.

A number of studies have probed the value of integrative and instrumental motivation, showing how each of these types of motivation appears to relate to second language proficiency. Whereas in the early studies it appeared that integrative motivation was superior to instrumental, later investigations demonstrated that in situations where the practical value of the second language is high, and frequent use of the second language is available and necessary, instrumental motivation may be a powerful spur toward second language proficiency.

It seems clear that both types of motivation can positively influence the rate and quality of L_2 acquisition; each is more effective under certain conditions. In terms of the filter, high motivation of either sort probably acts to let the learner absorb a maximal amount of the target language.

Gardner and Lambert conducted two studies of high school students learning French in Montreal. The first included seventy-five eleventh grade students (Gardner and Lambert, 1959), and the second (Gardner, 1960) included eighty-three tenth graders. In both samples they found integrative motivation to be more strongly related to French achievement than instrumental motivation. Moreover, Gardner pointed out that integrative motivation was especially important for the development of communication skills (p. 215). In a similar setting, Gardner, Smythe, Clement and Gliksman (1976) confirmed the importance of integrative motivation in Grades 7–11 French classes in Montreal. They also found that measures of integrative motivation tended to have higher correlations with oral communication measures than with grades.

Gardner et al. also studied factors related to "dropping out" of French, which was not a compulsory subject in schools which they studied. From their analysis, they concluded that those who dropped French were not simply the less able students. Dropouts did tend to get lower grades and show lower aptitude, but the primary motivation for the stay-ins appeared to be integrative, in addition to an overall motivation to learn French. Gardner et al. suggest that integrative motivation "provides students with the necessary motivation to persist in second language studies" (p. 200).

Integrative motivation also seems to affect actual behavior in the classroom. Gardner et al. found that those students whose test responses indicated the presence of integrative motivation volunteered to answer questions more often, made more correct answers in class, and received more positive reinforcement from their teacher. They were also perceived by observers to be more interested in the French lesson.

Integrative motivation has also been found to relate to proficiency in the United States for English as a second language. In this case, however, indirect methods of measuring integrative motivation have been necessary. Spolsky (1969) found that questionnaires as direct as those used in the Canadian studies were not appropriate for foreign students in the United States because such subjects may not want to "admit to motives which suggest they wish to leave their own country permanently" (p. 409). In his study of several hundred international students, Spolsky used an indirect measure of integrative motivation. He defined integrative motivation as the amount of agreement between subjects' views of themselves and their views of speakers of the target language for a variety of personality traits (e.g. stubborn, lazy, kind). Spolsky reported that direct means of measuring integrative motivation did not show any relationship between proficiency in English and scores on the questionnaires, but clear positive correlations were shown when the indirect method was used.

The effect of integrative motivation appears to be weaker in other situations; Gardner and Lambert (1972) investigated high school students learning French in three American communities in Maine, Connecticut, and Louisiana. Integrative motivation did *not* relate to proficiency in Maine or Louisiana, and only a weak relationship was found in Connecticut. Additionally, Chihara and Oller (1978) studied the acquisition of English in Japan by 123 adults in basic, intermediate, and advanced EFL courses. They found little relationship between attitude and proficiency.

Equally interesting are the findings of two studies that show *instrumental* motivation to be superior: Lukmani (1972) found that for Marathi-speaking women in Bombay "who belonged to the comparatively non-Westernized section of Bombay society," proficiency in English as measured by a Cloze test[2] was more related to instrumental motivation than to integrative motivation. Lukmani concluded that her subjects saw themselves "based in their own country but reaching out to modern ideas and life styles" (p. 272). Gardner and Lambert (1972) reached similar conclusions for English as a second language in the Philippines. In the Philippines, English is often the language of education and business, but it is rarely spoken in the home. Gardner and Lambert found that instrumental motivation was a better predictor of overall English proficiency, but they

2. A Cloze test is a test of second language ability, and is constructed by deleting every nth word (where n is usually between 5 and 10) from a reading passage. Students are then asked to fill in the missing word. Originally developed to assess readability in the native language, it has been claimed that the Cloze test is a reliable and valid measure of second language ability as well. For a summary of relevant research, see Oller (1973).

also found a clear relationship between the presence of integrative motivation and "aural-oral" skills.

Motivation may also act to filter out parts of the language that are not important to the learner, for example, the phonological aspects of American or British English for learners of English in the Philippines or Bombay. Another case where it is quite possible that language is filtered as a result of instrumental motivation is the development of pidgin languages by communities which learn a second language for purposes of commerce and other functional reasons, rather than for social contact (see Schumann, 1974, for discussion of pidginization). In such circumstances, only the minimum syntax and vocabulary necessary to communicate in limited domains would be learned. As Richards points out:

> We can predict, for example, the sort of English likely to be acquired by an immigrant who mixes exclusively with his own language group and who opens shop, catering largely, but not exclusively, to that language group. He will probably learn first to reply to a limited set of questions in English, to manipulate a closed class of polite formulae, the vocabulary of some food items, and perhaps the language of simple financial transactions . . .
>
> (Richards, 1974a, p. 66)

Social Group Identification   The language or language variety one speaks is often a signal to others that one belongs to a certain social group. The **social group identification motive** may thus be defined as the desire to acquire proficiency in a language or language variety spoken by a social group with which the learner identifies. Conversely, lack of identification with a given group may result in a learner not wanting to acquire the language or language variety spoken by that group. We saw in Chapter 2 that children tune in other children as L_2 models but often tune out the teacher or their parents. We also saw that the research strongly indicates that adult learners also prefer their peers as language models, and one study suggests that both child and adult learners who belong to a particular ethnic group prefer other members of that group as models.

The social group identification motive is similar to the integrative motive, but, in our interpretation, goes beyond it. Learners with an integrative motive for learning a new language would wish to participate in the social or cultural life of the target language speakers while retaining their identification with their own native language group. Learners who have a social group identification motive would want social and cultural participation, but they would also want to become members of the group that speaks the new language or language variety.

In other words, social group identification implies integrative motivation, but not vice versa. The social group identification motive would be particularly applicable to immigrants or migrants who may want to assimilate fully into the host society or community. Other immigrants or migrants have only integrative or instrumental motives for learning the host language.

The research findings regarding motivation and attitudes are not entirely clear with respect to distinguishing the effects of a limited environment from the effects of filtering. A learner may simply be processing all that is available given the limited environment. However, given the same language environment, differences between successful and unsuccessful learners in rate and quality of acquisition are most plausibly accounted for by some kind of internal selective mechanism, such as a filter that controls or selects what learners process depending on their particular motives, needs and desires. If, for example, instrumental motivation is narrow in scope, only a small subpart of the language heard will be of interest to the learner. If, on the other hand, instrumental motivation is wide in scope, such as the desire to work in a country where the target language is the official language, much of the language will be of interest and filtering will be minimal.

Emotional States

The learner's emotional states are also part of the filter. In combination with attitudes and motivation, they affect what the learner admits for further processing.

Research has shown, for example, the effects of various forms of anxiety on acquisition; the less anxious the learner, the better language acquisition proceeds. Similarly, relaxed and comfortable students apparently can learn more in shorter periods of time.

Relaxation   Techniques to induce in students a state of mental relaxation and comfort intended to maximize language learning have been developed and are currently being used with reported success by Georgi Lozanov in Bulgaria. The student's relaxed mental state, brought about by classical music, comfortable chairs, and the instructor's modulation of voice is believed to increase the receptivity of the student to the new material. Shearer (1978) describes the method, termed "suggestopedia," briefly:

The typical Lozanov classroom is like a comfortable living room. The *teacher reads a lesson dialogue in an expressive way* accompanied by *theatrical gestures* and the students repeat sentences after him, occasionally breaking into Bulgarian to ask a question. This finished, the teacher sits back in his armchair and closes his eyes. The students do the same and Vivaldi wafts softly into the room. While the students recline in their armchairs, trying to empty their minds and listen only to the music, *the teacher re-reads* the same lesson, this time to the rhythm of the classical music. A few minutes later, he stands and his class joins him in a few stretching exercises. He then *reads the lesson once more and the class is over for the day.*

Sessions like these continue four hours a day, six days a week. There is no homework. Lozanov claims that within a month, students with no prior knowledge of the language will have learned 2,000 to 3,000 words and have a good enough grasp of the grammar to use them in conversation. Western experts who have visited his institute support his claim.

(See also Stevick, 1976, pp. 155–158.)

In the United States, Elizabeth Philipov of Pepperdine University has adapted Lozanov's technique to teach Cyrillic languages. "A study comparing this method with traditional language instruction showed the suggestopedic students were more proficient with only one-third study time" (Budzynski, 1977, p. 42).

T. Budzynski, of the Biofeedback Institute of Denver, refers to a "twilight state"—a state between consciousness and sleep characterized by theta brainwaves—during which individuals become more receptive to absorbing certain kinds of information, including language. Budzynski reports case studies of people who have been helped by being placed in a twilight state and given information that had been previously blocked, including "students who have mental blocks for subjects such as foreign languages; fat people who are unable to comply with suggestions to eat properly; prejudiced people who find it hard to believe anything a member of a minority group says" (p. 41).

Ann Harriet Buck of "The Golden Door," a health resort in Escondido, California, who brought Budzynski's work to our attention, reports that basketball players who imagine practicing foul shots perform as well as players who actually practice them (Buck, 1981).

Research of this sort is still in its infancy; nevertheless, the little that is available seems to hold promise.

Anxiety A number of studies have shown a relationship between low anxiety and successful language acquisition. Carroll (1963) noted a small negative correlation (r= −.20, n= 68) between test anxiety and accomplishment in intensive foreign language courses. Gardner, Smythe, Clement and Gliksman (1976) reported that classroom anxiety negatively correlated with speech skill levels as well as with grades in French as a foreign language in grades 7–11 in Canada. Low anxiety tended to be more closely related to good scores on speech tests than to grades.

Naiman, Frohlich, Stern, and Todesco (1978) found that for their subjects (French learners in grades 8–12 in Toronto), "classroom anxiety, a high fear of rejection and similar feelings may be related to failure" (p. 289). They devised a composite variable consisting of certainty in hand-raising, reaction to being called on without hand-raising, and embarrassment in speaking French. This was called "overall classroom personality," and related to achievement on an imitation test (r= .361, p<.01) as well as on a listening comprehension test (r= .380, p.<.01).

Wittenborn, Larsen and Vigil (1945; cited in Pimsleur, Mosberg, and Morrison, 1962) studied college French and Spanish students and found that low and high achievers may be distinguished by level of anxiety as well as by degree of self-confidence. Dunkel (1947; also cited in Pimsleur et al., 1962) found that low achievers in Latin showed "emotionality, inner conflict, and anxiety" on a personality test. Oller, Baca, and Vigil (1977), in their study of Mexican-American females in New Mexico, reported that subjects who saw themselves as "calm," in addition to "conservative, religious, shy, humble, sincere," did better on a Cloze test of English as a Second Language than others who did not.

Chastain (1975) reported a significant correlation between test anxiety and success in audio-lingually taught French in an American university. The correlation was negative (r= −.48), indicating that low test anxiety was associated with greater success, which is consistent with the studies reported above. A positive correlation, however, was found between test anxiety and achievement in Spanish (r= .21) and German (r= .37) taught by traditional methods. Anxiety as measured by the *Taylor Manifest Anxiety* scale was positively correlated with Spanish achievement but showed no other significant relationships. One interpretation of the test anxiety result not discussed by Chastain is that the audio-lingual approach permits subconscious acquisition to some extent despite its announced intention to establish habits, while traditional methods focus on conscious learning. Perhaps low anxiety benefits subconscious acquisition, while at least a moderate degree of anxiety may be helpful for conscious learning.

Although the filter has visible effects on learning results, it is only the first processor. It is based on affective factors, while the next processor relates to analytical, or cognitive, aspects of language acquisition.

THE ORGANIZER[3]

The organizer is that part of the internal processing system that is responsible for the learner's gradual organization of the new language system. Its functioning is subconscious and is based on what psychologists call "cognitive" principles: analytical and logical criteria for the organization of knowledge and behavior.[4]

In examining the language that learners produce, researchers can see the functioning of the organizer reflected in three pervasive phenomena: (1) the systematic progession of changes in interim rules, or transitional constructions that learners use before a structure is finally acquired; (2) the errors that systematically occur in learner speech; and (3) the common order in which mature structures are learned. The relationship between these findings and the operation of the organizer is highly informative. Analyses of these aspects of the learners' developing L_2 system reveal different facets of the operation of the internal principles that govern the acquisition of language.

Transitional Constructions

A variety of rules have been found to characterize learners' second language speech. We have used the term **transitional constructions** (see Chapter 6) to refer to the interim structures learners regularly use during the acquisition of a particular target language structure.

The observation that many structures develop in a systematic manner for different students is one of the most important indicators of the force of the organizer in controlling the language acquisition process. Structures whose development has been studied so far include English and German negation, English and French simple *wh*-questions, English embedded *wh*-questions and reflexive pronouns, and German particles.

In the development of negation, for example, the learner's first attempts typically place the negator outside the rest of the utterance—either before or after it (e.g. *no sleeping*). In Step 2, the ne-

---

3. In previous writings, we used the term "cognitive organizer" instead of just "organizer."
4. The organizer is similar to Chomsky's (1975) "language acquisition device."

gator is placed inside the utterances, although the auxiliary is still absent (e.g. *I not dumb*) In Step 3, the "early" auxiliaries are used, the tense is regularly marked, and the negator is correctly placed to its right within the utterance (e.g. *No, they're not white*).

Of course, the beginning and end of developmental steps in the acquisition of a structure are not as abrupt as these characterizations suggest. Language development is not a series of plateaus, but a continuum made up of blending the beginning and ends of several successive phases.

The details of transitional construction development are presented fully in Chapter 6. What is important here is that the development of these structures can be characterized by general linguistic principles. These are organizational rules whose source must lie in the organizer, give the common appearance of the same steps in the developing language of learners of different language backgrounds and in the absence of such utterances in the language environment of students.

Error Types

Analyses of numerous errors in L_2 learners' speech and writing (discussed in detail in Chapter 7) have revealed systematic distortions of surface elements of the new language:

1. The **omission of grammatical morphemes**—omitting items that do not contribute much to the meaning of the sentence, as in *I buy some coloring book*, where past and plural markers are omitted.

2. The **double marking** of a given semantic feature—marking two or more items in an utterance when only one marker is required, as in *She didn't wented*, where the past tense is marked more than once.

3. The **regularization** of irregular rules, as in *That mouse catched him*, where the regular past tense marker -*ed* is used instead of the irregular *caught*.

4. The use of **archiforms**—using one form for the several required, as in the use of the accusative for both nominative and accusative pronouns, e.g. *Them going to town; I know them*.

5. The **alternating use of two or more forms** whose conditions for use are still being internalized, as in the random alternation of *much* and *many: too much dolls; many potteries*.

6. The **misordering** of items in constructions that require the reversal of word-order rules that have been previously acquired, as in *I don't know who is it*, where the placement of *is* erroneously follows the rule for simple questions rather than embedded questions.

The Acquisition Order of Structures

As we will see in Chapter 8, numerous research studies have revolved around the question: Is there a characteristic L_2 acquisition order for certain English structures?

Nearly every soundly designed study has answered this question in the affirmative. Researchers have discovered an L_2 acquisition order which is characteristic of both children and adults, and which holds for both oral and written modes, provided the focus of the learners is on communicating something. This general finding is one of the most exciting and significant outcomes of the last decade of second language acquisition research. (See Chapter 8 for specifics.)

The structures seem to fall into at least three or four groups, each of which is ordered with respect to the other groups. The acquisition groupings that have been observed seem to correspond to levels of linguistic development, and most learners pass through each in a fairly stable sequence.[5]

The organizer apparently guides the acquisition process, limiting what can be learned to new material that fits into the growing organization of the new language system, and rejecting material which does not yet fit into the emerging system. The result is that observers are actually able to witness groups of structures being acquired in the same fairly stable order in the new language systems of many learners of diverse first language backgrounds.

These observed learning hierarchies, together with the systematic nature of error types and transitional constructions, are among the most impressive evidence of the internal controls the organizer exerts in the development of a second language. All of the general observations indicate that the organizer functions as a guide and regulatory mechanism which permits the gradual and systematic growth that has been observed for L_2 acquisition in natural and formal settings.

Attempts to Characterize the Organizer

While it seems clear that some mental processor, which we have referred to as an organizer, is responsible for the learner's development of the new language system, we cannot yet fully specify its operational principles.

Attempts have been made to characterize organizational learning principles in L_1 research (Brown, 1973; Bever, 1970; Slobin, 1973;

5. While some learners may appear to skip some steps, they are not observed to pass through them in differing orders. That is, the structures in group III have not been observed to be acquired before those in group I or II, nor those in group II before I.

and Ervin-Tripp, 1973), and to a limited extent, for L_2 acquisition (Ervin-Tripp, 1974; Dulay and Burt, 1975). Most of these efforts have been more successful in determining what the principles are not, than in what they are. This is instructive, however, especially for those interested in advancing the theoretical state of the art.

Perhaps the most difficult problem in attempting to characterize the organizer has resulted from the tendency to equate principles which may *describe a developed* language system with those the mind relies on to *acquire* the system. As long as these principles are assumed to be the same, researchers will continue to hope that improved methods of describing mature language systems will bring us closer to discovering learning principles. This may be a false hope, however. For example, while it is true that the number of transformations in the derivation of a structure may be an accurate measure of the complexity of that structure, we do not know if the principles for acquiring it will be the same. Chomsky and Halle (1968) made a point of this when they wrote that their decision to focus on accurate linguistic descriptions had no bearing on the psychological reality of their linguistic descriptions (p. 331).

The disappointing results of Brown's efforts to use descriptive linguistic rules to explain learning order underscores this point. Brown (1973) proposed that the two major "determinants of acquisition" for the first language learning order he observed were semantic and grammatical complexity. Semantic complexity was defined as the number of major meanings of roughly equal weight expressed by a morpheme; the greater the number of major meanings, the more semantically complex that morpheme should be. He defined grammatical complexity in terms of "derivational complexity": the more grammatical transformations required in the derivation of a structure (according to the Jacobs and Rosenbaum [1968] analysis), the more grammatically complex that structure should be. Brown's analysis showed that neither grammatical nor semantic complexity alone explained the learning order he found, and he had to conclude that "the order of acquisition is dependent upon relative complexity, grammatical and/or semantic" (p. 255).

Even less encouraging results were obtained by Dulay and Burt (1975). They tested Brown's (1973) grammatical and semantic complexity predictions for the learning order of the structures in their data and found that neither grammatical nor semantic complexity, nor both combined, could explain the learning order found for L_2 learners.

Bever (1970) and Slobin (1971) have also pointed to the need to distinguish between learning complexity and linguistic or any other type of descriptive complexity. Bever discussed "learning strategies," while Slobin focused on "operating principles." While the learning strategies and operating principles proposed accounted for some of the data, they did not turn out to be universal. Bever and Slobin, however, were the first to recognize the need to distinguish between learning complexity and linguistic complexity.[6]

Linguistic complexity refers to the amount of linguistic knowledge in a structure. X is said to be more complex than Y if X involves more linguistic knowledge than Y. Perfect tenses, for example, require more morphemes than the simple tenses, and thus are considered more complex. Or, in reading, blends and diphthongs are considered more complex than simple vowels and consonants. In transformational grammar, the more transformations required to generate a sentence, the more complex the structure is said to be.

Learning complexity, on the other hand, refers to the degree of difficulty a learner experiences in acquiring a structure. The possessive -s marker, for example, is considered more complex in this sense than the progressive -ing because it is learned later. Research is in progress to determine the principles underlying L_2 learning complexity, but to date results are not conclusive enough to report.

Items which are linguistically complex may not be complex by learning standards. For example, the shortened passive sentence (*It was stolen*) is more complex, in transformational terms, than the full passive (*It was stolen by someone*), because an extra transformational rule is required to delete the agent (*by someone*). Yet, children learn to produce the shortened passive well before the full ones (Slobin, 1963; Bever, 1970).

We believe that the confusion of learning complexity and linguistic complexity has led to erroneous sequencing of second language lessons: items which are linguistically simple, such as the -s in *loves*, are often presented early despite their being one of the structures learned late.

The specification of principles governing learning complexity is probably one of the most important areas of theoretical research that remains to be undertaken. Describing such principles would describe the operation of the organizer.

THE MONITOR

The monitor is the part of the learner's internal system that appears to be responsible for conscious linguistic processing.[7] When a person tries to learn a rule by reading about it in a grammar book or

6. See Clark and Clark, 1977 for a discussion of how Slobin's principles might be ordered and see Dulay and Burt, 1975 for a review of Bever and Slobin's work in this area.
7. Conscious linguistic processing has been called "learning" in Krashen's previous work.

by attending a class session where the teacher explicitly describes the rule, the person is engaging in conscious language learning. Whenever conscious linguistic processing takes place, the learner is said to be using the monitor. Similarly, when a learner performs a drill that requires conscious attention to linguistic form, or when he memorizes a dialogue, conscious processing is taking place and the monitor is being used.

The linguistic knowledge that one gains through monitoring can be used to consciously formulate sentences and to correct one's own speech and writing. The editing function of the monitor comes into play when a student attempts to edit compositions and correct ungrammatical sentences in language test items, as well as when the student spontaneously self-corrects errors made during natural conversation.[8]

Conscious processing may also underlie a learner's use of his or her first language structure to formulate second language sentences in particular situations. When called upon to produce structures that are not yet part of the subconscious linguistic system, some learners—adults in particular—tend to plug second language vocabulary words into their consciously available first language syntax. This conscious word-for-word translation process may be a communication strategy of last resort.

The degree to which the monitor is used depends on at least the following: (1) the learner's age; (2) the amount of formal instruction the learner has experienced; (3) the nature and focus required by the verbal task being performed; and (4) the individual personality of the learner. For example, conscious concern over sounding grammatically correct is a personality trait of many adults. This often results in a great deal of self-correction and hesitation when speaking. Likewise, tasks which cause learners to focus on conscious linguistic analysis (such as fill-in-the-blank with the correct morpheme) invite monitoring; while tasks which cause the speaker to focus on communication (such as answering a real question) do not.

Krashen (1975, 1977) initially posited the construct of the monitor to account for a number of perplexing phenomena that have been observed in adult verbal performance. It is entirely possible, however, that children have access to it, especially if they are old enough to have attained what is called in Piagetian terms the concrete operations stage. Research along these lines has been, unfortunately, sparse.

Available research evidence suggests that conscious linguistic

---

8. The monitor is not the only source of self-correction; subconsciously acquired language may also be brought into play, as when one corrects a slip of the tongue "by feel" rather than by applying a rule.

knowledge is independent of the linguistic system that is built up subconsciously by the organizer. Young children may have virtually no conscious awareness of linguistic rules, yet they acquire languages easily and well. Conversely, some adults who may have elaborate conscious knowledge of the rules of a language may be at a complete loss when attempting to use that language for communication.

Despite the differences, both organizer and monitor are agents for the acquisition of linguistic knowledge. They interact, sometimes smoothly and in complementary fashion, at other times in conflict. Both affect, to different extents and in different ways, the verbal performance of the second language learner. Both are themselves affected by other factors such as personality and past experience.

While the organizer is probably language-specific—it processes only language (cf. Chomsky, 1964, 1975)—the monitor may be a general cognitive processor responsible for conscious learning in other areas (cf. Felix, 1981).

MONITORING AND THE ONSET OF FORMAL OPERATIONS

The capacity for grasping the conscious representation of abstract linguistic rules appears to emerge at about puberty and may well be a result of the adolescent's new ability to think abstractly in general. At around puberty, many adolescents pass through a developmental state Piaget calls "formal operations" (Inhelder and Piaget, 1958). Children (aged seven to about eleven), who are still "concrete" thinkers, may arrive at abstract concepts, but these abstractions derive directly from experience with concrete objects. The formal thinker, on the other hand, has the ability "verbally to manipulate relationships between ideas in the absence of prior or concurrent available empirical propositions" (Ausubel and Ausubel, 1971, p. 63). For formal thinkers "new concepts are primarily acquired from verbal rather than from concrete experience" (op.cit., p. 66).

In addition, the formal thinker has a meta-awareness of this developing system of abstractions: "the adolescent seems to reflect on the rules he possesses and on his thoughts" (*Developmental Psychology Today*, 1971, p. 336). The formal thinker can also develop general solutions to problems: "the adolescent organizes his [or her] operations into higher order operations, ways of using abstract rules to solve a whole class of problems" (op.cit., p. 336). A classic example of this is the solution to the problem of selecting which items from a group can float; the formal thinker will typically apply a general rule (i.e. objects that are made out of wood), while the concrete thinker may try out each item. Finally, the formal thinker can "conceptualize his own thought . . . take his mental constructions as objects and reason about them" (Elkind, 1970, p. 66).

The ability to think abstractly about language, to conceptualize linguistic generalizations, to mentally manipulate abstract linguistic categories, in short to construct or even understand a theory of a language, a grammar, may depend on those abilities that develop with formal operations. Of course, the capacity to process language consciously does not mean that it will always be done; other factors also come into play. The point is simply that the capacity for linguistic monitoring may be related to the onset of other developmental changes that occur at about puberty and which include the ability to formalize rules and concepts.

On occasion, young second language learners have demonstrated a quasi-awareness of language, especially with regard to the notion that two languages are being learned. Young bilinguals, for example, have been observed to keep their two languages separate. They tend not to mix the two (Lindholm and Padilla, 1978) and have been observed to resist mixing languages in conversation or "code switching" (Hatch, 1971). Children have also been observed to play with the language. For example, some children comment that they like certain sounds and one child asked whether *jeudi* was related to *jour de jeu* in French. Instances of a kind of rule-giving also occur; one child commented that the feminine gender in French referred to things that were good and beautiful (Kenyeres, 1938, cited in Hatch, 1978b).

While such examples indicate that some children have a certain awareness of the language, it does not compare with the depth and extent to which older students consciously grasp the grammar of the language. The in-depth knowledge adults possess is made possible by the onset of other developmental processes, such as formal operations, which are not yet available to young children.

The mere capacity for monitoring is not a guarantee that the learner will rely on it. The scope of monitor use depends on a variety of factors, including the learner's personality (see the next chapter), the focus of the linguistic task, and, of course, whether the individual has been exposed formally to the grammar of the language.

Focus on Linguistic Task

Tasks which focus on linguistic manipulation seem to encourage monitoring, while those which focus on communicating do not. A

linguistic manipulation task directs the student's attention to the linguistic operation required by the task. For example, asking a speaker to transform *Maria likes doughnuts* into a negative sentence requires manipulation of the elements in the sentence. A **natural communication task** focuses the student's attention on communicating an idea or opinion to someone rather than on the language forms themselves. In such situations the speaker subconsciously uses the grammar rules acquired to convey the message. (See Chapter 11 for further description of these types of tasks.)

As we will see in our review of acquisition order studies (Chapter 8), a fairly stable order of acquisition has been observed for adults learning English as a second language when the task subjects performed permitted a focus on communication. In a study which focused instead on linguistic manipulation (fill in the blank with the correct morpheme), we saw that a different order was obtained (Larsen-Freeman, 1975). This finding has been replicated by Houck, Robertson and Krashen (1978).

It appears that when individuals are focused on the form of the language, they may apply formally learned, consciously available rules to the language they produce. Thus, to the extent that consciously available rules come into play when speakers are concentrating on linguistic manipulation, the observed order will vary somewhat from the stable order obtained in most communication tasks.

The structures affected, of course, will be only those to which the learner has applied a rule. Other structures remain unaffected. For example, a student of ESL who has consciously learned the third person singular ending on regular verbs in English, but who has not yet subconsciously acquired it, can utilize this conscious knowledge on a grammar test and may perform relatively better in producing this item on a test than in a natural conversation.

Effects of Formal Instruction on Monitoring

It goes without saying that an individual cannot consciously apply rules unless they have been learned. The converse, however, is not true: knowledge of rules does not mean they will be applied. A recent study by Krashen, Sferlazza, Feldman and Fathman (1976) examined two groups of adult subjects who were labeled formal and informal learners. "Formal" learners were defined as those who reported a great deal of classroom ESL training (three to fifteen years) and little informal exposure. The "informal" group consisted of those who reported little schooling in ESL (none to a semester) and had lived in the United States from three months to fifty years. Despite the differences in formal training, the two groups agreed very closely (*rho* = .87, p<.001) in the order of structures observed in an oral task called the *SLOPE* test (cf. Fathman, 1975).[9] Mere conscious knowledge of rules, though necessary for monitor use, does not ensure that they will be applied to the language that learners produce.

It has also been shown that simply asking students to check their (written) work carefully does not guarantee the use of consciously learned rules. Krashen, Butler, Birnbaum, and Robertson (1978) compared orders of structures obtained in a writing task under two conditions. First, ESL students at the University of Southern California were asked to describe in writing a series of pictures under a "free" condition: They were told to simply write as much as possible in five minutes. To further discourage monitoring, they were told that they would be graded on the number of words they could get on paper during this time. In a second "edited" condition, students were asked to check their work carefully. Both a different-subjects and same-subjects design was used: In one version of the experiment, different students participated in each condition, while in another, the same students were used for both.

Two important findings emerged from this study. First, there was only a modest amount of improvement in the edited condition for the six grammatical morphemes that were analyzed (overall improvement was about 6%). Second, both groups showed the familiar stable communication order for the grammatical morphemes analyzed. The only clear difference between the free and edited conditions was that the third person singular morpheme rose in rank in the edited condition; however, it did not rise enough to disturb the overall order.

Thus, even when students were asked to check their work, they apparently chose to focus on its factual correctness, clarity of ideas, or other non-grammatical aspects of their compositions. Or, perhaps they simply rested. It appears that the task itself must force the typical learner to focus on form in order to bring conscious rule-knowledge into play.[10]

More typical, however, is the finding by Schlue (1976), who studied adult self-correction with three foreign students in the United States who were at an intermediate level of proficiency in English. She found that self-corrections in free speech (corrections initiated and made by the student while speaking), while helpful in increas-

9. See Fathman (1975) for details of the *SLOPE* test and test results.
10. See Table 10-1, p. 248 for a partial listing of such manipulation tasks. There are, of course, a few personality types who try to monitor their language while communicating.

ing accuracy, occurred on only about 10% of all errors. The students were generally able to correct most of the errors they detected. Schlue concludes that situations high in communicative urgency (such as natural conversation) find the language learner "attending to the accuracy of his message and the appropriateness of his utterance to the discourse rather than to his grammatical accuracy" (p. 134).

While the monitor makes conscious editing of one's own language possible, it is not the only source of self-correction. Subconsciously acquired grammar also plays such a role. This is most clearly seen when learners report that they correct themselves (or others) by "feel," and are unable to state the rule that has been violated. Though this phenomenon has been observed, very little is known about it.

M.J., an extremely competent free-lance editor we know, does most of her editing by feel. When she has to explain to her clients what grammatical or stylistic rule they violated, she usually asks one of her friends to remind her of the explicit rule. M.J. finds conscious rule-knowledge dispensable and even inadequate for comprehensive editing.

Linguistic Domain of the Monitor

It appears that the linguistic domain of the monitor in most L_2 learners is limited to lower-level rules of the language, those that are easy to conceptualize and do not require mental gymnastics. Conscious knowledge of a rule, however, does not guarantee the learner will use it. Learners have been observed to make many self-described "careless" errors, which they were able to correct themselves and for which they could state the rule violated. When asked to correct themselves, learners have increased their overall accuracy by 6% in some studies and up to 47% in others. The corrections were typically made for lower-level morphological rules.

Researchers have also found that learners are commonly able to produce fairly high-level constructions without being able to state any kind of relevant rule at all. Thus, the ability to produce many of the complex sentences and constructions of the language appears to be the result of subconscious processes rather than conscious ones.

These suggestions arise from observations of second language learners, but they have also been made as a result of experiments in related learning research. "Implicit" (subconscious) and "explicit" (conscious) learning were the focus of an interesting study conducted by A. Reber (1976). Reber asked American college students who were native speakers of English to look at cards with three to eight letters on them. The students were asked to reproduce the sequence of letters after the card was withdrawn. Half the students were told that "it will be to your advantage to figure out what the rules are." The other half were given no special instructions. Neither group was given specific error correction, but they were told whether the sequence they repeated was correct.

Reber reported that the group given no instructions performed better, both on the simple reporting task and on a subsequent test where they were asked whether a given sequence was correct. Reber concluded that "subjects who engaged in an explicit search for rules that define a complex structure performed more poorly in memorizing exemplars of the structure than subjects who operated in a more neutral, implicit fashion" (p. 92).

Reber noted that previous studies of this sort suggested that conscious rule-learning in such situations was helpful. The tasks involved, however, were considerably easier, indicating that conscious learning is only efficient when the task is simple, a conclusion supported by research in second language acquisition.

The instructions to search for rules "produced a strong tendency for subjects to induce or invent rules which were not accurate representations of the complex stimulus structures." Because the rule for the sequence of letters was *complex,* those who looked for rules often got them wrong.

Reber's study suggests that implicit learning is superior when complex rules are involved. Very easy rules, however, may be consciously learned. Reber notes that in situations where an easy rule was to be learned, subjects did not behave "like language learners at all, they operated like linguists" (p. 94).

The notion that complex aspects of grammar are difficult to teach through rule use is also shared by curriculum developers. Rutherford (1975), for example, in his *Modern English* text concerning English as a second lnguage, comments about a notoriously difficult-to-learn rule of English: "The way to learn the correct use of the articles is more through practice than close study of the rules and their many exceptions" (p. 127).

The direct evidence for our suggestion about which aspects of a second language are learnable and usable through conscious rule-learning comes from a variety of case studies. In all cases, we see that a subset of the errors learners make are easily self-correctable, given a focus on correction. In addition, many learners can state the rule violated.

One interesting case study is P., a native speaker of Chinese in her forties, who had come to the United States and began to learn

English when she was in her twenties (Krashen and Pon, 1975). Her errors in casual speech were transcribed during normal family activities over a period of about three weeks. Some 80 errors in all were tabulated.

The researchers report that she "was able to correct nearly every error in the corpus (about 95%) when the errors were presented to her after their commission. In addition, in nearly every case she was able to describe the grammatical principle involved and violated." What kinds of errors were involved? The authors found that "for the most part the rules involved were simple, 'first level' rules (e.g. omission of the third person singular ending, incorrect irregular past tense form, failure to make the verb agree with the subject in number (is/are), use of *much* with countable nouns, etc.)" (p. 126). Besides identifying the domain of the monitor, this study indicates that rules learned consciously are not necessarily incorporated into the language system a person uses when communicating.

Two similar cases are presented by Cohen and Robbins (1976). Two adult second language learners, Eu-lin and Eva, were observed to self-correct errors successfully when asked to do so. Eu-lin simply described her errors as "careless," since she knew the rules. Among Eu-lin's recurrent errors were "-s deletion . . . subject verb number agreement" (Cohen and Robbins, 1976, p. 55). Eva too, ascribed her errors to carelessness. She commented that

> ". . . sometimes I would write something the way I speak. We can say a word more or less in a careless way. But if I take my time, sometimes go over it, that would be much easier . . . Whenever I go over something or take my time, then the rules come to my mind."

Eva's errors were similar to Eu-lin's and P.'s in that they had to do with lower-level morphological rules.

Finally, Duskova (1969) reported that her college EFL students' written errors were also "self-correctable by rule" (p. 20). The error types made were in bound morphology, such as the omission of noun plurals and subject-verb agreement errors.

While many of these apparently easy to correct "careless" errors are recognized by learners, learners demonstrate a great deal of complex knowledge that they cannot possibly trace to any conscious rules they know.

Consider, for example, V., an adult ESL student studied by Stafford and Covitt (1978). Although this student ascribes great importance to the study of grammar (he wrote "grammar is the key to every language" on a questionnaire), and although V. thinks he uses conscious rules when speaking, careful examination by the authors revealed that V. knew hardly any grammar rules at all, speaking and self-correcting instead by "feel."

A similar example is described by Cohen and Robbins (1976), who provide this revealing quote by one of their adult ESL subjects: "I never taught any grammars. I guess I just never learned the rules that well. I know that everytime I speak it's pretty correct, so I never think about grammars. I just write down whatever I feel like it. Every time I write something I just stop thinking. I don't know which (rule) to apply. So I tried a lot of stuff to best fit in writing paragraph. If it fit—what's logical—you get a pretty good chance of getting it right . . ." (p. 59).

Clearly, learners such as this one illustrate that they have many complex constructions firmly under control in their casual speech for which they know no conscious rules at all.

The area of error correction also provides support for the suggestion that conscious rule-learning is limited to lower-level rules. White (1977), for example, allowed adult ESL students to self-correct written versions of their oral output. They managed to correct 47% of their errors successfully. Of these, White's subjects were more successful at correcting lower-level morphological errors (52%) than syntactic errors (27%).

Aptitude, Metalinguistic Ability and the Monitor

In the previous sections, we have seen that the monitor represents one's conscious knowledge of the rules and forms of the language— one's metalinguistic awareness. Obtaining such knowledge about the second language usually depends on formal training. We would expect that the more formal training one has had, the greater one's monitoring capacity will be. We have also seen, however, that the availability of conscious knowledge of the rules of a language does not predict it will be used. Thus, the role of this knowledge in producing a successful L_2 learner is not yet known; many learners are observed to produce quite complex language without being able to state any rules at all.

Given these findings, determining the relation of foreign language aptitude to metalinguistic awareness is a very important avenue for future research.

Foreign language aptitude, which Carroll (1973) defines as the rate at which persons at the secondary school, university and adult level learn a foreign language, has most recently been measured by standardized tests such as the *Modern Language Aptitude Test* (MLAT), and the *Language Aptitude Battery* (LAB). According to Carroll, there are three major components of modern aptitude tests. The first, phonetic coding ability, is the ability to store new language sounds in memory. The relationship between phonetic coding ability and the components of the organizer are not yet clear. This is not the case for the other two components, grammatical sensitivity and inductive ability.

Grammatical sensitivity is defined as "the individual's ability to demonstrate his awareness of the syntactical patterning of sentences in a language" (Carroll, 1973, p. 7). Carroll makes it clear that although performance on this component does not require the subject's actual knowledge of grammatical terminology, it does involve a conscious meta-awareness of grammar. Carroll discusses this in a comparison of conscious knowledge of a language with the subconscious or tacit knowledge entailed in Chomsky's term "competence":

> Although it is often said that linguistic "competence," in the sense defined by Chomsky (1965), involves some kind of "knowledge" of the grammatical rules of a language, "knowledge" is ordinarily out of conscious awareness . . . nevertheless, some adolescents and adults (and even some children) can be made to demonstrate an awareness of the syntactical structure of the sentences they speak . . . even among adults there are large individual differences in this ability, and these individual differences are related to success in learning foreign languages, apparently because this ability is called upon when the student tries to learn grammatical rules and apply them in constructing and comprehending new sentences in that language.
>
> (Carroll, 1973, pp. 7–8)

Grammatical sensitivity is tapped by the *Words in Sentences* subtest of the Carroll-Sapon MLAT, which asks the individual to pick out the word or phrase in one sentence that "does the same thing" in that sentence as a capitalized word in another sentence. Here is a famous example:

1. He spoke VERY well of you.
2. <u>Suddenly</u> <u>the music</u> became <u>quite</u> <u>loud</u>.
       1   2   3   4

Most readers will see that the correct answer is 3, regardless of whether they know the correct grammatical terminology or the grammatical role of "very" and "quite."

Inductive ability is defined as the ability to "examine language

material . . . and from this to notice and identify patterns of correspondence and relationships involving either meaning or grammatical form" (Carroll, 1973, p. 8).

A typical method of measuring this ability is "to present materials in an artificial language in such a way that the individual can
induce the grammatical and semantic rules governing that language" (Carroll, 1973, p. 8).

Inductive ability also appears to draw on conscious learning, since
its goal is the discovery of an explicit, abstract set of rules by means
of a problem-solving approach. (Linguists use a similar process in
writing a grammar.)

Pimsleur's summary of the components of language aptitude is
similar to Carroll's:

> . . . the 'talent' for learning foreign languages consists of three com-
> ponents. The first is verbal intelligence, by which is meant both fa-
> miliarity with words (this is measured in the *Language Aptitude Battery*
> by the "Vocabulary" part) and the ability to reason analytically about
> verbal materials (this is measured by the part called "Language Anal-
> ysis"). The second component is motivation to learn the language . . .
> The third component . . . is called "auditory ability" . . .
>
> (Pimsleur, 1966, p. 182)

The other parts of both Carroll's and Pimsleur's aptitude batteries
deal with auditory factors which are not discussed here. Pimsleur's
motivation component forms an additional part of the *Language Aptitude Battery*.

These descriptions of aptitude make it clear that in large part Carroll's "grammatical sensitivity" and "inductive ability," and Pimsleur's "verbal intelligence" tap conscious linguistic knowledge—
the metalinguistic ability or monitor capacity of learners.

It seems that most current measures of aptitude are more generally
related to the acquisition of metalinguistic skills than to the acquisition of communicative skills. The development of communicative
skills seems to be fairly independent of metalinguistic knowledge.
Thus, *aptitude measures such as the MLAT are probably better predictors of who will attain a high degree of metalinguistic skill
awareness than they are of who is likely to attain communicative
competence in the second language.*

Several studies support this suggestion. First, the validity of aptitude tests is usually determined by correlating scores with grades
in foreign language classes and/or with pencil and paper grammar
tests (Pimsleur, 1966; Carroll, 1963). Such correlations are often but

not always quite high. Pimsleur (1966), for example, reports validity coefficients for MLAT ranging from .13 to .78 for high school and college students (p. 181). Similarly, Gardner (1960) concludes that "language aptitude appears to be of major importance in the acquisition of second language skills acquired through direct instruction" (p. 124). In his study, three subtests of Carroll's *Psi-Lambda Aptitude Test* (*Words in Sentences; Paired Associates; and Spelling Clues*) related to several "school type" tests of French as a foreign language (reading, vocabulary, grammar, pronunciation accuracy, and phonetic discrimination). Gardner and Lambert (1959) presented evidence that "school French achievement," represented by grades in French as well as overall grades, is strongly related to performance on the *Words in Sentences* subtest of the MLAT, "suggesting that the student who is aware of grammatical distinctions in English will do well in French courses where the emphasis is on grammar" (p. 290). Gardner and Lambert also found a "linguistic reasoning factor": scores on the MLAT related to achievement in reading French, a French grammar test, and a test of phonetic discrimination. While these studies were carried out in Canadian English-speaking situations (Montreal), Gardner and Lambert's (1972) subsequent research in the United States confirm these findings. Gardner, Smythe, Clement and Gliksman (1976) also concluded that aptitude related more to classroom skills (grades) than to communicative skills (speech) in French as a foreign language in Grades 7–11 in various English-speaking communities in Canada. In general, the effect of aptitude on performance was stronger for older students, a not unexpected finding since the metalinguistic skills tapped are not usually available to younger students. Finally, in *The Good Language Learner*, Naiman et al. (1978) also reported that the study of grammar alone was not enough. "Several interviewees, who had achieved high marks in their language courses in school, now attached little significance to this aspect of success" (p. 34).

Research now suggests that *attitudinal and motivational factors have more to do with the successful attainment of communicative skills in a second language than metalinguistic awareness does.* In addition to reducing the amount of filtering, high motivation can "determine whether or not the student avails himself of . . . informal language contexts" (Gardner, Smythe, Clement and Gliksman, 1976, p. 200). (See also Oller's *Hypothesis 6* in Oller, 1977.) A similar observation is made by Fillmore in her case study of five children acquiring ESL in an American kindergarten. She describes the most successful English learner as a child who "was strongly motivated to be associated with English-speaking children . . . she sought them out to play with to an extent that none of the other children in the study did" (p. 706). Hatch (1976) too, has documented cases from diary studies where affective and attitudinal factors played a role in the success of child second language acquisition.

Much, if not most, foreign language teaching focuses on the acquisition of formal, conscious knowledge of the language—learning via the monitor. We have seen that such knowledge is not necessarily related to, and indeed is not needed for communicative fluency. Attitudinal factors related to subconscious learning are much better predictors of a student's eventual success in gaining command of a second language. An effort to structure second language teaching programs to enhance subconscious learning and to downplay reliance on metalinguistic skills could lead to second language teaching that takes advantage of the student's internal processors rather than working against them.

SUMMARY

Language learning ultimately occurs in the mind of the learner, where mental structures or mechanisms process and organize the language to which the learner is exposed. Systematic discrepancies between the language that learners produce and the language they hear or read provide the basis from which we can infer the characteristics of otherwise invisible mental structures.

Research suggests that three internal processing factors play a substantial role in second language acquisition: the *filter*, the *organizer*, and the *monitor*.

The **filter** appears to be the first major hurdle that incoming language data must pass. It screens all incoming language based on affective factors: the learner's motives, attitudes, and emotional states.

Three related types of motivation have been observed to affect second language learning: *integrative motivation,* or the desire to participate in the life of the community that speaks the language; *instrumental motivation,* or the desire to use the language for practical reasons such as getting a job; and the *social group identification motive,* which is the desire to acquire proficiency in a language spoken by a social group with which the learner identifies.

The learner's emotional states are also part of the filter. Research has shown that the **less anxious** and **more relaxed** the learner, the better language acquisition proceeds.

Filtering determines (a) which target language models the learner selects; (b) which parts of the new language the learner attends to first;

implies consciousness

(c) when language efforts cease; and (d) how fast a learner can acquire a language.

The *organizer* subconsciously processes data which the filter lets in. It is responsible for the learner's gradual organization of the new language system.

The functioning of the organizer is reflected in three aspects of learners' verbal performance: in the series of *transitional constructions* learners systematically use before a structure is acquired; in the *errors* that most L_2 learners regularly make; and in the common *order* in which L_2 learners acquire the structures of the new language.

While the imprint of the organizer on learners' behavior is clear, L_2 scholars have not yet succeeded in specifying its operational principles. Attempts to characterize the organizer in terms of *linguistic complexity* (the amount of discrete linguistic knowledge in a structure) have had limited success. An alternative approach using the concept of *learning complexity* (the degree of difficulty a learner experiences in acquiring a structure) is promising, but still being developed.

The *monitor* is responsible for conscious linguistic processing. Learners can use the linguistic knowledge they gain through monitoring to consciously formulate sentences and to correct or edit their speech and writing.

The degree to which the monitor is used depends on a number of factors: (a) *The learner's age or level of cognitive development.* It appears that monitoring is more easily done when learners have reached the formal operations stage, when they can manipulate abstract relationships between ideas; (b) *The verbal task being performed.* Tasks that focus the learner's attention of linguistic form bring monitoring into play; (c) *The learner's personality.* Learners who are insecure, self-conscious, and afraid to make errors tend to use the monitor more than others.

It appears that the use of the monitor is limited to lower-level rules of the language, those that are easy to conceptualize. Conscious knowledge of a rule, however, does not guarantee that a learner will use it. Conversely, many people can correct grammatical errors or stylistic flaws "by feel."

Research evidence indicates that the successful acquisition of communicative skills in the new language depends primarily on filtering and organizing factors rather than on monitoring (which linguists, in contrast, cannot do without).

STUDY QUESTIONS

1. It is the end of the year and, being a conscientious language teacher, you have diagnosed your students' verbal performance in terms of all the structures presented in class. You find that most students have not learned structures x, y, and z. Discuss briefly three factors you might consider to explain your finding.

2. The seven- and ten-year-old children of Turkish guestworkers in Munich are enrolled in a German public school. The children's father is working in an automobile plant and their mother keeps house. What would the primary motivation for learning German be:
   a. For the children?
   b. For the father?
   c. For the mother?

3. If a linguist has written a grammar of a certain language, would he or she necessarily be a fluent speaker of the language? Explain your answer.

4. Schumann, Holroyd, Campbell and Ward (1978) reported that subjects who reported greater depth of hypnotizability performed better on a pronunciation test of Thai words, a language previously unknown to them. Can this be related to the operation of the filter, the organizer, or the monitor? (Subjects heard the Thai words once and then repeated them.) Explain.

4

Effects of Personality and Age on Second Language Acquisition

Even within the same language environment, some learners acquire a second language better or faster than others. Although everyone has the same innate language processing mechanisms (described in the previous chapter), certain individual characteristics affect how much individual learners use each processor.

Researchers are now trying to pinpoint which aspects of the age and personality of the second language learner make a difference in the language learning process, and then to determine why those characteristics have such an effect. This research has important implications for pedagogy. If we understand why, for example, self-confident people are good L_2 learners or why children are ultimately more successful than adults in learning to speak a new language, it may be possible to alter curricula or to tailor programs to individual students in order to help otherwise unsuccessful L_2 students succeed.

EFFECTS OF PERSONALITY

The term "personality" is generally understood even though it is not defined to scientific satisfaction. When we ask questions such as: Is X an introvert or extrovert? Impulsive or reflective? Authoritarian or submissive? Charming or dull?, we believe that the answers reveal something about an individual's personality. Such personal characteristics, along with countless others, are what we consider to make up personality. Suffice it here to define personality informally as an aggregate of traits characteristic of a particular individual.

Although the construct itself is vaguely defined, the operation of personality factors in second language learning is quite evident. The personality traits researchers have so far studied in relation to language learning include self-confidence level, capacity to empathize, and the degree of logicality or tendency to analyze.

Self-Confidence

Not surprisingly, nearly all the available literature suggests that self-confidence is very much related to second language development. All things being equal, the self-confident, secure person is a more successful language learner.

Two measures of self-confidence are anxiety level and extroversion. In nearly all the studies conducted to determine the personality characteristics associated with successful L₂ learning, researchers have concluded that *lower anxiety levels* and a *tendency to be outgoing* were connected with successful L₂ acquisition.

Learners who are eager to try new and unpredictable experiences, and who are willing to guess before knowing for sure, are likely to seek out situations that require real communication in the new language. These people have been observed to use a larger range of forms in the target language than those with "wait and see" personalities who are at the same level of L₂ development. The adventuresome have been observed to find language learning relatively painless and to learn fairly quickly.

The studies that led to these conclusions were described in the previous chapter in the section on the filter. They do not show precisely how self-confidence and language learning relate, but they do demonstrate the existence of the relationship. We suggest that self-confident people have the advantage of not fearing rejection as much as those with high anxiety levels and are therefore more likely to put themselves in learning situations and to do so repeatedly. They are thrown into less personal turmoil when they make mistakes than those who are more self-conscious. This probably enhances subconscious language learning because they are more able to take in and process what they hear at any given moment. To use our terms, the filter of the self-confident person has a larger screen. In addition, self-confident people are less hampered by the conscious operation of the monitor because they are not so worried about how they appear.

Empathy

Webster's defines empathy as the "capacity for participation in another's feelings or ideas." A number of investigators have attempted to relate an individual's capacity for empathy to language learning success, but the results have been inconclusive. It has been observed, however, that learners with authoritarian dispositions do not seem to learn a second language as easily as less rigid personalities. Learning a language requires careful listening to others and caring more about communicating ideas than about avoiding speech errors. Neither of these characteristics is typical of authoritarian personalities.

Because of the ambiguity of the research findings on the relationship between empathy and L_2 learning, we will not summarize them here. The interested reader may refer to them directly (Schumann, 1975; Naiman et al., 1978; Guiora et al., 1972 and 1972a; and Guiora et al., 1975). We would like to point out, however, that while one might expect a strong relationship between an individual's degree of empathy and his or her success in L_2 performance, it is unlikely that someone's "capacity for participation in another's feelings or ideas" would be measured by linguistic manipulation tasks of the sort most investigators have used to determine success in L_2 learning. If empathy is indeed an important factor in L_2 success, it is more likely to be manifested in the development of communication skills, which enable participation in another's feelings and ideas far more than linguistic manipulation tasks do. Researchers might find that studies using communication tasks as indicators of L_2 success would yield a more systematic and positive relationship between characteristics such as empathy and L_2 acquisition.

Analytical Tendencies

A certain highly rational, "analytic personality" has been identified in the L_2 research literature. According to the literature in experimental psychology, "field independent" persons are able to perceive individual items that may be relatively difficult to distinguish from their visual background. This ability is thought to be associated with a more analytical (left-brained) cognitive style. The "field dependent" person, on the other hand, "perceives all parts of the organized field as a total experience" (Naiman et al., 1978). Field dependence has been associated with the empathic and open personality.

A predictable relationship between field dependence, field independence and successful language learning seems to be emerging from the little research that has been done so far. More analytical, field independent characteristics appear to be related to the acquisition of metalinguistic skills through conscious learning, while the field dependent person seems to be more apt to acquire communication skills through subconscious learning.

Naiman et al. (1975), for example, reported findings that appear to confirm this for students learning French as a second language. Another team of researchers, Tucker, Hamayan, and Genesee (1976) reported some relationship between field independence and performance on an overall test of French in grade 7, but they did not find any relationship for this characteristic with other, more communicative measures of French proficiency.

H. D. Brown (1977) has also suggested that field independence may be related to conscious learning, while field dependence may be related to subconscious acquisition. He notes that the field dependent person, "with his empathy and social outreach, will be a more effective and motivated communicator" (p. 350).

Personality and Monitor Use

The monitor appears to be the only fully conscious internal mechanism learners use as they acquire a second language. The available data suggest that the degree to which monitoring is used depends primarily on personality characteristics, especially self-confidence and self-consciousness. The more self-confident and the less self-conscious a learner is, the less reliance he or she places on the monitor.[1]

Researchers have identified three types of monitor users: overusers, underusers and optimal users.

A great concern with correctness and a hesitance about one's control over the new language seems to bring out analytical characteristics which are manifested through consciously edited and monitored speech. Overusers rely a great deal on their consciously acquired rule knowledge when they speak, and they tend to place correctness ahead of communication.

More self-confident learners rely on selective monitoring or no monitoring at all. Selective monitoring can increase accuracy without significantly interfering with communication. Such "optimal" monitor users have generally acquired a substantial amount of the L_2 subsconsciously.

1. When learners are asked to perform non-communicative linguistic manipulation tasks, however, monitor use is more likely, as metalinguistic skills are called for.

Krashen (1978) and Stafford and Covitt (1978) also report examples of successful L_2 learners who make virtually no use of monitoring, relying totally on their subconsciously acquired system as children do. People who make little use of the monitor appear to have a more outgoing, less inhibited personality than the self-conscious and introverted personalities of people who rely heavily on the monitor. Underusers are typically not embarrassed at their own errors.

EFFECTS OF AGE

The belief that children are better at language acquisition than adults is supported by both scientific and anecdotal evidence. Children acquiring second languages in natural environments are more likely to eventually sound like native speakers than adults are. Adults may appear to make greater progress initially, but children nearly always surpass them. The turning point in language acquisition ability seems to occur at about puberty. Children under ten who experience enough natural communication in the target language nearly always succeed in attaining native-like proficiency, while those over fifteen rarely do, although they often come very close. Between these ages, about half are completely successful and about half are not.

The reasons for child-adult differences in L_2 acquisition are not well understood. The assumption has been that adults do not learn languages as well as children because they are not able to. Research evidence shows, however, that the language environment typically provided for adult second language learners tends to be impoverished in the natural communication and the concrete referents which foster subconscious language learning.

Research findings regarding age are especially important when educational policy decisions must be made concerning the age or grade level at which students are offered second language instruction. How soon can one begin or how late can one wait before introducing L_2 instruction? Although definitive answers cannot be given without considering the socio-political situation and the goals of parents and students, the research on the effects of age should provide some assistance in making such decisions.

The available research comparing aspects of L_2 performance in children and adults is basically of two types: (1) that which compares the level of proficiency eventually attained by learners who arrived in the host country at different ages, comparing especially those who arrive before and after puberty, and (2) that which compares the rate at which aspects of language are acquired by younger and older L_2 learners.

Proficiency and Age of Arrival

Most of the studies comparing attained L_2 proficiency and age of arrival in the host country have focused primarily on pronunciation.

Pronunciation It has been said that "Almost everyone learns the sound patterns of a language perfectly as a child, and yet, almost no one can learn the sound patterns of a language perfectly as an adult" (Scovel, 1969, p. 245). While some adults do achieve very high levels of proficiency in pronouncing a second language, they seem to be the exception rather than the rule.

Oyama (1976), for example, studied a group of Italian-born male immigrants who had lived in the United States from five to eighteen years and who had learned English as a second language. In general, they were well educated; nearly all reported that they had had "some college." Each subject was asked to read a paragraph and tell a story in English; the latter task was to describe a situation in which you felt you were in danger of losing your life, a technique first used by Labov as a method eliciting natural casual speech. The speech samples were recorded and played to a panel of native speaker judges (graduate students in linguistics), who rated them on a five point scale (1 = no accent, and 5 = heavy accent).

Oyama found a high degree of consistency among her judges (obtaining reliability coefficients of .80 for the story and .87 for the paragraph). The results for the paragraph are given in Table 4–1.

TABLE 4-1 Mean Accent Scores on Paragraph Reading as a Function of Immigrants' Age of Arrival and Number of Years in the United States*

Number of Years in the United States	Age of Arrival		
	6–10	11–15	16–20
12–18	1.27	2.27	3.72
5–11	1.37	2.58	3.50

Scale ranged from 1 (no foreign accent) to 5 (heavy foreign accent).

*Adapted from S. Oyama (1973), *A Sensitive Period for the Acquisition of a Second Language.* Ph.D. Dissertation, Harvard. Also adapted from Oyama, 1976. Reprinted by permission of the author.

As the table indicates, she found the subjects' age of arrival had the most effect on the degree of accent. Youngest arrivals had the least accent, but the amount of time the subjects spent in the United States did not influence the accent. The results for the story-telling task were quite similar.

Seliger, Krashen, and Ladefoged (1975), present results that agree with Oyama's concerning the relationship of age of arrival and pronunciation proficiency. In this study, undergraduate linguistics students of UCLA, Queens College, and Bar Ilan University were asked to interview immigrants who had lived in the United States or Israel for many years. Subjects were asked whether they felt that most ordinary, native target-language-speakers (English or Hebrew) could tell that they were not native speakers of those languages. The results, which clearly agree with Oyama's, are given in Table 4-2.

Seliger et al. found that those in the ten-to-fifteen-year-old group who reported a "conscious effort" to lose their foreign accents were not significantly more successful than those who said they made no such effort. A subsequent paper by Krashen and Seliger (1975) reported that length of time spent in the new country bore little relationship to accent acquisition; in fact, there was a slight tendency for those who reported the presence of a foreign accent to have lived in the new country longer. These results are quite consistent with what Oyama found in her study.

A third study examining this question was conducted by Asher and Garcia (1969). They investigated age of arrival in the United States and second language accent in seventy-one Cuban immigrants, aged nine to seventeen. Their subjects were asked to read four sentences in English and were allowed to rehearse the material

TABLE 4-2   Number of Immigrants to the United States and Israel Reporting Degree of Foreign Accent by Age of Arrival*

Age of Arrival	Accent	Don't Know	No Accent
	N	N	N
9 and under	5†	4	47
	2‡	3	30
10 to 15	37†	6	27
	9‡	1	20
16 and over	106†	4	7
	50‡	1	5

*From H. Seliger, S. Krashen and P. Ladefoged (1975), "Maturational Constraints in the Acquisition of a Native-Like Accent in Second Language Learning." *Language Sciences 36*, pp. 20–22. Reprinted by permission of the authors.
†English
‡Hebrew

TABLE 4-3   Percentage of Cuban Immigrants Judged on English Pronunciation, by Age of Arrival in the United States*

Degree of Pronunciation	Age of Arrival	Percent of Subjects
Near Native	1–6	68%
	7–12	41%
	13–19	7%
Slight Accent	1–6	32%
	7–12	43%
	13–19	27%
Definite Accent	1–6	0%
	7–12	16%
	13–19	66%

*Adapted from Asher and Garcia (1969), "The Optimal Age to Learn a Foreign Language." *Modern Language Journal 53,* pp. 334–341. Reprinted by permission of the publisher.

in advance. Judges were a group of American junior high school students who rated the samples on a four point scale (A= native speaker of English, B= near-native, C= slight accent, D= a definite accent). Asher and Garcia reported that their judges agreed with each other perfectly 70% of the time. Table 4–3 shows their results.

While the previous studies found little relationship between years in the U.S. and acquisition of a native-like accent, Asher and Garcia noted an interaction between years in the U.S. and age of arrival, concluding that "a Cuban child had the greatest probability of achieving a near-native pronunciation of English when he was six or younger and lived in the United States five years or more. A child who came to America when he was thirteen or older had a small chance of acquiring a near-native pronunciation even if he lived here five years or more. The child who was between seven and twelve when he arrived here and then lived here five years or more had a fifty-fifty chance of achieving a near-native pronunciation" (p. 339).

These three studies concluded that age of arrival is a powerful determinant of ultimate success in accent acquisition, and all confirm that puberty is an important turning point with respect to this aspect of language learning.

Scovel (1977) conducted a different kind of study dealing with the question of age and the acquisition of phonology. He found an interesting relationship between age and the ability to distinguish native from non-native English. His subjects were asked to listen to tapes of native and non-native speakers of English (the non-natives, however, were pre-selected; only those with "excellent pronunciation" were used), and to indicate whether the speakers were native speakers of English. Scovel found that his adult subjects were nearly completely successful. His child subjects got better with age, the youngest (ages five and six) getting about 75% correct. Interestingly, he notes that "the adult criterion is reached by the nine and ten years olds . . ." (p. 7), approximately the age at which foreign accents emerge. This seems to link production and recognition: "It is . . . possible," Scovel reports, "that the competence to recognize non-native speech is simultaneous in its development with the performance limitations which account for the production of non-native speech" (p. 11).

Still another phenomenon related to child-adult differences in the acquisition of phonology has been suggested by Labov (1966), who proposes that similar constraints exist with respect to the acquisition of a second dialect. "New York speech," according to Labov, is acquired by non-New Yorkers if they move to New York before puberty. To test this hypothesis, Krashen and Seliger (1975) asked linguistics students to interview people living in the New York City area who were not born in New York. Subjects were first asked if they recognized "New York speech." All did, confirming Labov's claim that there is an agreed-upon recognized dialect spoken in New York. Then the subjects were asked whether non-New Yorkers took them for New Yorkers from their speech when they traveled outside New York. The results of this survey are given in Table 4-4, which shows trends similar to those seen in the Seliger et al. second lan-

TABLE 4-4 Answers to the question: "When you travel outside New York, do people think you are a New Yorker by your speech?"*

Age of Arrival in New York	Yes	No
3–9	31	16
10–15	20	25
16 and over	11†	36

*From S. Krashen and H. Seliger (1975b), "Maturational Constraints in the Acquisition of a Second Language and Second Dialect." *Language Sciences 38*, pp. 28–29. Reprinted by permission of the authors.

†Two of these subjects arrived in New York at age 16.

guage survey, but with less sharp breaks between the groups. Again, years lived in New York had no effect. The data thus confirm Labov's suggestion and further implicate puberty as an important turning point in dialect acquisition as well, at least as far as pronunciation is concerned.

Grammar   Unfortunately, there is less available on child-adult differences in the degree of proficiency ultimately attained in grammar. Oyama's work is again useful here. In addition to the two tests of accent described earlier, Oyama's Italian-born subjects also took several tests involving the syntactic and semantic components of the grammar. In two of these, a clear effect of age of arrival was observed. In the "sentence through noise" task (a test first used in Spolsky, Siguard, Sako, Walker and Arturburn, 1968), subjects heard twelve sentences that were masked by white noise. Each subject's score was the total number of words correctly reproduced. Oyama suggests "that it may be this highly coordinated interpretive skill . . . that is lacking in the person who complains that he [or she] understands speech in [the] second language perfectly well under normal circumstances, but comprehension drops drastically in noisy environments or on the phone." The Italian-born subjects' performance on this test was similar to that seen earlier in the paragraph and story-telling tests used to probe pronunciation ability. Age of arrival and performance were significantly correlated ($r = .57$, $p < .001$), indicating that those who arrived earlier scored higher on the test.

Similar results were obtained from Oyama's "anomalous sentences" task, in which subjects were asked to decide which of two sentences was grammatically acceptable. Again, those who arrived earliest did best and years spent in the United States had no effect. (Performance on the other tests used by Oyama probing syntactic and semantic abilities in English [detection of ambiguities and "inventions," that is, making up meanings for noun compounds] did not show significant correlations with age of arrival or with years spent in the United States. This failure to produce significant results may be due to their lack of validity as language tests rather than to the lack of relationship between age of arrival and competence.)

In a more recent report, Patkowski (1980) also found evidence that age of arrival is related to syntactic proficiency. Patkowski tested sixty-seven immigrants who had come to the United States before age fifteen, and who had lived in the United States for at least five years. Interviews between these subjects and native speakers were tape recorded and transcribed. The written transcripts were then rated by two trained judges, who rated them on a zero to five scale, where 0 = unable to function in the language, and 5 = native control of grammar. Patkowski found that the younger the students were when they arrived, the higher the judges' rating. Further statistical analysis showed that the amount of exposure to English did not relate to proficiency.

From these investigations, it seems clear that the degree of native-like pronunciation ultimately attained, whether in a second language or a second dialect, depends largely on the age of arrival of the learner in the host country. The younger the learner upon arrival, the more likely that native-like pronunciation will be attained, and the available data suggest that this is also true for syntax (Patkowski, 1980).

Rate of Acquisition

The evidence we have reviewed indicates that children are more successful than adults in learning a second language. They are not, however, always faster. Several studies suggest that adults seem to progress faster, especially in the very early stages.

Snow and Hoefnagel-Hohle (1978) tested native speakers of English living in Holland, including children and adults. Their "beginners" had been in Holland less than three months, while "advanced" subjects had been living in Holland at least one year. Tests included pronunciation of Dutch (imitation of a native speaker), auditory discrimination, morphology (subjects were asked to inflect nonsense words, as in Berko, 1958), the *Peabody Picture Vocabulary Test*, a sentence repetition test, and a translation test. The beginners were scored for tests given four-and-a-half months apart; the advanced subjects were tested once. While no age differences were apparent in the pronunciation tests, older subjects did indeed do better in syntax and morphology tests.

Snow and Hoefnagel-Hohle summarize their results as follows: "(1) Considerable improvement occurred in all aspects of knowledge of Dutch for subjects of all ages. However, this improvement occurred at different rates for the different aspects and the different age groups. (2) Older learners seemed to have an advantage over younger learners in acquiring the rule-governed aspects of a second language morphology and syntax . . . the teenagers did better than the adults . . . (this) reflected simply rate of acquisition, not an upper limit on ability, since age differences on these tests diminished and disappeared with longer residence in Holland; (3) There were no or very small age differences for tests reflecting control of the phonetic system . . ."(p. 552).

Further evidence for older children's faster rate of grammatical learning is seen in Fathman (1975). Fathman administered her *SLOPE* test, an oral measure, to about 200 children acquiring English as a second language in Washington, D.C. Her results "indicated that there was some relationship between age and rate of learning. Among children exposed to English the same amount of time, the older (11–15) children scored higher on the morphology and syntax subtests, whereas the younger (6–10) children received higher ratings in phonology. There were, however, no major differences observed in the *order* in which children of different ages learned to produce the structures included in the test"(p. 245).

Ervin-Tripp (1974) reports similar findings for syntax acquisition. She tested American children, ages four through nine, who were acquiring French as a second language through "peer interaction" and French language schooling in Switzerland. Her tests included syntax comprehension (children acted out the sentences they heard with dolls or animals), morphology (pronoun gender and number), as well as imitation and translation tests. With respect to accent, Ervin-Tripp found that "for most features of segmental phonology the children above seven learned faster than the younger children" (p. 123). The older children were also better at morphology and syntax: "On virtually all the tests the nine-year-olds were always correct in French, including a child in Geneva for only six months" (p. 124). (No child had been in Switzerland more than nine months at the time of testing.) The morphology and syntax results are consistent with Fathman's and with Snow and Hoefnagel-Hohle's; however, the pronunciation results are not.

Krashen, Long, and Scarcella (1979) suggest that the difference in the length of residence of subjects in the Fathman and Ervin-Tripp studies may be responsible for these differences. Krashen et al. hypothesize that older children do in fact acquire pronunciation more rapidly, but that younger children catch up to them and eventually surpass them. Children in the Ervin-Tripp study had been in the country for a maximum of nine months, while the minimum length of residence in Fathman's study was one year. Snow and Hoefnagel-Hohle (1977), in a laboratory study, also confirm that older children acquire pronunciation skills more rapidly.

On the other hand, Yamada, Takatsuka, Kotake, and Kurusu (1980) report that younger children are more successful at memorizing vocabulary and pronouncing new words in a second language. Their subjects were seven-, nine-, and eleven-year-old Japanese children who were asked to learn four English words. They were taught the words by being shown a picture, while the experimenter named the item shown. Yamada et al. found that the younger children not only learned the items faster, but also had the impression that "the pronunciation of the first graders was generally better than that of the fifth graders" (p. 246). This question, clearly, is far from settled.

It appears that for syntax and morphology, adults, at least in early stages, proceed faster than younger children, although older children, around ten years of age, may be the fastest of all.

Sources of Age Differences

A number of suggestions have been made concerning the sources of the observed child-adult differences in L_2 acquisition. While no single source by itself appears to be adequate to explain the available findings, each holds promise in accounting for the differences between children and adults learning a second language.

The first proposal focuses on *biological factors.* This explanation revolves around the question of whether the adult brain is fundamentally different from the child brain, and whether this accounts for the differences observed. A second explanation focuses on the learner's *cognitive developmental stage,* suggesting that the onset of "formal operations," the ability to formulate abstract hypotheses, is a major determinant of child-adult differences observed. A third explanation proposes differences in the affective *filter* as a source of child-adult differences. This explanation addresses the question of whether the adult is generally less able to achieve the affective mental state necessary for acquisition. Factors such as self-consciousness and hesitance are suggested as causing significantly more filtering of what the learner hears, thus reducing what can be processed by the organizer and, consequently, acquired. The fourth proposal, and the last we shall consider, suggests *differences in the language environment* for children and adults as a source of difference for L_2 acquisition. Children appear to receive much more concrete here-and-now language than adults, who are typically talked to about things for which referents are often not clear or obvious from the non-linguistic environment. This difference, it is proposed, affects adults' and children's ability to process and, hence, acquire language.

As we shall see from the more detailed discussion of each of these proposals below, it is very likely that several of these factors interact to cause the differences that have been observed between young children and adults who are learning a second language.

Biological Factors

Development of Cerebral Dominance

Lenneberg (1967) hypothesized that the development of specialization of functions in the left and right sides of the brain ("cerebral dominance" or "lateralization") begins in childhood and is completed at puberty. Puberty is the time when foreign accents emerge and when "automatic acquisition from mere exposure to a given language seems to disappear" (Lenneberg, 1967, p. 179). In our terms, Lenneberg hypothesized that the ability of the organizer to subconsciously build up a new language system deteriorates after puberty, when the brain's left and right hemispheres have developed specialized functions.

For most people (nearly all right-handers and most left-handers), language and other "analytic" functions are located on the left side of the brain,[2] while spatial and configurational abilities are located on the right side.[3] There are several methods for determining which side of the brain is used. We know that the left side of the brain is involved in the language function in adults for the following reasons (from Krashen, in Wittrock et al., 1977):

1. Loss of speech caused by brain damage occurs far more frequently from leftsided lesions than from rightsided lesions.

2. When the left hemisphere is temporarily anesthetized, loss of speech results; but when the right hemisphere is anesthetized this generally does not happen.

3. When competing simultaneous verbal material is presented to the two ears (a procedure called "dichotic listening"), the words or digits presented to the right ear are more often recalled correctly and subjects can react to them faster than those presented to the left ear. This right-ear advantage presumably results from better right-ear connections to the left hemisphere.

4. During verbal tasks, whether performance is overt or covert, researchers have found signs of greater electrical activity in the left hemisphere. This is shown by analysis of brain waves; for example,

2. Recent research has conclusively shown that the left hemisphere is specialized for more than language. For discussion of these left brain mental abilities and their relation to language and language acquisition, see Krashen (1973a, 1976a) and Wittrock, Beatty, Bogen, Gazzaniga, Jerison, Krashen, Nebes and Taylor (1977).
3. For review of the "other side of the brain," see Bogen (1969, 1969a)

the more active side of the brain produces less "alpha," the brain wave associated with resting states.

Lenneberg (1967) presented the hypothesis that the potential for the language function is in both hemispheres in very young children. With increasing age, the left hemisphere assumes more and more of the responsibility for language until around puberty, when the adult level of cerebral asymmetry is reached. Lenneberg based this hypothesis on the following evidence:

1. Right hemisphere damage occasionally causes speech deficits in children, while it rarely does in adults. This indicates a greater right hemisphere role for language in children as compared to adults.
2. When the left hemisphere is removed in an adult, total aphasia (loss of language) results. In children, this does not occur. This also means that the right hemisphere in children is more active in the language function.
3. Children appear to recover from aphasia resulting from damage to one side of the brain, after language development has already begun, much better than adults do.

Lenneberg suggested that the transfer of the language function from one hemisphere to another was related to the "plasticity" required to acquire language naturally and completely. Scovel (1969) states this explicitly with respect to accent acquisition: ". . . the same plasticity that accounts for the ability of the child's brain to relocate speech to the non-dominant hemisphere accounts for the plasticity that must be evident in the neurophysiological mechanisms underlying the production of the sound patterns of a second language" (p. 252).

Lenneberg's arguments are impressive. There is, however, evidence that the development of lateralization occurs much earlier than puberty. Some researchers have argued for a "lateralization by five" position, while others hold a "lateralization by zero" position, that is, cerebral asymmetry is present at birth or even before.

Before reviewing these positions, we must make one more point clear. The demonstration that lateralization is complete by a certain age x, does not demonstrate that learners younger than x can acquire second languages perfectly while learners older than x cannot. The association of cerebral dominance with language acquisition ability has never been substantiated. Lenneberg and Scovel both noted the coincidence of the lateralization by puberty hypothesis and the age of the emergence of foreign accents. In Scovel's words, "the simultaneous occurrence of brain lateralization and the advent of foreign accents is too great a coincidence to be left neglected" (p. 252). Evidence showing that the completion of the development of lateralization occurs at a different age, however, would indicate that lateralization and the ability to acquire a second language completely are *not directly related.* Observed child-adult differences might have another or various sources.

The "lateralization by five" hypothesis was proposed by Krashen (1973; also Krashen and Harshman, 1972), who re-analyzed Lenneberg's data and presented new evidence. Referring back to Lenneberg's three arguments, Krashen showed that the data Lenneberg used to support points (1) and (2) were also consistent with lateralization by five. Right hemisphere brain damage producing speech disturbance appears to be limited to ages five and under in the studies Lenneberg cites. A review of the hemispherectomy literature shows that in the vast majority of cases, the brain damage occurred before age five. Moreover, additional cases of childhood aphasia, that were not available to Lenneberg at the time his book was written, clearly show that the percentage of cases of speech disturbance associated with right hemisphere damage in children older than five is about the same as that seen in adults, a result that is inconsistent with lateralization by puberty.

Thus, Lenneberg's data were shown to be consistent with lateralization by five, as well as with lateralization by puberty, and new data on unilateral brain damage pointed exclusively to age five. The ability of children to recover from brain damage, Lenneberg's third point, may be due to factors other than the presence of right hemisphere language. In addition, most dichotic listening studies done in recent years supported the lateralization by five position, showing no development in right ear advantage in children after age five (Berlin, Hughes, Lowe-Bell and Berlin, 1973; Dorman and Geffner, 1973). One study, by Satz, Bakker, Teunissen, Goebel, and Vander Vlugt (1975), claims a different developmental course for longer and more complex stimuli. (See Krashen, 1975.)

More recently, clear signs of hemispheric asymmetry have been found in newborns and very young children. Molfese (1972) and Gardiner, Schulman and Walter (1973) found evidence of more electrical activity over the left hemisphere in infants presented with speech stimuli. Anatomical asymmetries similar to those seen in the adult brain have been reported in both full-term and premature infants (Witelson and Pallie, 1973; Teszner, 1972). Wada, Clarke and Hamm (1975), moreover, reported such asymmetries in fetal infants as young as twenty-nine weeks post-gestational age. From this sort of evidence, it has been proposed that there is no development of cerebral dominance at all (Kinsbourne, 1975).

The controversy over the developmental course of cerebral dominance and its significance continues to rage. Krashen (1975a) proposed that a small degree of lateralization exists in babies, with the adult level being achieved by around five, synthesizing the age five and age zero positions. Related to this, Krashen and Harshman (1972) proposed that the development of cerebral dominance and the maturation of mental abilities necessary for first language acquisition go hand in hand. Brown and Jaffe (1975) have argued that lateralization may continue throughout life, with greater specialization developing with age (see also Seliger, 1977). What must be emphasized, however, is that nearly all of the evidence shows that the development of cerebral dominance is complete well before puberty, and is thus probably not responsible for changes in second language acquisition ability associated with this age.

Of course, there may be some as yet undiscovered neurological basis for linguistic puberty. It seems unlikely now, however, that cerebral dominance, once the leading candidate for an explanation of child-adult differences, is responsible. Moreover, if such an obvious change in the brain did take place at this time, and if it were related to language acquisition, one might expect child-adult differences to be greater than they are.

Even those who accepted the completion of cerebral dominance as a biological barrier to adult language acquisition acknowledged that many adults might succeed in the acquisition of a second language. Nevertheless, the belief that such a deep-seated difference between children and adults exists discourages not only investigation into other possible causes for child-adult differences, but also individual effort in teaching and learning. The evidence for subconscious acquisition by adults, and the demonstration that lateralization does not set up a rigid obstacle to adults' second language achievement, is encouraging for both the learner and the teacher. These results suggest that the organizer functions in the acquisition process for both adults and children. Observed child-adult differences, therefore, may have their bases in other domains.

Cognitive Factors   With the lack of convincing evidence for a "biological barrier" to second language acquisition by adults, but allowing, at the same time, that real child-adult differences in second language acquisition do exist, we turn now to other possible explanations for the observed child-adult differences.

One alternative explanation that has been proposed for child-adult differences is Piaget's "formal operations" stage (Inhelder and Piaget, 1958) which was discussed in Chapter 3, p. 60. To summarize, it has been suggested that (1) the formal thinker thinks in terms of general solutions to problems, in terms of rules rather than in terms of *ad hoc* solutions; (2) he or she can arrive at abstract ideas without necessarily working through concrete objects; and (3) he or she can "step back" from his or her ideas and have "ideas about ideas."

How do formal operations influence language acquisition and how do they predict child-adult differences? Interestingly, several scholars have argued that the adult's cognitive superiority should make adults better than children at language acquisition. Genesee (1977), while not referring specifically to formal operations, notes that "the adolescent's more mature cognitive system, with its capacity to abstract, classify, and generalize, may be better suited for the complex task of second language learning than the unconscious, automatic kind of learning which is thought to be characteristic of young children" (p. 148). In support of his argument, Genessee cites several studies that indicate a superior *rate* of second language achievement in classroom studies for older learners, concluding "there is a rather noteworthy consensus among these studies concerning the learning rates of students at different ages—older students seem to be more efficient learners than younger students. That is to say, given the same amount of instruction, or even less, adolescents will learn as much or more than younger children" (p. 150).

Taylor (1974) also makes the point that adults' cognitive maturity should allow them to deal with the abstract nature of language better than children. Taylor suggests that cognitive differences between children and adults could not account for observed child-adult differences, because adults have a cognitive superiority rather than a cognitive deficiency.

The available evidence suggests, however, that formal operations relate directly to *conscious* language learning, which, as we have seen, apparently plays a minor role in learning to speak a new language.

The suggestion that formal operations allows the development of the conscious grammar clarifies the insights of the researchers cited above: it helps explain the findings that adults are better and faster conscious learners than children. Adults can talk about rules like subject-verb agreement, or relative clause formation. Some children do have some degree of meta-awareness of language, but it is typically restricted to the most elementary rules of grammar (e.g. singular-plural differences, gender distinctions) and, as far as we know, is rarely applied to actual performance. The availability of conscious rules, however, permits very early production. Adults can use the patterns of their first languages and insert L_2 vocabulary words in the slots. This allows immediate participation in simple conversations. Using such unnatural means for producing language has its limitations, however, and learners who acquire the new language system subconsciously will eventually surpass those who are dependent on conscious rules, despite the conscious learner's head start.

It appears that cognitive differences between children and adults can explain some child-adult differences. Hypothesizing a relationship between formal operations and conscious learning successfully predicts (1) the age at which the capacity for extensive metalinguistic awareness develops; and (2) adult initial advantages in rate of learning. Cognitive considerations, however, do not address the fact that, in the long run, children typically outperform adults in second language production. To account for this, we turn to a discussion of affective explanations for child-adult differences.

Affective Factors   It has been argued that the adult is more self-conscious than the child, is less able to identify with other groups, and is, in general, less able to achieve the open mental state necessary for language acquisition to take place. According to this view, a greater amount of affective filtering by adults explains children's ultimately superior performance: the adult tunes out various aspects of the language environment and ceases language acquisition efforts prematurely. Schumann's (1975) review of the literature on the relationship of affective variables and adult L_2 acquisition lends support to this view.

David Elkind (1970) proposes that the onset of formal operations leads to affective differences between children and adults. According to Elkind, the ability to think abstractly leads the adolescent to "conceptualize his own thought . . . (and) to take his mental constructions as objects and reason about them" (p. 66). Earlier, we suggested that this new ability leads to the capacity and perhaps to the requirement to create a conscious grammar of a second language. Another consequence, according to Elkind, is that the adolescent can now also "conceptualize the thought of other people":

> . . . this capacity, however, is the crux of adolescent egocentrism. This egocentrism emerges because, while the adolescent can now cognize the thoughts of others, he or she fails to differentiate between the objects toward which the thoughts of others are directed and those which

are the focus of his or her own concern. The young adolescent, because of the physiological metamorphosis he or she is undergoing,
believes that others are preoccupied with his or her appearance and
behavior.

(Elkind, 1970, p. 67)

In other words, adolescents who have passed through formal operations gain a greater ability to imagine what other people are
thinking about. This ability, however, may lead them to believe
that others are thinking about the same thing they are most concerned with, namely, their own appearance and behavior. This state
of mind, according to Elkind, leads to the increased self-
consciousness, feelings of vulnerability, and lowered self-image that
are associated with this age, and that contribute to an increase in
strength of the filter.

Differences in Language Environment   A fourth position is that
child-adult learning differences are due to differences in the kind of
language children and adults hear. It has been shown that many
mothers (and fathers) modify their speech to their children in order
to help them understand what is being said. Among other things,
they use simpler and shorter sentences (that get progressively longer
and more complex as the child matures), and they tend to talk about
the "here-and-now," providing extra-linguistic context as an aid to
comprehension. Several of the studies we reviewed in Chapter 2
have shown that the child second language learner also receives this
kind of "motherese," while the adult second language learner often
does not.

Simplified input does not always mean comprehensible input,
however. In a very recent study, Scarcella and Higa (in press) compared child and adolescent second language learners in a task that
required interaction with a native speaker (block building). They
noted that while the language directed at the younger learners was
"simpler," the older learners were more adept at "conversational
management," that is, they were better at indicating to the native
speaker whether they understood what was said, they were better
at keeping the conversation going, and were more proficient at
changing the topic of conversation. This suggests that one reason
older learners are faster in early stages is that they obtain more *comprehensible* input via better conversational management, even though
the input directed at them appears to be more complex.

Each of the explanations mentioned above focuses on one dimen
sion of language acquisition. Most likely, some aspect of all or sev-

eral of the explanations taken together are required to completely understand the effects of age on second language acquisition. Research on this important question is just beginning. The study of factors such as those described here will no doubt cast some light on the forces which interact to account for both similarities and differences in the way children and adults learn second languages.

SUMMARY

Age and personality are individual characteristics of individual learners which have been shown to have a marked effect on second language development.

Personality refers to an aggregate of traits characteristic of a particular individual. Research indicates that low anxiety level and a tendency to be outgoing, both expressions of **self-confidence,** have a positive effect on second language acquisition. It appears that self-confident people are more willing to take risks, to place themselves in unfamiliar learning situations, to guess or experiment with new forms, and to make mistakes, all of which contribute to their increased ability to learn.

The research on **empathy,** an individual's capacity for participation in another's feeling or ideas, has been inconclusive. Researchers' prevalent use of linguistic manipulation tasks (rather than communicative tasks) may be masking a positive correlation between empathy and L_2 acquisition.

Finally, investigations of L_2 learner's **analytic tendency** indicate that the "field independent" personality, characterized by a left-brained, analytical cognitive style, tends to be successful at acquiring conscious metalinguistic skills; while the "field dependent person," a more empathic type, seems to achieve greater success in the subconscious acquisition of communication skills.

Personality characteristics have also been observed to affect an individual's use of the monitor. A self-conscious learner, more concerned with correctness than communication, is likely to rely heavily on use of the monitor, whereas self-confident learners rely on selective monitoring or no monitoring at all.

Much research has focused on the effect of age on the rate of quality of second language acquisition. Evidence points to the following:

1. Children appear to be much more successful than adults in acquiring the phonological system of the new language; many eventually attain native-like accents.

2. Most children are ultimately more successful than adults in learning a second language, but they are not always faster. Adults appear to pro-

gress faster than children in the areas of syntax and morphology, at least in the early stages of learning.

Several plausible sources for the observed differences have been proposed. The **biological explanation,** namely, that the adult brain is fundamentally different from the child's brain with respect to language acquisition mechanisms, was a popular thesis until it was called into question by neurolinguistic research on cerebral dominance. The **cognitive explanation** suggests that the onset of "formal operations" (the ability to formulate abstract hypotheses) is a major determinant of child-adult differences. **Affective factors** too, may play a role, especially in causing adults to filter out more of the available language input than children do. Finally, **differences in the language environment** of children and adults may also result in differences in the success attained by children and adults. Children receive much more concrete "here-and-now" input, which facilitates language acquisition; in contrast, adults typically are exposed to conversation about topics whose referents are not obvious from the nonlinguistic context. On the other hand, older students may be better at "managing conversations."

Each of the explanations mentioned above focuses on one aspect of language acquisition. It is most likely that a combination of several explanations is required to completely understand the effects of age on second language acquisition.

STUDY QUESTIONS

1. Have you met anyone who began second language acquisition as an adult and who appears to perform like a native speaker of a language that you know well? What would you predict about such an individual with respect to personality type?

2. If you were planning a foreign language program for a school system, at what age would you recommend it begin? Provide a justification for the recommendations that you would give to the school personnel and parents.

3. Imagine that you want to learn Japanese as a second language. You are twenty-eight years old and living in New York. What factors unique to **adult** (as opposed to child) language learning situations would you try to take into account when planning your Japanese language learning efforts? Given you are a self-confident and relaxed person, is there reason to be pessimistic about the results of your efforts? Explain.

5

The Role of the First Language

The first language has long been considered the villain in second language learning, the major cause of a learner's problems with the new language. In recent years, however, data have accumulated that place the L_2 learner's first language in a more respectable, sometimes even valuable, place in the scheme of things. The first language is no longer considered an annoying "interference" in a learner's efforts to acquire a second language, and when an individual finally becomes bilingual, the availability of both the first and second languages is recognized as an enrichment of the individual's communicative repertoire.

To a large extent, controversies over the role of the first language in second language acquisition have resulted from vague and varying uses of the terms "interference" and "transfer." When the terms are clarified and when empirical data is assembled, there appears to be a convergence of opinion on the role of the first language in second language acquisition. Despite a long history of assumption to the contrary, present research results suggest that the major impact the first language has on second language acquisition may have to do with accent, not with grammar or syntax.

THE CONTRASTIVE ANALYSIS HYPOTHESIS

The contrastive analysis hypothesis held sway over the field of applied linguistics and second language teaching for over two decades. Even though it is currently giving way to a more positive view of the role of the first language in second language acquisition, it is useful to understand the theories which shaped so much early linguistic research and which therefore underlie much current L_2 teaching methodology and materials.

Contrastive analysis (CA) took the position that a learner's first language "interferes" with his or her acquisition of a second language, and that it therefore comprises the major obstacle to successful mastery of the new language. The CA hypothesis held that where structures in the L_1 differed from those in the L_2, errors that reflected the structure of the L_1 would be produced. Such errors were said to be due to the influence of the learners' L_1 habits on L_2 production. For example, in Spanish the adjective is usually placed after the noun; according to the CA hypothesis, therefore, Spanish-speaking learners should tend to say *the girl smart* instead of *the smart girl* when attempting to communicate in English. This process has been labelled "negative transfer" in the psychological literature.

By the same token, "positive transfer" refers to the automatic use of the L_1 structure in L_2 performance when the structures in both languages are the same, resulting in correct utterances. For example, the use of the Spanish plural markers -s and -es on English nouns should yield a correct English plural noun (e.g. niña-s and mujer-es in Spanish; girl-s and dress-es in English), if positive transfer were operating in L_2 production.

Following this reasoning, linguists thought a comparison of a learner's L_1 and L_2—contrastive analysis—should reveal areas of difficulty for L_2 students, thereby providing teachers and developers of L_2 materials with specific guidelines for lesson planning.

Apparently, this theory so appealed to the common sense of researchers and teachers alike, that a large body of data challenging it was ignored for years. We know that an examination of the available empirical data that addresses the CA hypothesis has revealed that:

1. In neither child nor adult L_2 performance do the majority of the grammatical errors reflect the learners' L_1.

2. L_2 learners make many errors in areas of grammar that are comparable in both the L_1 and L_2—errors that should not be made if "positive transfer" were operating.

3. L_2 learners' judgments of the grammatical correctness of L_2 sentences are more related to L_2 sentence type than to their own L_1 structure.

4. Phonological errors exhibit more L_1 influence than do grammatical errors, although a substantial number of the L_2 phonological

errors children make are similar to those made by monolingual first language learners, and only a small proportion of phonological errors in reading are traceable to the learner's L_1.

From these findings, we can conclude that at the level of performance (or *product*), the CA hypothesis has emerged as a weak predictor of learner performance, accounting only for a small portion of L_2 performance data.

At the level of *process*, the constructs of negative and positive transfer must be seriously questioned. Obviously such processes do not operate much of the time or systematically.

The enthusiasm for contrastive analysis in foreign language teaching can be traced to Charles Fries who wrote in 1945: "The most effective materials are those that are based upon a scientific description of the language to be learned, carefully compared with a parallel description of the native language of the learner" (p. 9). Further, in a foreword to Lado's famous treatise on the topic (Lado, 1957), Fries stated: "Learning a second language therefore constitutes a very different task from learning the first language. The basic problems arise not out of any essential difficulty in the features of the new language themselves but primarily out of the special "set" created by the first language habits" (Fries, 1957, Foreword).[1] A large part of the rationale for the CA hypothesis was drawn from principles of behaviorist (stimulus-response) psychology that were the accepted learning principles at that time, but which have since been shown inadequate to explain language learning. (Chomsky, 1959; R. Brown, 1973; Fodor, Bever, and Garrett, 1974, among others.) Empirical data was also called upon as support. Unfortunately, the data used—that of linguistic "borrowing" and "switching" described later—has since been shown to be inapplicable to the issue of L_1 interference in L_2 acquisition.

ON THE TERMS "INTERFERENCE" AND "TRANSFER"

Interference has been used to refer to two very distinct linguistic phenomena, one that is essentially psychological and another that is essentially sociolinguistic. The *psychological* use of the term interference refers to the influence of old habits when new ones are being learned, whereas the *sociolinguistic* use of interference refers to language interactions, such as linguistic borrowing and language switching, that occur when two language communities are in con-

1. See also Lane (1962); Upshur (1962); Stockwell and Bowen (1965); Banathy, Trager and Waddle (1966); Nickel and Wagner (1968); and Jakobovits (1970).

tact. Such a distinction had not been made clear during the heyday of CA, and data documenting these sociolinguistic phenomena, gathered by linguists such as Weinreich (1953) and Haugen (1953), were used by CA proponents as empirical support for the psychological phenomenon of negative transfer (see Lado, 1957, p. 1).[2]

Upon close examination, it became evident that the phenomenon of "interference," which Weinreich has documented, and that of "linguistic borrowing," which Haugen has documented, are similar sociolinguistic phenomena. They are, furthermore, quite different from "first language interference" as conceived by CA proponents. This led to great confusion when linguists relied on Weinreich's and Haugen's work. The differences are easily seen when we compare Weinreich's and Haugen's definitions.

Weinreich defines interference as:

> Those instances of deviation from the norms of either language which occur in the speech of bilinguals as a result of their **familiarity**[3] with more than one language, i.e., as a result of languages in contact (p.1).

Haugen defines linguistic borrowing as:

> An example of cultural diffusion, the spread of an item of culture from people to people. Borrowing is linguistic diffusion, and can be unambiguously defined as the attempt by a speaker to reproduce in one language, patterns which he has learned in another (p. 363) . . . **it is the language of the learner that is influenced, not the language he learns** (p. 370).[4]

The CA hypothesis, on the other hand, states that interference is due to unfamiliarity with the L_2, that is, to the learner's not having learned target patterns. Further, it is manifested in the language the learner learns, not the first language of the learner: "We know from the observation of many cases that the grammatical structure of the native language tends to be transferred to the foreign language . . . we have here the major source of difficulty or ease in learning the foreign language . . . Those structures that are different will be difficult" (Lado, 1957, pp. 58–59).

Further, Weinreich's definition of interference is not based on which language was learned first: "Throughout the analysis of the forms of linguistic interference, conventional terms like 'mother

2. Note that work written more than twenty years ago may no longer reflect the author's current views. Therefore, comments referring to such work should be seen in the context of the time of its writing. This comment applies to all such references in this book.
3. Emphasis added.
4. Emphasis added.

tongue,' 'first,' 'second,' or 'native' language were avoided; for from the structural point of view the genetic question . . . is irrelevant" (p. 74).

On the contrary, the native/second language distinction is central to Lado's statement.

Weinreich's and Haugen's specification of when and why interference occurs is also different from that of CA. Weinreich's observations of conversations between a bilingual and a monolingual, and between bilinguals, led him to state that when both speakers are bilingual, interference in the bilingual's speech is uninhibited: "When the other interlocutor is also bilingual, the requirements of intelligibility and status assertion are drastically reduced. Under such circumstances, there is hardly any limit to interference" (p. 81).

Similarly, Haugen writes: "Linguistic borrowing . . . is something that has happened wherever there have been bilinguals. It is, in fact, unthinkable without the existence of bilinguals, and apparently inevitable where there is a considerable group of bilinguals" (p. 263). However, "in speaking to a unilingual, the bilingual often tends to limit interference and to eliminate even habitualized borrowings from his [or her] speech . . ." (p. 81). Apparently, the bilinguals Weinreich refers to here know two codes—one that includes interference structures and one that does not. Furthermore, they are able to code switch when the situation demands it.

The CA notion of interference applies to quite different circumstances: the less bilingual speakers are, the more interference there will be when they attempt to communicate with speakers of the target language.

Haugen also mentions the deliberate use by a bilingual of loan translations "for the sake of enriching his [or her] language" (p. 459).[5] This use of interference is quite different from the CA notion of interference structures as unwanted forms which the L_2 learner cannot help but use.

Clearly, the work of Weinreich and Haugen was fundamental to research in language shift (and we shall discuss it in that context later in this chapter), but it does not speak to the phenomenon of first language interference as defined by the contrastive analysis hypothesis.

The same sort of problems with the simultaneous use of several meanings for **transfer** have created further confusion with CA theoretical accounts of the role of the L_1.

Behaviorist psychologists, who first defined "transfer" techni-

---

5. This seems similar to the notion of "foregrounding" suggested by Gumperz and Hernández-Chávez (1971) in their discussion of Chicanos speaking Enlish.

cally, used it to refer to a process described as the automatic, uncontrolled, and subconscious use of past learned behaviors in the attempt to produce new responses. In this sense, transfer may be of two types: "negative" and "positive."

"Negative transfer" refers to those instances of transfer which result in error because old, habitual behavior is different from the new behavior that is being learned. For example, if one has regularly driven a car where the gear shift is on the floor, one will invariably reach for the floor when first attempting to drive a new car whose gear shift is on the steering column.

In contrast, "positive transfer" results in correct performance because the new behavior is the same as the old. In our gear shift example above, positive transfer would operate if the new car also had its gear shift on the floor—the old and new gear shifting would be the same. Both types of transfer refer to the automatic and subconscious use of old behavior in new learning situations.

Transfer has also been used by educational psychologists and educators to describe the use of past knowledge and experience in new situations. If, for example, one already knows how to read in one language, one does not have to learn anew that written symbols represent sounds when learning to read in a second language. Thus the basic concepts and skills involved in reading are said to "transfer" to the new language. This view of transfer is not predicated on stimulus-response nor on any other clear theoretical principles. Although it seems superficially similar to the first notion of transfer, there are critical differences, in particular with respect to *what* is transferred. As this is a highly tentative theoretical area, we do not address it further in this book.

Yet another use of "transfer" refers not to any underlying process, but simply to a characteristic of the learner's performance. Thus, errors that reflect the structure that the first language also happens to have are often referred to in the literature as "transfer errors" no matter what the real source of those errors might be. Such errors may be the result of the negative transfer process described by behaviorist psychologists, or they may be the result of some other internal process, or some factor in the learner's language environment.

Because of the potential for misinterpretation and confusion, we have refrained from using the term "transfer" to describe surface characteristics of errors. Transfer is used in this book only in the context of the theoretical constructs of "negative transfer" or "positive transfer," two terms that are clearly associated with their technical definition from habit theory in psychology. Errors that reflect the learner's first language structures have been labelled "interlingual errors."

This distinction is essentially between process and product; that is between the processes hypothesized to underlie verbal performance (e.g. negative transfer) and the characteristics of the performance itself, in this case, the characteristics of errors. The distinction is analogous to that between explanation and description. One may describe an error without implying an explanation of the error; moreover, several explanations may be offered, of which only one is correct.

The empirical research available on the role of the first language covers different aspects of L_2 learners' verbal performance. These aspects include:

1. Grammatical Errors
2. Non-use of L_1 rules similar in L_2
3. Judgments of grammatical correctness
4. Avoidance

Grammatical Errors

The change in the perceived role of the first language began with the observation that the number of errors in second language performance that could be attributed to first language influence was far smaller than had been imagined previously.

In the area of grammar, including syntax and morphology, the incidence of errors that are traceable to characteristics in the first language is relatively low—around 4% to 12% for children, and from 8% to 23% for adults. Of these interlingual errors, most tend to be limited to word order and are not made in the morphology of the language.

Child Studies   In Dulay and Burt's (1974) initial study of the natural speech of children, an analysis of over 500 grammatical errors made by 179 children learning English in United States schools (in New York and in Northern California) revealed that less than 5% of the errors observed reflected the children's first language, Spanish. Since then, other empirical studies have shown that children place limited reliance on the structure of the mother tongue when learning the second language in a host environment. Studies of Japanese-speaking children learning English in the United States (Milon, 1974; Gillis and Weber, 1976), or Spanish-, French- and Greek-speaking children learning English in the

United States (Gonzalez and Elijah, 1979; Venable, 1974) are typical examples of empirical studies in which the actual incidence of interlingual errors observed was negligible. Such findings are not limited to children who are learning English as a second language. Native English-speaking children have been observed acquiring languages as diverse as Welsh in Wales (Price, 1968), French in Geneva, Switzerland (Ervin-Tripp, 1974), Spanish in an immersion program in the United States (Boyd, 1975), German in Kiel, West Germany (Wode, 1976), and Urdu in Pakistan (Hansen-Bede, 1975).

The researchers just mentioned all made a point of commenting on the very low incidence of interlingual errors. Instead, most of the errors observed appeared to be developmental—of the sort that might be made by children learning those languages as their first language.[6] (See Chapter 7 for detailed descriptions of studies mentioned in this and the following section.)

Adult Studies   Studies conducted on the speech and writing of adults learning English as a second language have reached similar conclusions, namely, that the majority of non-phonological errors observed for adults do not reflect the first language. The proportion of errors that reflect the first language, however, is somewhat larger than that which has been observed for children. Approximately 8% to 23% of the adult errors may be classified as interlingual. Though this proportion is larger than it is for children, it still represents a minority of the total errors adults make. Researchers studied the speech of adults learning English in the United States (White, 1977), and the compositions of native English-speaking adults enrolled in Spanish and German foreign language university classes in the U.S. (LoCoco, 1975, 1976).[7]

Other researchers (who did not conduct complete counts but who nevertheless examined error types) have also commented on the relatively small numbers of interlingual errors in their observations. An Arabic speaker learning English in the U.S. (Hanania and Gradman, 1977) and French speakers learning English in Quebec (d'Anglejan and Tucker, 1975) have been studied, as have native English-speaking students observed in a French foreign language class in a Midwestern university (Valdman, 1975). Even studies which appear

6. In a study conducted by Politzer and Ramirez (1973) the incidence of interlingual errors was said to be "considerable." The authors point out, however, that these errors by no means comprised the majority of the error types found. More importantly, the majority of errors they counted as interlingual were omissions of the past tense -*ed* marker, an error that most L$_2$ researchers have classified as developmental since L$_1$ learners also make such errors.
7. Studies that suffer from serious methodological flaws (e.g., the use of timed translation tests which encourage heavy reliance on the first language) have not been included here, because their results cannot be reported with confidence.

to emphasize the description of interlingual errors did not find a majority of that error type (e.g. Scott and Tucker, 1974, who studied Arabic-speaking students learning English at the American University of Beirut).

The adult studies were conducted in both host and foreign language environments. It seems likely that a foreign environment should be more conducive to L_1 influence than a host environment because of the lack of sufficient natural exposure; however, the available data do not permit such a generalization to be made.[8]

Teachers might be interested to know that the available research on error correction suggests that neither correction techniques nor heavy drilling does much to affect the quality of student speech (Hendrickson, 1977; Plann, 1977; Cohen and Robbins, 1976). Thus, whatever attention is given the small number of interlingual errors that do appear to occur, it is not likely that the correction or drilling procedures suggested by contrastive analysis tenets are likely to lead to much change in the students' verbal performance.

Non-Use of L_1 Rules Similar in L_2 (Lack of Positive Transfer)

In addition to the finding that relatively few of the errors learners have been observed to make can be traced unambiguously to their native language, the data show that learners make a number of grammatical errors which they would *not* have made if they had used the same rule they were already using in their L_1.

According to one study, 5% to 18% of errors would not have been made had the learners resorted to rules they were already using in their native languages (LoCoco, 1975). This study included monolingual English-speaking university students learning Spanish and German in the U.S.

Another example of the limited use of the L_1 is evidenced in the learning of plural allomorphs. An allomorph is a variant of a morpheme in English. The plural morpheme has three predictable allomorphs—it is pronounced /s/ after voiceless consonants, such as /p/, /t/, and /k/ (*cats*); /z/ after voiced consonants, such as /b/, /d/, /g/ (*bags*); and /iz/ after sibilants, such as the last sounds in the words *fish* and *church*. Using a test similar to the Berko (1958) "wug" test (e.g. "this is a wug; here are two _____."), Natalicio and Natalicio (1971) found that native Spanish speakers aged six to sixteen acquired the /-s/ and /-z/ plural allomorphs before the /-iz/. If transfer from Spanish

---

8. Some researchers of adult L_2 acquisition in a foreign environment have noted the incidence of interlingual errors (e.g. Duskova, 1969; Grauberg, 1971; Scott and Tucker, 1974), but have not provided any indication of the proportion of those errors relative to other types they observed.

to English had been operating, the order of acquisition would have been /s/ only first, then /z/ and /iz/ together, because Spanish plurals are all voiceless, and voicing is the new feature English requires.

Similarly, Hernández-Chávez (1972) has observed that his Spanish-speaking subject Guero omitted the plural /-s/ and /-es/ endings in the early stages of English acquisition, even though Guero used the same rules productively in his native Spanish.

And finally, Richards (1971) provides an example of this phenomenon from a French-speaking adult learning English, who produced the utterance *composed with* (instead of *of*). He remarks, "Had the French speaker followed the grammar of his mother tongue, he would have produced the correct English form!" (p. 16).

These findings provide additional evidence for L_2 learners' lack of reliance on the specific grammatical rules and structures of their mother tongues. There seems to be little natural predisposition to mix the rules and structures of the two language systems when learners have the opportunity to learn and use the new language in even a partially natural setting.

Judgments of Grammatical Correctness

Another kind of study that attempts to explore the role of the L_1 in L_2 performance focuses on judgments of grammatical correctness. The basic question asked is: Will judgments of grammatical correctness be affected by the differences between one's first and second languages? If so, one should detect similar patterns of responses for students from the same language backgrounds. If not, there should be no systematic relationship between errors made and the first language of the learners.

Schachter, Tyson and Diffley (1976) conducted one such investigation involving Arabic, Persian, Japanese, Chinese and Spanish students. The investigation elicited grammaticality judgments from some fifty students on relative clause constructions in English. The researchers constructed a variety of misformed English sentences based on a one-to-one translation from the native languages of the students. For example, a sentence based on Chinese structure would be:

Most of the people live in Hong Kong are Orientals.

One based on Arabic or Farsi would be:

The problem that a tourist guide must face them are numerous.

Sentences such as these were mixed in with correctly formed English sentences such as:

Two cities that have similar smog problems are Tokyo and Los Angeles.

The person that you should see is the dean of the college.

Students were then asked to indicate which of the sentences on the list were grammatical.

Mixed results were obtained. Only in the Persian groups did a majority judge misformed relative clauses based on their first language to be correct. These students, however, also judged the correctly formed relative clauses to be correct. No significant majorities in the other three language groups[9] judged the misformed relative clauses based on their respective first languages to be correct. Thus, the students' first language could not consistently be inferred from the errors they made in grammaticality judgments.

In another study, Ioup and Kruse (1977) also elicited grammar judgments on various relative clause constructions from students who represented the same five language groups studied by Schachter et al. Again, misformed sentences containing relative clauses were constructed so that they corresponded to the structure of the student's native languages. Grammatical and ungrammatical sentences were presented in random order in a written list, and the subjects were asked to mark those which they deemed incorrect in English. (The study included eighty-seven students enrolled in ESL classes in American universities—eighteen Spanish, sixteen Chinese, eighteen Persian, ten Japanese, and twenty-five Arabic.)

A number of analyses performed on these data again revealed no significant relationship between the student's language group and his or her judgments about the correctness of English sentence types (which were based on the native language word order of each language group). Instead, Ioup and Kruse state that "contrary to the contrastive analysis hypothesis, sentence type rather than native language background is the most reliable predictor of error" (p. 165). Ioup and Kruse devote the rest of their article describing and analyzing the sentence types which seem to cause the most difficulty generally, testing recent hypotheses based on the structure of English itself, in particular those regarding the linguistic complexity of embedded sentence types which have been proposed by Kuno (1974), Keenan (1975), and Sheldon (1973).

9. The researchers did not find any Spanish specific non-native relative clauses, so the question could not be addressed.

These two studies, then, do not lend much support to the notion of L_1 influence. Where judgments of grammatical correctness are concerned, factors other than the structures and rules of the L_1 seem to be operating.

Avoidance

An interesting area of second language acquisition research that may also bear on the question of L_1 influence pertains to the avoidance of certain structures by L_2 learners. Schachter (1974) analyzed relative clause production in university-level students of ESL and found that Persian and Arabic speakers produced about twice as many relative clauses in their compositions as did Japanese and Chinese students, but they made nearly twice as many errors in the relative clauses, as compared to Japanese- and Chinese-speaking students. Schachter believes that contrastive analysis helps to explain these results. Persian (Farsi) and Arabic relative clauses are similar to English relative clauses, in that they are formed with the head noun phrase to the "left" (". . . *the boy* who I saw . . ."). Japanese and Chinese relative clauses are quite different, however, in that the head noun phrase appears to the "right" of the subordinate clause. Schachter concludes that "the students may have had so much trouble with these constructions that they refused to produce them."

Kleinman (1978) presented results using Arabic, Spanish, Portuguese, and American students that essentially support Schachter's view, but also show that contrastive analysis alone cannot predict when structures will be circumvented or produced. Kleinman's research suggests that personality factors, such as anxiety, confidence, and willingness to take risks, provides information on which students are likely to avoid various structures. Also, Madden, Bailey, Eisenstein, Anderson (1978), in a detailed investigation of the acquisition of four auxiliaries in forty-six adult ESL students, distinguish "avoiders" and "guessers." Avoiders "appeared to avoid responding to items they did not know well and were willing to imitate a sentence only when they felt the likelihood of making errors was small" (p. 112). Guessers "were willing to try . . . even when there was little likelihood of being correct" (p. 112).

We have seen that the contrastive analysis hypothesis has received little empirical confirmation in the area of L_2 syntax and morphology. Given its base in habit formation theory, the CA hypothesis can be seriously questioned also on purely theoretical grounds. Not only have the general premises of habit theory been shown to be inadequate to account for language acquisition (Chomsky, 1959;

Fodor, Bever, and Garrett, 1974, among others), but general psycho-logical interference theory derived from verbal learning and memory research is also being seriously questioned by psychologists themselves. (See Tulving and Madigan, 1970; Shiffrin and Schneider, 1977; and Schneider and Shiffrin, 1977 for the literature on this issue.)

SOURCES OF INTERLINGUAL ERRORS

Even though interlingual errors of syntax and morphology occur in relatively small numbers in the verbal performance of L_2 learners, a comprehensive account of L_2 acquisition should be able to accommodate them. Unfortunately, virtually no work has been done to probe the conditions under which interlingual errors are made. Most of the available research, including our own, has focused on the less refined question of proportion or mere occurrence of such errors. We can thus offer only our best educated guesses, gleaned from a close review of the current literature.

There are indications that interlingual errors are occasioned by at least two environmental factors: (1) conditions that result in premature use of the L_2, and (2) certain elicitation tasks.

Conditions that Result in Premature Use of the L_2

Pressure to Perform   A tourist in a foreign country, equipped with a few hundred vocabulary words and perhaps a few structures, is likely to fall back on the L_1 when attempting to communicate a message that is far beyond his or her knowledge of the new language. This is premature use of the L_2, triggered by a need to communicate in the target language before one has been exposed to enough of it for meaningful processing.

Adults often have to produce the new language long before they have been exposed to a sufficient amount of it to internalize the rudiments of its basic structure. If the learner lives in the country where the second language is the major language of communication, many jobs and social activities will require sophisticated verbal interaction in the new language. In foreign language situations the pressure to produce the new language stems from requirements of classroom performance—writing compositions, oral classroom exchanges, or taking tests.

Children, who have been observed to make fewer interlingual errors than adults, are not usually subjected to such pressures to perform in the second language. As we have seen in Chapter 2, children in natural host language contexts have been observed to go through a silent period of two or three months, during which they limit their speech to brief imitations and a few routines. The silent period is believed to help build up some competence through listening—enough to permit some spontaneous speech production without relying on the first language.

It seems then, that conditions that exert pressures on the learners to produce or communicate too soon in the second language will encourage conscious use of the first language as an aid in communication. As Newmark (1966) has pointed out, learners fall back on the first language when they have not acquired enough of the second language.

Limited L_2 Environments.   Ervin-Tripp (1974) has noted that L_1 influence in learner performance has been found for "learning conditions in which the second language was not the language of the learner's larger social milieu so that the learning contexts were aberrant both in function and frequency of structures" (p.121). As we mentioned earlier, environmental factors that apparently limit the scope and quality of second language learning include: (1) the absence of peers who speak the language natively; and (2) severely limited and often artificial conditions under which the language may be learned (such as, for example, two hours a week spent largely memorizing vocabulary or dialogues, doing audiolingual drills, answering unreal questions, or trying to simulate conversation with speakers who themselves are not proficient in the language).

These unfortunate conditions are often inevitable, however, in foreign language learning contexts because the target language is not a language used for communication in such situations. The total burden to provide a target language environment falls on the teacher in the often difficult environment of the classroom. Under these conditions, learners have little recourse but to fill the vacuum of second language knowledge with the structures of their first language. (Surprisingly enough, errors resulting from first language influence still represent only some 8 to 23% of all errors made in natural production.)

As had been pointed out previously, foreign language immersion programs rectify some of the shortcomings of the foreign language context by offering students real and extended communicative experiences in the second language through the presentation of subject matter in the new language. The one apparent hiatus in immersion programs is the lack of peers who speak the target language natively. In these programs, second language input is restricted to the teacher's proficient speech and the less-than-proficient speech of the other children in the class. Since teachers do not seem to be children's first choice for language models, the students rely on themselves and their classmates, all of whom are also still grappling with the task of learning the second language. Although it has been suggested that the incidence of interlingual errors in immersion speech is higher than that of children in host environments, unfortunately, no actual empirical error counts have been made to date. No firm comments, therefore, can be made at this time regarding this suggestion.

The Elicitation Task

Elicitation task refers to the manner in which spoken or written performance is elicited from the second language learner. For example, we could ask a student to translate a paragraph written in his or her native language, or we could ask the student to describe a picture, or we could construct a fill-in-the-blanks test. Elicitation task has a little-discussed, but extremely important, influence on a learner's verbal performance.

The proportion of interlingual errors changes with the elicitation task, translation in particular. Lado (1978) asked 15 Spanish-speaking university students learning English to translate a 150-word text, while another 15 such students were asked to interpret that same text after a day's delay. The students who performed the translation task made a significantly greater number of interlingual errors than those who performed the "delayed interpretation" task. A replication of the experiment using the oral mode and a much shorter delay again yielded similar though less dramatic results.

Translation tasks artificially increase the L_2 learner's reliance on first language structures, masking processes the learner otherwise uses for natural communication. For this reason, studies that rely exclusively on translation and strict linguistic manipulation to elicit language cannot be used validly in formulating accounts of L_2 learners' acquisition of communicative skills.

Monitor Use and the Use of the L_1

The conditions under which the L_1 grammar is used in L_2 performance coincide to a certain extent with conditions in which **conscious** language processing is in effect. This suggests the monitor as an important factor associated with L_1 use in L_2 acquisition.

When learners use first language structures in second language performance, they in effect plug lexical items (vocabulary) of the second language into the surface structure of the first language. In other words, they "think" in the first language and use words from the second language, much as one would handle word-for-word translations. In situations where the surface structure of both languages is similar, this is not a problem. In fact, when this happens, use of the L_1 can be considered an asset. Languages do, however, differ considerably with respect to surface syntax. When learners try to use first language structures that are not identical to second language structures, they make interlingual errors, and it is up to the Monitor to repair these errors.

The ability to monitor allows some people to speak second languages with little, if any, naturally acquired competence. While it allows for very early performance (a good student of languages can begin to speak second languages nearly instantly using this system), it has real limitations. It requires constant vigilance, constant attention to form, and it is limited by the amount of conscious knowledge the learner has. Also, while monitor use may be relatively straightforward in parts of grammar like bound morphology, the monitor may not be adequate to handle complex word-order changes and permutations.

Phonological Performance

We have seen that the grammar rules and structures of the learner's first language are for the most part held in abeyance in the acquisition of a second language by children as well as adults. However, the L_1 does have one significant influence on the L_2, particularly for adults, and that is seen in the learner's pronunciation. Theoretical tenets aside, the contrastive analysis of the phonological systems of the learner's two languages is a useful predictor of a substantial portion of the phonological performance of L_2 learners, in particular that of adults and beginning level children.

Though much of the available evidence is observational or anecdotal, studies conducted on children acquiring a second language have suggested that for a time, children process the sound system of the new language through that of their first language. (For literature review see Dulay, Hernández-Chávez and Burt, 1978.) Gradually, however, children begin to rely more and more only on the L_2 sound system with the result that the "accent" largely or entirely disappears. Many if not most adults, however, process the L_2 sound system through their L_1 system throughout most of their lives. The mechanisms underlying this singular influence of the L_1 on the L_2 are not yet known.

Haugen (1978) reported that he had become quite successful in determining the various first languages of L_2 learners he had encountered during his extensive investigations of bilinguals. A great many non-linguists believe they can identify a Spanish, Russian or other accent, and many indeed can do so. Moreover, others who are monolingual are talented at producing accented speech, producing quite a variety of foreign "accents" with ease and success.

The widespread familiarity with these phonological phenomena, as well as constant exposure to the accented speech of well-known politicians, actors, and others, has given the notion of L_1 influence on L_2 acquisition its greatest credibility and may have been an underlying reason for the unexamined acceptance of the CA hypothesis as "self-evident" in all areas of language.

The processes used in children's acquisition of L_2 phonological structures appear to be similar in many respects to those children use in learning their L_1, suggesting the existence of a set of natural processes of phonological acquisition. In contrast to the acquisition of grammar, however, the learner makes extensive use of first language phonological structures as a communicative strategy in the early stages of L_2 acquisition. The new phonology is built up using L_1 phonology as a base. Because the L_2 learner already has an L_1 phonology, and uses it as a foundation for further learning, the learner's L_2 speech will have a substratum of L_1 sounds.

Research investigating the internal dynamics underlying the localization of L_1 influence to phonology has not yet been undertaken. The prevalence of numerous individuals with accented speech is evidence that the development of the lexicon and grammar are somewhat independent of that of phonology. In fact, persons have been known to develop an accent or maintain one for various social reasons, such as to mark membership in a certain group. Such phenomena point to the special status of pronunciation in language learning and language use. Furthermore, it is clear that communication is not seriously impeded by an accent (e.g. Henry Kissinger or Greta Garbo), while an underdeveloped lexicon or lack of control over basic aspects of grammar precludes meaningful communication.

THE INTERACTION OF A BILINGUAL'S FIRST AND SECOND LANGUAGES[10]

There is one other area where the L_1 and L_2 clearly interact. The cultural and linguistic contact inherent in societal bilingualism gives rise to two major phenomena that are sometimes subject to misin-

10. Most of this section has been reprinted from Dulay et al., 1978, with permission of University Park Press.

terpretation: "borrowing" and "code switching" (also called "language switching" or "code alternation"). These are often erroneously believed to symptomize serious language abnormalities or, at the very least, to signal a linguistic and mental confusion or interference that is deleterious to learning. A description of the linguistic and sociolinguistic processes involved in these phenomena, however, can provide a clearer understanding of their structure and function.

Borrowing

Linguistic borrowing is the incorporation of linguistic material from one language into another. It is a normal consequence of the natural contact of languages in multilingual societies. Borrowing is extremely widespread in social groups around the world and is characteristic of socially and economically subordinate linguistic minorities in the United States (Weinreich, 1953; Haugen, 1953, 1956; Vildomec, 1963, among others).

Common sorts of borrowing are individual lexical items that express either cultural concepts that are new to the borrowing group, or notions that are particularly important in a given contact situation.[11] For example, the languages of the Old World, upon coming in contact with the cultures and the fauna and flora of the New World, borrowed many hundreds of words from the American languages such as *maize, tomato, igloo, skunk*, etc. The native American languages, in turn, borrowed many words from European culture. Similarly, a great many items from Spanish have come into English by way of the Southwestern cattle-raising culture, e.g. *corral, lasso, arroyo*, and many more.

The extent to which borrowing can take place under conditions of cultural contact is evidenced by the case of English, a Germanic language, which, as a consequence of the Norman conquest, borrowed thousands of French words, opening the doors for a virtual flood of Latin-based borrowing. It is estimated that more than half of the English lexicon is derived from Latin (Baugh and Cable, 1978).

Similarly, the non-English languages in the United States borrow many words from English. Some of these represent cultural concepts that were previously unfamiliar to the speakers of those languages, as when Spanish borrows *queque* (cake), *béisbol* (baseball), or *lonche* (lunch). A great many words, however, are borrowed

11. Borrowing may take a number of other forms such as "loan shifts," "loan translations," and the like. See Weinreich (1953) and Haugen (1956) for discussion of these and other categories of complex lexical borrowing.

mainly because of their constant and intensive use by Spanish speakers as they come into necessary contact with English-oriented commercial and educational institutions (Espinosa, 1917). Such words as *traque* (track), *cheque* (check), *espeliar* (to spell), and *juipen* (whipping) illustrate these kinds of borrowing.

As one may infer from the examples in the above paragraphs, words borrowed into a language maintain the general sound pattern of the original word but modify it to conform with the phonetic and phonological system of the borrowing language. Thus, the words *cake* and *lunch* in English end in obstruent consonants. Since no word in Spanish may end in these sounds, the words are modified in the process of borrowing by the addition of the epenthetic vowel *e*. In addition, the word *lunch* contains a "short u" (schwa [ə]), which is not used in Spanish, and it is therefore changed to the phonetically similar [o].

Words, once borrowed, are incorporated into the grammatical structure of the borrowing language. They become, in effect, new words in the language. The words *maize* and *tomato*, for example, obey the English grammatical rules for co-occurrence with articles: *tomato* may be used with the indefinite article *a*, although *maize* may not. Similarly, the Spanish word *espeliar* forms its infinitive with an ending and is conjugated like all Spanish verbs of the same class.

Borrowed words may have such widespread use within a community that speakers of the borrowing language may learn them from each other, not needing to have knowledge of the original in the other language. When this occurs, it is said that the words are "integrated borrowings." On the other hand, bilingual speakers commonly learn to use a set of interlinguistic rules of "creative borrowing" during an act of communication. If, for example, in using the native language, the speaker wishes to express a concept that is closely associated with activities or cultural values of the other language, an appropriate foreign word not usually borrowed by the bilingual community (e.g. *experienciar*) may be brought into play and incorporated into the communication by means of the productive rules of correspondence. Such creative borrowing provides an additional linguistic resource on which bilinguals may draw to enhance their communication.

Code Switching

Code switching, too, is an active, creative process of incorporating material from both of a bilingual's languages into communicative acts. It involves the rapid and momentary shifting from one language into another. This alternation may occur many times within a single conversation and is not uncommon within single sentences.

The rapidity and automaticity with which the alternations take place often give the impression that the speaker lacks control of the structural systems of the two languages and is mixing them indiscriminately. However, quite the contrary is true. Code switching is most often engaged in by those bilingual speakers who are the most proficient in both their languages. Moreover, as we shall see, code switching itself obeys rather strict structural rules in addition to the grammatical rules of each of the component languages.

Many alternations within a single sentence involve the insertion of a word or a short phrase that makes reference to a single, unified notion. The following examples are taken from the speech of adults reported by Aurelio Espinosa (1917). Espinosa recorded these forms using the conventional Spanish orthography for colloquial speech.

1. *Ayer juimos a los* movies

We went to the movies yesterday.

2. *Comieron* turkey *pa'* Christmas?

Did you eat turkey for Christmas?

3. *No andes ahí de* smart Alek.

Don't go around as a smart aleck.

4. *Vamos a ir al* football game *y después* . . .

We're going to go to the football game, and then . . .

Code alternation may also involve entire phrases or clauses with a complex internal grammatical structure. For example,

5. He is doing the best he can *pa' no quedarse atrás, pero lo van a fregar* (Espinosa, 1917).

He is doing the best he can in order not to be kept back, but they're going to mess him up.

6. *Te digo que este dedo* has been bothering me so much (Lance, 1975).

I'm telling you that this finger has been bothering me so much.

7. Those are friends from Mexico *que tienen chamaquitos* (Gumperz and Hernández-Chávez, 1971).

Those are friends from Mexico who have little kids.

8. The type of work he did *cuando trabajaba,* he . . . what . . . that I remember, *era regador* at one time (Gumperz and Hernández-Chávez, 1971).

The type of work he did when he worked, he . . . what . . . that I remember, he was an irrigator at one time.

The languages may shift back and forth several times within a single sentence. Within each stretch of speech the grammatical structure belongs completely to the particular language being used. (This includes forms such as *pa'* and *juimos* which, although they are nonstandard forms, adhere to monolingual adult grammatical norms.) That is to say, the word order, morphology, syntactic processes, etc., are all those of the language of the particular stretch of speech. Furthermore, the phonetic and phonological structure of a given unilingual segment is systematic and conforms to the structure of the language in question. At the point of alternation, the entire structure—syntactic, morphological, phonological—shifts to that of the other language. Each unilingual segment thus retains an internal structural consistency that shows all of the complex grammatical and phonological characteristics of monolingual speech.

In addition to adhering to the linguistic structures of each of the languages, code alternation is not a random, uncontrolled process. Rather, alternations occur only at specific, definable syntactic junctures. For instance, in examples 5–8 above, the alternations may occur at relative clause boundaries (e.g. *que tienen chamaquitos*), before adverbial clauses (e.g. *cuando trabajaba; pa' no quedarse atrás*), at the beginnings of verb phrases (e.g. *that I remember*), etc. Alternations may also occur at other junctures: noun qualifiers, verb complements, parts of a noun phrase, or the predicate portion of an equational sentence (Gumperz and Hernández-Chávez, 1971).

Alternations that are made at unpermitted junctures are considered ungrammatical by persons proficient in code alternation (Aguirre, 1975). The exact specification of the restrictions on alternations will require further detailed investigation, but it is possible to make a few tentative observations. For example, constructions like the following are rejected by speakers as ill-formed and have not been observed to occur in natural code alternation:

que have *chamaquitos*	who have little kids
he *era regador*	he was an irrigator
cuando did you arrive?	when did you arrive?

Not enough research has been conducted to permit us to specify why these alternations do not occur.

Finally, code switching has a number of specific sociolinguistic functions. First, it is used to symbolize ethnic identification. Persons who alternate languages do so only in speaking with other members of the group or to indicate (symbolic) acceptance of a nonmember into the group. Even in essentially unilingual conversations, in either language, the occasional use of such terms as *OK, you know, and then, ándale pués, híjole!, digo,* etc. function to symbolize the intra-ethnic character of the interaction.

Related to this usage are those situations in which code switching functions to permit the precise expression of ethnically or culturally relevant information. For example in the following sentences the alternations to Spanish express certain nuances of meaning that are not available to the speaker in English.

1. I got to thinking, *vacilando el punto este,* . . .	I got to thinking, mulling that point over . . .
2. And my uncle Sam *es el más agabachado.*	And my uncle Sam is the most Americanized.
3. There are no children in the neighborhood. Well, *sí, hay criaturas.*	There are no children in the neighborhood. Well, there are kids.

In Example 1, the word *vacilando* connotes informality, the fact that the "mulling over" is "the fun of it." *Agabachado* in Example 2 not only means "Americanized," it also includes the idea of rejection of one's own Chicanismo. And, in Example 3, the word *criaturas* carries with it the implication of "Spanish-speaking children" rather than just any children.

In the last examples, we see that the very act of code switching itself carries a potential meaning. *Criaturas* by itself does not mean "Spanish-speaking children." But in Example 3, the contrast of *criaturas* with *children* and the concomitant phrasal switch provides the term with an unmistakable nuance of meaning. The alternation from English to Spanish, then, not only functions as an ethnic marker, as described above, it also functions to symbolize those values that are most closely associated with Spanish-speaking community. Two final examples illustrate this point:

1. In talking about whom a certain friend's children play with, a speaker says, (they play) *with each other. La señora trabaja en la canería orita, you know.* ("The mother works in the cannery now, you know.") The mother is a Spanish speaker and "working in the cannery" is a seasonal activity that is part of the local Chicano community's social and economic system. Only Chicana women work in this particular cannery. The switch to Spanish symbolizes all these values.

2. Reminiscing about the frustrations of smoking, an ex-smoker says, *I'd get desperate, y ahí voy al basurero a buscar, a sacar, you*

know. ("I'd get desperate, and there I go to the wastebasket to look for some, to get some, you know.") The juxtaposition of the two codes here is used with great stylistic effect in depicting the speaker's attitudes. The Spanish conveys a sense of personal feeling, even one of intimacy in revealing such a private act. We can compare these kinds of effects to the changes in intonation, loudness, rate of speech, vocabulary choice, etc. that occur in stylistic switching within a single language (Cook-Gumperz and Gumperz, 1976).

It is very clear that code switching, far from constituting a breakdown of a bilingual's grammatical system or being an uncontrolled and meaningless *Mischsprache,* is a systematic and meaningful mode of communication for many bilingual communities. It is not "interference" or an abnormality in the speech of a person. On the contrary, code alternation represents the creative use of both languages by the bilingual community. As bilinguals learn the usage norms of two languages within the community, they use them to facilitate the total act of communication.

SUMMARY

Before much empirical work had been conducted, it was widely believed, following behaviorist learning theory, that most second language learners' errors would result from their automatic use of L_1 structures when attempting to produce the L_2. According to the **Contrastive Analysis (CA) hypothesis,** the automatic "transfer" of L_1 structure to L_2 performance is "negative" when L_2 and L_1 structures differ, and "positive" when L_2 and L_1 structures are the same. Negative transfer according to the CA hypothesis would result in errors, while positive transfer would result in correct constructions.

A decade of psycholinguistic research has instead revealed the following:

1. Children who are learning the second language in the host country, and who are exposed to peers who speak the target language natively, make very few errors that unambiguously reflect the grammatical structure of their first language.

2. Adults make relatively more use of their native language than children, although the total proportion of errors that reflect the first language are in the minority.

3. Most of the errors that reflect the first language are those that involve word order rather than morphology.

4. Learners make grammatical errors which they would not have made had they used the rules of their first language.

5. First language background has little influence on L_2 learners' judgments of grammatical correctness in the second language.

6. The first language has a substantial influence on the second language in the area of pronunciation, especially for adults and beginning level children.

The available empirical data indicate that L_2 learners do not automatically use their L_1 grammar rules when attempting to produce L_2. What then causes the small number of interlingual errors (those that reflect the L_1) that do occur? Some possible explanations are **environmental**: (1) Learners will fall back on their L_1 if they are forced to use the L_2 before they are ready. Thus, environmental conditions that result in premature use of the L_1, such as pressure to perform or lack of natural L_2 exposure, may result in interlingual errors; (2) The use of timed translation tasks to elicit language also increases the number of interlingual errors.

Borrowing and code switching are additional areas where L_1 and L_2 interact. Borrowing, the incorporation of linguistic material from one language into another, is an extremely common phenomenon observed in languages throughout much of the world. Code switching refers to alternating between one language and another among bilinguals. It is a normal consequence of the natural contact of languages in multilingual societies.

STUDY QUESTIONS

1. Imagine that you heard a French-speaking person saying *I have 17 years* (J'ai 17 ans). Would that indicate that the contrastive analysis hypothesis is correct? Explain.

2. A new wave of immigrants from X-land has settled in Y-land. They work mainly in the micro-computer industry and have no access to grocery stores that sell their native food. What interactions between language X and language Y would you expect to observe in the adult immigrants:

a. During the first two months in Y-land?

b. During the first 5–10 years of life in Y-land?

c. At a party in their community held about 50 years after the first X-ish settlements were established in Y-land?

d. If you collected y speech from the children of the X-ish immigrants, would you expect to find many errors that reflect x structure? Explain your prediction.

3. The research evidence indicates that relatively few interlingual errors are made by L_2 learners. If somebody asked you whether this meant

that relatively little borrowing and code switching should occur, how would you respond? Persuade the person of your position.

4. In which of the following L_2 performance situations would you expect an L_2 learner to make use of his or her L_1 structures?:

   a. An adult who has been in the L_2 host country for 3 years, reading aloud.

   b. A child who has been in the L_2 host country for 3 years, reading aloud.

   c. An American tourist in Germany for the first time.

   d. An adult who has lived in the host country for a year, conversing with an acquaintance at a party.

   e. A child playing with L_2-speaking friends.

   f. A university student taking an L_2 test.

6

Transitional Constructions

Transitional constructions are the language forms learners use while they are still learning the grammar of a language.[1] A student who is still learning English might say for example: *Why you no come?* or *Why you get mad?* or *Who you calling?* These imperfect sentences are transitional constructions—indicators of the progress learners have made in deciphering and producing a new language system.

The studies that look at transitional constructions indicate that children and adults go through a number of key steps before mastering a structure. For example, during the earliest stage of learning English negatives in a first or second language, a child might be heard saying *No sleeping* or *No play baseball.* After a while, these transitional constructions become *She no sleeping* and *I no play base ball.* And finally we hear *She is not sleeping* and *I don't play baseball.* Analysis of these and numerous other similar kinds of sentences have made it possible for researchers to describe in some detail the intermediate steps involved in learning some basic second language structures.

Much of the work in this aspect of second language (L_2) acquisition has involved comparing the grammatical constructions used by second language learners with those made by young children acquiring their *first* language. At one time much more work had been done in first language (L_1) acquisition research than in second lan-

---

1. The term "developmental sequences" is used by Wode (1976) and his colleagues in Germany (Felix 1978a, 1980a; Meisel, 1980), to refer to transitional constructions and the orders in which they appear.

guage research. Subsequently, researchers assumed that discovered similarities between L_1 and L_2 development would give them a shortcut by permitting them to draw on the theoretical advances that had been made to describe the process of first language acquisition.

The research conducted had indeed documented striking similarities between the transitional constructions produced by first and second language learners, although some differences were also noted. Second language learners appear to produce a wider variety of forms in one developmental phase than do L_1 learners (e.g. *this* and *these* rather than just *this* in the beginning), evidence of the greater mental sophistication of older second language learners.

Researchers also found that many of the errors in transitional constructions produced by second language learners bore no relation to their native languages. For example, a Hispanic child learning English omitted the plural -s in *two boy* even though when speaking his native Spanish he supplied the plural -s, as in *casas* or *mesas*. It is is not surprising, therefore, to find that second language learners with native language backgrounds as diverse as Japanese, Spanish, Norwegian and Arabic, exhibit the same kinds of transitional constructions while learning English as a second language. These observations comprised one of the first indications of the existence of universal mental mechanisms involved in learning a second language.[2]

Most of the studies that have been undertaken along these lines have looked at children learning a second language in a host country, where that language is the official or major language of communication. Of the thirteen studies available, two investigate adults and one examines transitional constructions produced in a foreign language setting.

The structure types studied so far include English negation, *wh*-questions, *yes/no* questions, embedded *wh*-questions, and reflexive pronouns. The learners' first languages include Norwegian, Japanese, Spanish, Arabic, German and Keres.[3] In addition to English, L_2 transitional constructions in German and French have been investigated. These findings are presented below.

---

2. As in all types of learning, there is individual variation among second language learners, in particular, with respect to the number of different forms the learner attempts to use while learning a structure. For example, one learner might use *no* and *not* as negative words, while another might use only *no*. Such variation occurs within developmental steps and may be indicators of differences in learning style or in the quality of language the learners hear. (See also Pienemann, 1980.)

3. Keres is a language spoken by Pueblo Indians in New Mexico.

THE DEVELOPMENT OF NEGATION

English Negation

Researchers have observed that second language learners commonly pass through systematic and ordered stages in the acquisition of English negation.

Basic sentence negation in English (such as the *not* in the English auxiliary) is the aspect of negation that has been most studied by psycholinguistic researchers. For example: *He doesn't know how to paint; She is not a very interesting person.*

The acquisition of sentence negation of this sort has been elegantly described for English L₁ acquisition by Klima and Bellugi (1966). Their raw data were the voluminous recordings of three unacquainted children whose speech was regularly taped over a period of four years by Roger Brown, Ursula Bellugi, Courtney Cazden and their colleagues at Harvard. Klima and Bellugi's analysis and description of the transitional steps in the acquisition of negation have been used as the basis for comparison by all L₂ researchers who have investigated its development in English.

Seven research studies representing five language backgrounds have been completed to date. The types of transitional constructions reported in these studies are compiled and summarized in Table 6–1.

Column 1 presents representative examples of the children's utterances and the general rules Klima and Bellugi formulated to describe the developing speech of their three first-language learners. In the succeeding columns, we have summarized the transitional structures observed by the second language researchers who studied the acquisition of English negation for children speaking a variety of first languages: *Spanish* (Hernández-Chávez 1972; Cazden et al., 1975), *Japanese* (Milon, 1974; Gillis and Weber, 1976), *Norwegian* (Ravem, 1968), *German* (Wode, 1976, 1980a); and *Arabic* (Hanania and Gradman, 1977). Since all researchers compared their developing structures to Klima and Bellugi's, with similar results, we have reproduced only the general rules proposed by Klima and Bellugi to characterize the learners' development.

The table represents the major steps that have been observed during the acquisition of basic English negation: first attempts (Step 1) generally place the negator (e.g. *no, not*) outside the rest of the utterance—either before or after it. In Step 2, the negator is placed inside the utterance between the subject and verb, although the auxiliary (e.g. *is, are, do*) is still absent. In Step 3, the early auxili-

TABLE 6-1 Some Intermediate Steps in the Acquisition of Negation*

First Language Acquisition	Second Language Acquisition				
(Klima & Bellugi, 1966)	L₁=NORWEGIAN (Ravem, 1974)	L₁=JAPANESE (Milon, 1974; Gillis & Weber, 1976)	L₁=SPANISH (Hernández-Chávez, 1972; Cazden et al., 1975)	L₁=GERMAN (Wode, 1976, 1980a)	L₁=ARABIC (Hanania & Gradman, 1977)
Step 1† $S \rightarrow \left(\left\{ {no \atop not} \right\} \right) - Nucleus - \left(\left\{ {no \atop not} \right\} \right)$					
Examples: No wipe finger. Not a teddy bear. Wear mitten no.	Not like it now. Not ready. No, no like it.	Not me. Not dog. Not cold.	No milk. No sleeping.	No, you. No play baseball. No catch it.	No, English. Not raining. Not here.
Step 2 $S \rightarrow Nom - Aux^{neg} - \left\{ {Predicate \atop Main\ Verb} \right\}$ $Aux^{neg} \rightarrow \left\{ {No \atop Not \atop Don't} \right\}$					
Examples: I don't sit on Cromer coffee. He not little, he big. He no bite you.	I not this way. I not like that. Dolly "er" not here.	I no queen. I not give you candy. I no more five. Don't tell teacher, ok?	I no like this one. I no know it. I not dumb. I don't can explain.	Me no close the window. You not shut up. You no swim.	—
Step 3 $S \rightarrow Nom - Aux - \left\{ {Predicate \atop Main\ Verb} \right\}$ $Aux \rightarrow T - V^{Aux} - (Neg)$					
Examples: No it isn't. That was not me.	No, I didn't. I haven't seen this afore. You can't have this back.	You're not playing it. No, they're not white.	I'm not scare ghost. They didn't have time.	Lunch is no ready. I didn't can close it. I cannot hit the ball.	—

*The acquisition of negation does not preclude errors in other structures. Hence, errors in other structures appear even in Stage 3.

†While Klima & Bellugi's "Stages" for L₁ learners are defined by Mean Length of Utterance (MLU), L₂ researchers have not usually done so. Instead, they report the "steps" observed as learners acquire the second language, regardless of MLU.

Heidi Dulay and Marina Burt, 1978. From research to method in bilingual education. In: *Georgetown University Round Table on Languages and Linguistics, 1978.* Edited by James E. Alatis. Washington, D.C.: Georgetown University Press. Copyright © 1978 by Georgetown University. Pp. 551–575.

aries are used, and the negator is correctly placed to the right of the auxiliary.

Some Caveats

Blending of Transitional Steps   The beginning and end of developmental steps in the acquisition of a structure are not as abrupt as the table suggests. Language development is not a series of plateaus, but a continuum. Learners typically use transitional constructions representative of one step while they try out forms representing the next step. The "steps" presented in Table 6-1, then, indicate the major types of changes that negative structures undergo during the learning process, and the order in which these transitions have occurred.

Skipping a Step   All three steps were not always apparent in the speech of the L_2 learners studied. For example, some data showed utterances characteristic of just Steps 1 and 3, others just Steps 2 and 3, and still others showed all three. It is difficult to ascertain whether the step was actually skipped by the learner. As Cazden (1972) points out in her discussion of research methods, learners may very well produce structures when researchers aren't there to collect them. We can conclude, however, that whether or not steps were skipped, the types of transitional constructions observed appeared in the same order for all subjects, indicating that the structure develops systematically.

Variability of Forms   Learners may differ in the number and type of forms they produce during a given stage of language development. Second language learners, who are mentally more mature than first language learners, exhibit quite a variety of forms in their speech. In the acquisition of negation, both the negator and the auxiliary are expressed in various ways by different learners. For the negator in Step 2, for example, some used just *no* or *not;* others used one of these (or both) as well as *don't;* while others used *can't* in addition to *no, not* and *don't.* All these variations are consistent with the general characteristic of Step 2, namely, that the negator was usually placed after the subject, and the auxiliary and the negator were treated as a single unit regardless of which auxiliary the learner apparently mistook as part of the negator (*can't, don't* or both).[4]

4. One may conclude that *can* and *do* are acquired as auxiliaries when they are produced without the contracted negative morpheme. In the available data, Step 2 is characterized by the appearance of *can't* and *don't* as unanalyzed, rather than as segmented, elements (see Chapter 9 for further discussion of wholes in learner speech), suggesting that these forms are used as negators rather than as auxiliaries.

Similarly, Felix (1977, 1980c) found that German high school students who were exposed to English only during their formal ESL classes placed *don't/doesn't* rather than the negative morphemes *no/not* in sentence-initial position. After detailed explanations of the *do*-insertion rule, the students obviously knew that they were supposed to use *don't/doesn't* for sentence negation; however, as they were unable to apply the rule correctly, they did exactly what language learners in a natural language environment do as a first approximation, namely, place the negator external to the remaining sentence.

This type of variability within learning steps appears to characterize the acquisition of other structures as well. Madden, Bailey, Eisenstein and Anderson (1978), for example, in a study of forty-six adults learning English as an L₂, found that in the acquisition of auxiliaries (*is, are, do* and *does*), learners alternated different auxiliaries for each other. They also noted that some students tried to use all the auxiliaries while others attempted only one or two. The use of more than one form within a step, then, appears to characterize the acquisition of structures, with some learners alternating more forms for a structure than others. This variation does not, however, alter the place of the step in the total sequence.[5]

German Negation

Researchers have compared the transitional constructions used by children learning German as a first and as a second language. Felix (1978a) and Lange (1979) studied English-speaking children who were acquiring German as their second language in Kiel. Wode (1976) looked at the development of negation in children learning German as their first language, and compared the results of the two groups of learners. Table 6-2 lists utterances that exemplify the developmental sequence observed.

As the table makes clear, the development of negation in German is orderly and strikingly similar for first language learners and child second language learners. The negator *nein* (*no*) is used alone first and is placed before the utterances produced (I-IIb). Next, *nicht* (*not*) appears, both before, within, and after the utterances produced. Finally, the placement of the negative *nicht* begins to stabilize, appearing after the verb (in declarative utterances). Park (1979) notes

5. Why some learners use more or fewer alternating forms in the acquisition of structures may be related to personality factors discussed in Chapter 4 or to affective filtering factors discussed in Chapter 3.

TABLE 6-2 Development of Negation in German as a First Language and Second Language for Children

First Language Acquisition (Wode, 1976)	Second Language Acquisition $L_1 = ENGLISH$ (Lange, 1979)
I *nein* (no)	*nein* (no)
II *nein, Milch* (no, milk)	*nein, da* (no, there)
IIb *nein hauen* (no bang = don't bang)	*nein helfen* (no help = don't help)
III *Heiko nicht essen* (Heiko is not to eat anything)	*Milch nicht da* (milk not there)
nicht Rasen (not step on the lawn)	*nicht fahren* there (not drive there)
Britta nicht (Britta not = Britta is not to do it)	*nein, das nicht* (no, that not) *das nicht ein Schaf* (that not a sheep)
IV *Holger kriegt nicht ein Lutscher* (Holger is not to get a lollipop)	

some variation in his subjects: within Stage II, IIb may precede IIa, and that the negation marker in Stage III may be *nein* in some cases.

Findings such as these will no doubt continue to appear for other languages, adding to the mounting evidence which demonstrates that language learners systematically develop transitional constructions as they acquire fairly complicated structures such as negation.

THE DEVELOPMENT OF INTERROGATIVES

English *Wh*-Questions

Wh-questions require, first of all, that the speaker place a *wh*-word (*what, why, who, how,* etc.) before the rest of the question. At the same time, if there is an auxiliary in the statement form of the sentence, it must exchange places with the subject noun. The following illustrates these requirements:

Statement: *Those are mangos.*
Wh-word placed at the beginning: *What those are?*
Auxiliary inversion: *What are those?*

If no auxiliary is present, as in *They cook rice every day*, then *do* must be inserted in the spot where an auxiliary would have gone.

Statement: *They cook rice everyday.*
Wh-word placed at the beginning: *What they cook everyday?*
Do insertion: *What do they cook everyday?*

Given that *wh*-constructions require the coordination of several kinds of knowledge, various things may be overlooked by beginning learners:

1. Learners may not have learned to exchange the places of the auxiliary (e.g. *are*) and the subject (e.g. *those*).
2. Learners may not have acquired some or any of the auxiliaries yet. For example, in *What he done?* the learner does not use the auxiliary *has*.
3. Learners may not insert *do* as the tense-carrying element, which is required in cases where no auxiliary is available. For example, in *How they get it all the time?*, *do* should have been inserted before the statement.

These errors occur in the developing speech of both first and second language learners acquiring English. The transitional constructions observed seem to fall into four major ordered steps:

STEP 1:   *Wh*-words appear before the rest of the statement form of the utterances, which is otherwise left unchanged. Utterances have virtually none of the little grammatical words and endings required, in particular auxiliaries such as *is* and *do*. A typical Step 1 question is:

What you study?

STEP 2:   Some early auxiliaries (e.g. *is, are, was*) appear, along with some modals (*can* and *will*). The auxiliaries are not yet systematically inverted with the subject. A typical Step 2 question is:

What she is doing?

STEP 3:   The early auxiliaries, which are acquired in Step 2, are regularly inverted. On the other hand, in the *wh*-questions that require *late* auxiliaries such as *do* and *am*, the auxiliaries are still omitted. In this stage, therefore, the learner produces *wh*-questions in which the auxiliary is inverted resulting in a correct sentence, along with those in which the auxiliary is omitted resulting in an incorrect sentence.[6] Typical Step 3 questions are:

What are they?
Where I put the man?
What he did?

STEP 4:   The late auxiliaries (e.g. *has, been, am*) are acquired and are inverted with subjects. *Do* is inserted between the *wh*-word and the subject, although it may still be misformed, as in *Do he make that?*

As with the development of negation, researchers compared *wh*-question development for L_2 learners to that reported by Klima and Bellugi (1966) for first language acquisition. Table 6-3 summarizes these comparisons in terms of the developmental steps observed. As we noted about negation, not all of the researchers' data we reviewed contained examples of all four steps. In most instances, this was simply because the writers presented few actual examples (only three or four in some cases), focusing instead on discussion of the characteristics of the examples. Further, as Table 6-3 indicates, Step 3 is characterized by the obligatory occasions for *late* auxiliaries. Learners typically omit these, consequently they cannot demonstrate subject-auxiliary inversion in these utterances. In producing utterances that contain occasions for *early* auxiliaries, however, learners produce the auxiliaries and invert them with the subject. Schumann (1976) has suggested that such data indicate that the inversion rule is applied arbitrarily, and therefore that there is not a systematic development in the L_2 acquisition of *wh*-questions. Such an inference seems premature, however, since the operation of an inversion rule can be demonstrated *only with items that have been acquired.* One can invert if the pieces to invert are both present; however, if the piece to be inverted is omitted, inversion is impossible. Similarly, the failure to insert some form of *do* between the *wh*-word and the subject (e.g. *where you get that?*) cannot speak to the presence, absence, or arbitrary application of an inversion rule in a learner's syntactic repertoire.

---

6. The *do* insertion rule does not operate regularly yet, although *don't* appears in non-question utterances and is inverted in *yes-no* questions.

TABLE 6-3   Some Intermediate Steps in the Acquisition of *Wh*-Questions by Children and One Adult: L₁ and L₂*

	L_1 = ENGLISH (Klima & Bellugi, 1966)	L_1 = NORWEGIAN (Ravem, 1974)	L_1 = JAPANESE (Gillis & Weber, 1976)	L_1 = SPANISH (Cazden et al., 1975)
Step 1 Virtually no auxiliaries.	Who that? Where milk go?	Where find it? Where "er" hers Mommy?	—	What you study?
Step 2 Some auxiliaries; plus modals (*can*, *will*). No inversion rule.	What he can ride in? Where the other Joe will drive?	What she is doing? Whosis that is?	. . . What's that is?	—
Step 3 Inversion (of acquired auxiliaries); *Do*-insertion for WH-questions not in control yet.	—	What are they? What are he doing now? Why can't you touch with your—with your hand?	Where's the start? What you did? Where I put the man?	How can you say it? Where you get that?
Step 4 Inversion of all acquired auxiliaries; *Do*-insertion for *Wh*-questions under control	—	What did you talk to them?	How can I get this in? How do you do it?	Where do you live?

*Heidi Dulay and Marina Burt. 1978. From research to method in bilingual education. In: *Georgetown University Round Table on Languages and Linguistics, 1978.* Edited by James E. Alatis. Washington, D.C.: Georgetown University Press. Copyright © 1978 by Georgetown University. pp. 551–575.

German *Wh*-Questions

Wh-question data from native English-speaking children learning German in Germany shows similar development (Felix, 1976, 1978a). Earliest examples (Step 1) show few or no auxiliaries; *wo zwei (where two); wo meine (where mine)*. Subsequent examples show that the children do not use the required verb inversion rule: *wo Sascha kommt (where Sascha comes); warum Guy machen das (why Guy do that); wohin du geht (to where you goes)*. Later, the correctly inverted *wh*-questions were used.

French and English *Wh*-Questions in a Foreign Environment

Valdman (1975) reported on the acquisition of French *wh*-question forms by American students learning French at a university in the United States. After a semester of instruction, Valdman asked his sixteen students to formulate *wh*-questions in French (a written task). He discovered something very interesting: a significant number of students (30%) actually produced a form to which they had never been exposed. Although only inversion questions (*Où va Jean?*) and *est-ce que* questions (*Est-ce que Jean va?*) were taught during this period, these students produced questions of the form *Où Jean va?* (which Valdman referred to as "*wh*-fronting").

This is an especially impressive finding, because the students had no exposure to French outside the classroom, where, according to Valdman, the intermediate form produced by the students had not been used. This suggests that transitional constructions are not limited to language learning in a host language environment; they appear in foreign language environments as well.[7]

Felix (1979, 1980c) reported similar findings with respect to German high school students studying English as a second language without any exposure to English outside of the classroom. These students, too, used uninverted *wh*-questions (e.g. *What they are picking? How many turkeys she is feeding?*), even though they were never exposed to such forms nor does German allow comparable structures. Felix observed that the students continued to use uninverted *wh*-questions for a period of roughly three weeks despite

7. He also points out that the corresponding structure in the first language can be rapidly eliminated as a potential source: "the EST-CE QUE construction provides the best one-to-one matching of the surface structure features of the English construction" (Valdman, 1974, p. 15). He compares:

| Où | est-ce que | Jean | travaille? |
| Where | does | John | work? |

pointing out that both languages have semantically empty elements occurring in the same linear order. The same observation holds for "semantically full" auxiliaries.

intensive daily practice of the correct forms. Furthermore, both in interrogation and negation (and a few other structural domains), students made the same developmental errors that have been found in L_1 and natural L_2 acquisition environments. Apparently, in both host and foreign language environments, practice and drill do not affect the learners' use of systematic transitional constructions.

English *Yes/No* Questions

The acquisition of English *yes/no* questions (questions that can be answered with a *yes* or *no*, e.g. *Is she very fat? Do you want some?*) has also been investigated, though much less systematically.

Some studies (Klima and Bellugi, 1966, for L_1 acquisition; Ravem, 1968; Gillis and Weber, 1976, for child second language acquisition) show clearly that *yes/no* questions first appear uninverted (*This is a face?*), and without *do* (*Daddy go yesterday?*). Then the auxiliaries that have been acquired are inverted and *do* is used.[8]

From the available data, scanty though they are, it appears that for some subjects at least, the auxiliary inversion rule is applied to *yes/no* questions somewhat before it is applied to *wh*-questions. Likewise, the *do*-insertion rule seems to begin operating on *yes/no* questions before it operates regularly in the *wh*-questions.

English Embedded *Wh*-Questions

The steps in the development of certain higher level structures, such as embedded *wh*-questions (also called "indirect *wh*-questions") have also been the subject of recent investigations.

This particular construction is of special interest because it requires that the learners *not* apply rules which they have already learned to apply correctly to simple questions—the auxiliary inversion and *do*-insertion rule. When questions are embedded in phrases such as *We don't know*, the auxiliary remains in the same place as it is in the statement e.g. *We don't know why she is sad.* It is ungrammatical to say *We don't know why is she sad.* Likewise, *do* is not inserted, as in *I wonder if she likes him.* We don't say *I wonder does she like him.* Before learners discover this kink, we regularly see errors due to the overapplication of rules otherwise well learned.

The converse also happens. Some learners attempt embedded question constructions early, even before they have mastered the

---

8. We do not include *don't, didn't* or *doesn't* in our *wh*-question *do*-insertion rule, as *do* + negative may already be present before inversion takes place (e.g. *He doesn't like it. What doesn't he like?*) We refer only to the *do*-insertion which is required when there is no auxiliary in the original utterance to invert (e.g. *He goes. Does he go?*).

auxiliary inversion or *do*-insertion rules. The resulting embedded constructions then look right, for example, *I don't know what he is doing*. We know, though, that they are not holding back on the inversion rule because we also hear *what he is doing?*, making it clear that they don't control the inversion rule at all.

The transitional embedded *wh*-constructions that learners use show how learners rely on previously acquired rules when they try out new related second language structures. Table 6-4 illustrates the transitional constructions observed in the acquisition of these structures by Spanish-, Keres- and Japanese-speaking children, and by one Spanish-speaking adult.

As Table 6-4 illustrates, learners begin by using the inversion rule from the simple *wh*-questions. Next, we see examples demonstrating that sometimes the learners try it both ways at once—inverted and uninverted. Finally, learners withhold the auxiliary inversion and *do*-insertion rules when the questions are placed into embedded contexts.

REFLEXIVE PRONOUNS

The development of the reflexive pronouns *herself, himself,* and *themselves* was investigated in a recent study of 175 Spanish-speaking students in the United States (grades 3–8) by Dulay and Burt (1977). The transitional constructions observed were compared with observations made of the acquisition of some of these complex pronouns by first language learners (R. Brown, 1973), a well as with observations of their development for a second language learner (Hakuta, 1976).

Although data on the acquisition of the whole set of reflexive pronouns is not yet available, what has been observed presents an orderly picture of the development of these pronouns for both first and second language learners. Table 6-5 summarizes the transitional constructions observed so far.

The developmental steps observed provide an interesting example of how learners try to fit new data into their existing (but not yet mature) language system. Once they begin to systematically combine a pronoun form with *self*, we see that they use the possessive pronoun forms—*my, your, her,* to do so. All of these lead to correctly formed reflexive pronouns: *myself, yourself,* and *herself*. *His* and *their*, however, are exceptions; their possessive forms are not combined to form reflexives, and this is the source of the erroneous forms *hisself* and *theirself(ves)*. The preferred forms are the exceptional *himself* and *themselves*.

TABLE 6-4 Some Intermediate Steps in the Second Language Acquisition of Embedded *Wh*-Questions*

Intermediate Steps	L_1 = SPANISH (Dulay & Burt, 1977; Cazden et al., 1975)	L_1 = KERES (Dulay & Burt, 1977)	L_1 = JAPANESE (Hakuta, 1975)
Step 1 [S] + [WH-word – Aux – NP]	I don't know where's the food. I don't know what are those. I know where are you going.	I don't know what's that.	I don't know where is it.
Step 2 [S] + [WH-word – Aux – NP – Aux]	I don't know where's the food is. †	I know what's that is.	I don't know where is the woods is.
Step 3 [S] + [WH-word – NP – Aux]	I don't know where the food is. I don't know what those are. I don't know what he had.	I know what that is.	I know where it is.

*Heidi Dulay and Marina Burt, 1978. From research to method in bilingual education. In: *Georgetown University Round Table on Languages and Linguistics*, 1978. Edited by James E. Alatis. Washington, D.C.: Georgetown University Press. Copyright © 1978 by Georgetown University, pp. 551–575.

†No example for Step 2 involving the plural copula was found in the children's speech protocols.

TABLE 6-5 Some Intermediate Steps in the Acquisition of Reflexive Pronouns for First Language and Second Language*

Intermediate Steps	L_1 = ENGLISH (Brown, 1973)	L_1 = SPANISH (Dulay & Burt, 1977)	L_1 = JAPANESE (Hakuta, 1975)
Step 1 Refl. Pron→ { self pronoun	—	(She see(s)) her (He see(s)) him (They see) them	You have to make it self.
Step 2 Refl. Pron→ Pron + self [+ poss]	*hisself*	. . . herself . . . hisself . . . theirself	You can write it with yourself. They have to do it with theirself.
Step 3 Refl. Pron→ Pron + self [+ accus]	—	. . . herself . . . himself . . . themself(s)/ves or . . . theirself(s)/ves†	—

*Heidi Dulay and Marina Burt, 1978. From research to method in bilingual education. In: *Georgetown University Round Table on Languages and Linguistics*, 1978. Edited by James E. Alatis. Washington, D.C.: Georgetown University Press. Copyright © 1978 by Georgetown University, pp. 551–575.

†*Theirselves* is a mature form in some varieties of English.

"Children [and older second language learners], by inventing *his-self* (and *theirself*), and often insisting on it for quite a period, iron out or correct the irregularity of language. And, incidentally, they reveal to us the fact that what they are learning are general rules of construction—not just the words and phrases they hear" (R. Brown 1973, p. 98). The general rule of construction learned is that "possessive pronoun form + self = reflexive pronoun." Overapplying this rule to exceptions produces the transitional constructions observed in Steps 2 and 3.

SUMMARY

Transitional constructions are the interim language forms learners use while they are still in the process of learning the grammar of a second language. Although imperfect, transitional constructions are indicators of progress rather than failure.

The numerous studies that focus on transitional constructions all indicate that L_2 learners, like L_1 learners, acquire grammatical structures in an ordered series of key steps. The structures examined in the literature include English negation, *wh*-questions and reflexive pronouns, along with some German negative and interrogative structures and French interrogatives. Most of the studies have investigated child second language acquisition in a host environment, although a few have investigated adult second language acquisition in host as well as foreign language settings.

Striking similarities between the systematic transitional constructions produced by first and second language learners have been documented, although some differences are discernible. A wider variety of forms produced by second language learners in a single developmental phase is one difference. There may be others, but more research is required to pinpoint them accurately. The greater mental sophistication of older L_2 learners probably underlies the differences.

Individual variation among L_2 learners has been observed with respect to the number of alternating forms used while a structure is being acquired, in particular in the acquisition of negative markers and auxiliaries. Such variability in performance occurs within developmental steps and does not alter the sequence of transitional constructions learners pass through during the acquisition of syntactic structures.

Finally, most of the researchers noted that the errors observed bore no relation to the first language of the students.

STUDY QUESTIONS

1. Speaker No. 1 said: "I don't know why *Omar is* not here."
   Speaker No. 2 said: "I don't know why *is Omar* not here."
   a. Can you conclude that Speaker No. 1 is more advanced than Speaker No. 2 in the acquisition of embedded questions?
   b. Explain your answer.
   c. How would you expect a beginning learner of English to express the question?

2. Nelson's (1980) subject Giovanni, an adult ESL learner in Canada, produced the following negative utterances:

Utterance	Frequency	Developed Form
I don't know	6	I don't know
I de see	23	I don't see
I no see	27	I don't see
I not here	54	I'm not here
I'm no here	15	I'm not here
I no here	31	I'm not here

   a. Would you say Giovanni is at the beginning, intermediate or advanced stage in acquiring English negation?
   b. Is there a discernible construction that characterizes the stage Giovanni is in? Explain.
   c. Does Giovanni's use of a variety of negative markers affect your answer in b. above? Explain.

7

Errors

Errors are the flawed side of learner speech or writing. They are those parts of conversation or composition that deviate from some selected norm of mature language performance. Teachers and mothers who have waged long and patient battles against their students' or children's language errors have come to realize that making errors is an inevitable part of learning. People cannot learn language without first systematically committing errors.

Studying learners' errors serves two major purposes: (1) it provides data from which inferences about the nature of the language learning process can be made; and (2) it indicates to teachers and curriculum developers which part of the target language students have most difficulty producing correctly and which error types detract most from a learner's ability to communicate effectively.

Error analysis has yielded insights into the L_2 acquisition process that have stimulated major changes in teaching practices. Perhaps its most controversial contribution has been the discovery that the majority of the grammatical errors second language learners make do not reflect the learner's mother tongue but are very much like those young children make as they learn a first language. Researchers have found that like L_1 learners' errors, most of the errors L_2 learners make indicate they are gradually building an L_2 rule system. Among the most common errors are:

Omitting grammatical morphemes, which are items that do not contribute much to the meaning of sentences, as in *He hit car.*

Double marking a semantic feature (e.g. past tense) when only one marker is required, as in *She didn't went back.*

Regularizing rules, as in *womans* for *women*.

Using archiforms—one form in place of several—such as the use of *her* for both *she* and *her*, as in *I see her yesterday. Her dance with my brother.*

Using two or more forms in random alternation even though the language requires the use of each only under certain conditions, as in the random use of *he* and *she* regardless of the gender of the person of interest.

Misordering items in constructions that require a reversal of word-order rules that had been previously acquired, as in *What you are doing?*, or misplacing items that may be correctly placed in more than one place in the sentence, as in *They are all the time late.*

The norm used to identify errors may be any one of the dialects or other varieties of the language the speaker uses. One might, for example, look at errors with respect to a nonstandard language variety such as Maori English. Using that norm, the utterance *Who's your name?* is well formed. If, however, the norm selected is British or American English, the use of *who* for *what* would be considered an error.

Sometimes researchers distinguish between errors caused by factors such as fatigue and inattention (what Chomsky, 1965, called "performance" factors), and errors resulting from lack of knowledge of the rules of the language (what Chomsky, 1965, called "competence"). In some of the second language literature, performance errors have been called "mistakes" while the term "errors" was reserved for the systematic deviations due to the learner's still-developing knowledge of the L_2 rule system (Corder, 1967). The distinction between performance and competence errors is extremely important, but it is often difficult to determine the nature of a deviation without careful analysis. In order to facilitate reference to deviations that have not yet been classified as performance or competence errors, we do not restrict the term "error" to competence-based deviations. We use *error* to refer to *any* deviation from a selected norm of language performance, no matter what the characteristics or causes of the deviation might be.

THE ERROR ANALYSIS MOVEMENT

If a popularity contest were held among the various aspects of verbal performance, errors would surely make off with first prize. The study of learners' errors has been a primary focus of L_2 research during the last decade. Since S. Pit Corder's initial arguments for the significance of learners' errors appeared in the Winter 1967 issue of the *International Review of Applied Linguistics*, researchers and teachers in numerous countries have spent countless hours extracting errors from student compositions and conversations, submitting them to close scrutiny, and using them as a base for theory construction and classroom practice.

The instant and widespread appeal of error analysis (EA) stemmed perhaps from the refreshing alternative it provided to the then prevailing but more restrictive "contrastive analysis" approach to errors. The contrastive analysis (CA) treatment of errors, which was popular up through the 1960's, rested on a comparison of the learner's native and target languages. Differences between the two were thought to account for the majority of an L_2 learner's errors. The associationist or behaviorist view of learning prevalent at that time provided the theoretical justification for CA. It held that learning was basically a process of forming automatic habits and that errors should therefore result from first language habits interfering with the learner's attempts to learn new linguistic behaviors. It was thought that contrastive analysis of the learner's two languages would predict the areas in the target language that would pose the most difficulty. (See Chapter 5 for a more detailed discussion.)

Attentive teachers and researchers, however, noticed that a great number of student errors could not possibly be traced to their native languages. For example, although Spanish plurals are formed almost exactly like English plurals, Spanish-speaking children still go through a plural-less stage as they learn English (Hernández-Chávez, 1972). This and other similar observations documented in journal articles pointed out an embarrassing gap between theory and reality and set the scene for the acceptance of a more comprehensive approach to errors.

The theoretical climate of the late fifties and the early sixties provided the ultimate rationale for the EA approach. Chomsky's "Review of B.F. Skinner's Verbal Behavior" (1959) questioned the very core of behaviorist habit theory as an account of language learning. Two years in the writing, the paper provided the catalyst for efforts that virtually turned the field of developmental psycholinguistics around overnight. Chomskyan generative linguistics, along with Piagetian psychology, have succeeded in highlighting the previously neglected mental makeup of learners as a central force in the learning process. As a consequence, error analysis came away with a rich source of explanation for the many as yet unexplained but frequently observed student errors.

The EA movement can be characterized as an attempt to account for learner errors that could not be explained or predicted by CA or behaviorist theory, and to bring the field of applied linguistics into step with the current climate of theoretical opinion. In these respects EA has been most successful. It has made a significant contribution to the theoretical consciousness-raising of applied linguistics and language practitioners. It has brought the multiple origins of learners' errors to our attention. Finally, it has succeeded in elevating the status of errors from complete undesirability to the relatively special status of research object, curriculum guide, and indicator of learning stage.

On the debit side of the EA balance sheet, however, are at least three major conceptual [1] weaknesses that seem to have impeded the potential contributions it might have made to the field. They are: (1) the confusion of error description of errors with error explanation (the process and product aspects of error analysis); (2) the lack of precision and specificity in the definition of error categories; and (3) simplistic categorization of the causes of learners' errors. (The discussion of these weaknesses is fairly technical. Some readers may, therefore, wish to skip to the next section.)

Weakness 1:   Confusion of explanatory and descriptive (process and product) aspects of error analysis

The description of an error refers to the product of language acquisition, whereas the *explanation* of an error—the determination of its origins—refers to the language of acquisition process.

The *process* of language acquisition consists of the interaction between the learner's internal processing mechanisms and the external environment. The *product* of acquisition, on the other hand, consists of the results of the learning process, namely, the learner's verbal performance. Verbal performance may be described in terms of errors, transitional constructions, acquisition orders and other aspects of a learner's linguistic product.

Determining the processes that underlie errors entails at least two steps: (1) describing the error categories in terms of precise, theoretically motivated, observable characteristics; and (2) formulating causal inferences about the learning process from the descriptive

---

1. The methodological problems of research design and analysis are discussed in later sections.

error data and any other data that might be brought to bear on the issue.

For example, if one notices that a Spanish speaker omits *does* in English negative sentences, as in *Lily no have money*, one might describe such an error as a word-for-word equivalent of a semantically similar sentence in the learner's native Spanish (*Lily no tiene dinero*). Such a description does not refer to the cause of the error; it refers to surface characteristics of the error, which can be determined simply by comparing the error structure with its equivalent in the native language.

Determining the processes responsible for the error is, on the other hand, a matter of inference, involving yet another step. Once we know the error's surface characteristics, we might ask: Is the error a manifestation of the process of negative transfer? Is it a reflection of some conscious translation strategy the learner has adopted as a modus operandi in certain situations? Or, is it due to some other factor or aggregate of factors as yet not conceived?

The answer to such questions are matters of inference reached by reasoned argument and empirical probe. One might, for instance, determine the relative frequencies of such errors in one's error sample and study selected features in the learning environment of the student. Additionally, one might examine other aspects of the learner's verbal performance, such as transitional constructions and acquisition orders, to see what additional light can be shed on the matter. The process of inferring the cause(s) of certain observed behavior consists of formulating hypotheses about the cause(s) and gathering enough confirming evidence to persuade oneself, as well as one's colleagues, that the hypothesized cause(s) are correct.

(We are not suggesting that teachers are responsible for carrying out such detailed analyses. Rather, materials and methods should be based on the results of such analyses.)

The EA literature is rife with studies that confuse the cause of error with their description. For example, most of the studies that report the incidence of *do* omission by Spanish speakers simply declare that such an error is due to "transfer." Transfer is rarely defined meaningfully, however, which leads one to wonder what the researcher is proposing. Does transfer refer to the technical definition of the transfer process in behaviorist psychology? Or to the nontechnical use of the term in education (meaning use of previously learned knowledge or skill)? Or simply to the surface characteristics of the error?

The lack of such distinctions in the EA literature has caused needless controversy as well as stagnation in two important areas of error research: (1) the development of descriptive criteria to delimit different error types; and (2) the formulation of theories to account for the appearance of a variety of error types in L_2 learner speech and writing.

Weakness 2: Lack of sufficient precision and specificity in the definition of error categories.

Virtually no effort has been made to define error categories precisely and in such a manner as to allow replication or comparative studies to be conducted with scientific rigor.

Consider, for example, the following definitions of "intralingual error":

> Intralingual errors are those which reflect the general characteristics of rule learning, such as faulty overgeneralization, incomplete application of rules, and failure to learn conditions under which rules apply.
>
> (Richards, 1974a, p. 174)

> Intralingual errors occur when L_1 does not have a rule which L_2 has; the learner applies an L_2 rule, producing an error.
>
> (LoCoco, 1976, p. 99)

Obviously, these are two quite different definitions, and would lead researchers to report different findings for the same data with respect to types and frequencies of intralingual errors.

In another study, the intralingual error category was not defined at all (nor were any of the other categories), even though overlap was a clear problem, as the following excerpt from the report shows:

> . . . The regularization of the irregular pattern in verb inflection is due to intralingual interference, but it is also a learner characteristic. The s-ending added to the verb is here considered to be conditioned both by the s-passive in Swedish and by overgeneralization of the -s in the third person singular in English. Consequently, it has been subsumed under the two headings Intralingual interference and Interlingual interference. . .
>
> (Olsson, 1974, p. 67)

It would not be constructive to expand further upon the many problems of definition in the currently available error studies. We simply wish to bring them to the reader's attention as one of the major obstacles to reporting findings across studies concerning the frequencies of variously defined error types.

Weakness 3: The inappropriate use of simplistic classifications to explain learners' errors

The development of error classification based on sources of errors has taken up a good portion of the error analysis research literature. Although this use of error taxonomies has led to a great deal of discussion and debate, much of it has generated more heat than light. This may be because explaining error types is not simply a matter of assigning a single source to each error that occurs. Language learning is an interaction of internal and external factors and explanation of errors must reflect that interaction. Nevertheless, in the literature we find many error categories that refer to (hypothesized) sources of origins of learners' errors. These include a number of environmental factors (training procedures, communication situations, sociocultural factors), and a number of *internal processing factors* (first language "transfer," "simplification," generation of "false hypotheses" by the learner, and others). Even factors that have to do with how speech was elicited from the learner can be sources of error.

An adequate explanation of language learners' verbal performance seems much too complex to be squeezed into taxonomic formats which were originally designed to classify rocks, flowers and other concrete observable phenomena. Taxonomies might more appropriately be used to organize errors according to *directly observable* characteristics.

The use of a taxonomy to delineate sources of error entails at least two assumptions: (1) that a particular error has a single source, and (2) that the specification of the source(s) of an error is a relatively straightforward descriptive task. Unfortunately, neither of these assumptions seems to hold up. For example, an error that reflects the structure of the learner's first language might have been triggered by at least three sources: by pressure to communicate, by the conscious use of a word-for-word translation strategy, and perhaps even by the manner in which the learner was initially exposed to the structure in question. If language acquisition is indeed an interaction between internal and external factors, then the end-products of the acquisition process—errors, for example—must have at least two major sources: one in the environment and one internal to the learner. Within those, multiple subsources can be delineated.

Any researcher who attempts to use an error taxonomy to posit sources of errors must make a number of difficult and ultimately arbitrary decisions in order to attribute a singular source to an error. Even if one classifies one error simultaneously into two source categories, the task would not be straightforward. Some errors that look like a structure in the learner's native language cannot automatically be attributed to transfer of the first language to the second; they may have been caused by some other mental process. Conversely, an error that seems to look like one made by children during first language acquisition may have been influenced in some way by the learner's first language.

Additionally, categories that have been proposed as different sources of error turn out to be subsets of each other. Consider, for example, Richards' "intralingual" and "developmental" (1971a) categories. Intralingual errors "reflect the general character of rule learning such as faulty overgeneralization, incomplete application of rules, and failure to learn conditions under which rules apply" (1974). Developmental errors, on the other hand, are, according to Richards, those which "illustrate the learner attempting to build up hypotheses about the [target] language" (1974, p. 174).[2] An examination of learners' developing speech, however, reveals that most developmental errors are intralingual. No published effort to date has been made to clarify the boundaries of these categories, and error analysts continue to use them as separate error types within a single taxonomy. In the absence of clear boundaries, arbitrary classification decisions are unavoidable.

In this chapter, we will limit our discussion to the descriptive aspects of error taxonomies on the assumption that *the accurate description of errors is a separate activity from the task of inferring the sources of those errors.* We have focused on error taxonomies that classify errors according to some observable surface feature of the error itself, without reference to its underlying cause or source. We have called these *descriptive taxonomies.* Error analysis, from this perspective, is an analytical tool, as are the specification of transitional constructions, the computation of acquisition orders, and the delineation of special utterance types.

In the interest of clear discussion, we have left the explanation of errors, which involves a specification of processes underlying language acquisition itself, to four earlier chapters (2, 3, 4 and 5). They deal with the learner's environment and internal processing factors, two major process dimensions in language acquisition which include all the sources of error so far postulated.

2. These categories derive from Selinker's (1972) proposal that there are five processes central to second language learning, among which are "overgeneralization of target language rules" (intralingual) and "strategies of second language learning" (developmental). Like Richards, Selinker proposed two processes, one of which is a subset of the other. Overgeneralization is one of the strategies of L₂ learning, and thus when one uses overgeneralization as well as strategies of L₂ learning as error categories, there is a great overlap.

We have also attempted to take a first step in making clear the great need in linguistic research for a sound and systematic methodology of error analysis. The descriptive classification of errors is often the first step a researcher takes in developing a hypothesis or inference about L_2 learning processes. Similarly, it is sometimes the first step in a teacher's development of a curriculum plan, or a textbook writer's organization and selection of material. Enormous problems have been caused, however, because idiosyncratic definition of error categories and error types has prevented meaningful cross-study comparisons or validation of results. In this chapter, we have attempted to begin to fill this need by specifying the major taxonomies used, stating their purposes and defining their categories.

We have reviewed the literature in order to present the most useful and commonly used bases for the descriptive classification of errors. They are (1) linguistic category; (2) surface strategy; (3) comparative analysis; and (4) communicative effect. Discussion of these descriptive taxonomies is guided by two major purposes: to present error categories which rely solely on observable (rather than inferred) characteristics for their definition; and to report the findings of research conducted to date with respect to error types observed. Such findings may assist teachers in their instructional efforts and theoreticians in their formulation of L_2 theory.

We strongly believe that each component of language should be studied separately and thoroughly before conclusions can be generally applied across components. Much psycholinguistic research has focused on syntax and morphology, permitting a synthesis of empirical findings from which certain conclusions may be drawn with some confidence. To our knowledge, no such extensive work has focused on semantic or phonological error analysis, although scattered findings are available. We leave the reporting of these for future efforts.

ERROR TYPES BASED ON LINGUISTIC CATEGORY

Many error taxonomies have been based on the linguistic item which is affected by an error. These linguistic category taxonomies classify errors according to either or both the language component or the particular linguistic constituent the error affects.

Language components include phonology (pronunciation), syntax and morphology (grammar), semantics and lexicon (meaning and vocabulary), and discourse (style). Constituents include the elements that comprise each language component. For example, within syntax one may ask whether the error is in the main or subordinate clause; and within a clause, which constituent is affected, e.g. the noun phrase, the auxiliary, the verb phrase, the preposition, the adverb, the adjectives, and so forth. A full presentation of language components and constituents would require a summary of descriptive linguistics, an undertaking much beyond the scope of this book. (See, for example, Gleason, 1951; and Long, 1961.) Here we simply assume that the reader has a basic understanding of them, and will later present two linguistic category taxonomies that are representative of others in the literature.

Curriculum developers have long used linguistic category taxonomies to organize language lessons in student textbooks and workbooks. While second language textbooks are increasingly organized according to content topic, such as renting an apartment or going to market, many are still organized according to linguistic category.

Such materials permit teachers and students to feel that they have covered certain aspects of the language in their classes. They also allow users to find easily those parts of the language they are most interested in studying or teaching.

Many researchers use the linguistic category taxonomy as a reporting tool which organizes the errors they have collected. Although some use it as the only classification scheme offered, many use it to add to the description of errors provided by other taxonomies. For example, if researchers have classified their errors as interlingual and developmental, they often additionally report the linguistic categories into which these major error types fall, e.g. developmental errors in the auxiliary, in the noun phrase, in the complement system; interlingual errors in phonology, in word order, and in vocabulary. We present below the results of two error analyses that used linguistic category as the primary classification scheme.

Politzer and Ramirez (1973) studied 120 Mexican-American children learning English in the United States, taping their narrative of a short, silent animated cartoon. Errors were extracted for analysis from this body of natural speech.

Politzer and Ramirez introduce their classification as follows:

> The errors were categorized as an aid in presenting the data rather than to create a basis for extensive speculation concerning the sources for the errors. For this reason they were categorized along fairly traditional lines into errors in morphology, syntax, and vocabulary . . . The three main categories were further subdivided according to different parts of speech or parts of the sentence . . .
>
> (Politzer and Ramirez, 1973, p. 41)

TABLE 7-1   A Sample Linguistic Category Taxonomy*

Linguistic Category and Error Type	Example of Learner Error†
A. *Morphology*	
1. Indefinite article incorrect	
• *a* used for *an* before vowels	*a ant*
• *an* used for *a*	*an little ant*
2. Possessive case incorrect	
• Omission of *'s*	*the man feet*
3. Third person singular verb incorrect	
• Failure to attach *-s*	*The bird help man.*
• Wrong attachment of *-s*	*The apple fall downs.*
4. Simple past tense incorrect	
a. Regular past tense	
• Omission of *-ed*	*The bird he save him.*
• Adding *-ed* to past already formed	*He calleded*
b. Irregular past tense	
• Regularization by adding *-ed*	*He putted the cookie there.*
• Substitution of simple non-past	*He fall in the water.*
• Substitution of past participle	*I been near to him.*
5. Past participle incorrect	
• Omission of *-ed*	*He was call.*
6. Comparative adjective/adverb incorrect	
• Use of *more + er*	*He got up more higher.*
B. *Syntax*	
1. Noun Phrase	
a. Determiners	
• Omission of the article	*He no go in hole.*
• Substitution of definite article for possessive pronoun	*He fall down on the head.*
• Use of possessive with the article	*He put it in the his room.*
• Use of wrong possessive	*The little boy hurt its leg.*
b. Nominalization	
• Simple verb used instead of *-ing*	*by to cook it*
• Preposition *by* omitted	*The dove helped him putting leaf on the water.*
c. Number	
• Substitution of singulars for plurals	*He got some leaf.*
• Substitution of plurals for singulars	*He stab him in the feet.*
d. Use of pronouns	
• Omission of the subject pronoun	*(He) pinch the man.*
• Omission of the "dummy" pronoun *it*	*Is nice to help people.*
• Omission of object pronouns	*I don't know (it) in English.*

Linguistic Category and Error Type	Example of Learner Error†
• Subject pronoun used as a redundant element	*My brother he go to Mexico.*
• Alternating use of pronouns by number as well as gender	*So he can eat it (referring to apples).*
• Use of *me* as subject	*Me forget it.*
e. Use of prepositions	
• Omission of preposition	*He came (to) the water.*
• Misuse of prepositions	*He fell down from (for on, into?) the water.*

2. Verb Phrase
   a. Omission of verb

• Omission of main verb	*He (fell?) in the water.*
• Omission of *to be*	*He in the water.*

   b. Use of progressive tense

• Omission of *be*	*He going.*
• Replacement of *-ing* by the simple verb form	*The bird was shake his head.*
• Substitution of the progressive for the simple past	*Then the man shooting (shot?) with a gun.*

   c. Agreement of subject and verb

• Disagreement of subject and verb person	*You be friends.*
• Disagreement of subject and number	*The apples was coming down.*
• Disagreement of subject and tense	*I didn't know what it is.*

3. Verb-and-Verb Construction

• Embedding of a noun-and-verb construction in another noun-and-verb construction	*I go to play. (I go and I play.)*
• Omission of *to* in identical subject construction	*I go play.*
• Omission of *to* in the verb-and-verb construction	*I see a bird got the leaf.*
• Attachment of the past marker to the dependent verb	*He was going to fell.*

4. Word Order

• Repetition of the object	*The bird (object) he was gonna shoot it.*
• Adjectival modifiers placed after noun	*He put it inside his house a little round.*

5. Some Transformations
   a. Negative transformation

• Formation of *no* or *not* without the auxiliary *do*	*He not play anymore.*
• Multiple negation	*They won't have no fun.*

TABLE 7-1   *(continued)*

Linguistic Category and Error Type	Example of Learner Error†
b. Question transformation	
• Omission of auxiliary	*How the story helps?*
c. *There* transformation	
• Use of *is* instead of *are*	*There is these hole.*
• Omission of *there*	*Is one bird.*
• Use of *it was* instead of *there was*	*It was round things.*
d. Subordinate clause transformation	
• Use of *for* for *so that*	*For the ant could get out.*
• Use of indicative for conditional	*So he don't kill the bird.*

*From R. Politzer and A. Ramirez (1973), "An Error Analysis of the Spoken English of Mexican-American Pupils in a Bilingual School and a Monolingual School." *Language Learning, a Journal of Applied Linguistics* 23, 1. Reprinted by permission.
†The errors in this taxonomy refer to Standard English usage.

The Politzer and Ramirez taxonomy for morphology and syntax summarized in Table 7-1 is a fairly traditional descriptive taxonomy.

Burt and Kiparsky (1972) developed another linguistic category taxonomy into which they classified several thousand English errors made by students learning English in foreign as well as host environments. Their work, including some of the concepts introduced in the table, is described in greater detail later in this chapter. For now, we present their linguistic category taxonomy (Table 7-2) as another example of this type of error classification.

SURFACE STRATEGY TAXONOMY

A surface strategy taxonomy highlights the ways surface structures are altered: Learners may *omit* necessary items or *add* unnecessary ones; they may *misform* items or *misorder* them. Researchers have noticed, however, that surface elements of a language are altered in specific and systematic ways which we enumerated briefly at the beginning of this chapter.

Analyzing errors from a surface strategy perspective holds much promise for researchers concerned with identifying cognitive processes that underlie the learner's reconstruction of the new language. It also makes us aware that learners' errors are based on some logic. They are not the result of laziness or sloppy thinking, but of the learner's use of interim principles to produce a new language.

TABLE 7-2   A Sample Linguistic Category Taxonomy*

Linguistic Category and Error Type	Example of Learner Error
A. *The Skeleton of English Clauses*	
1. Missing parts	
a. Surrogate subject missing: *there* and *it*	*Was a riot last night.*
b. Simple predicate missing: *be*	*We too big for the pony.*
c. Object pronoun missing	*I bought in Japan.*
d. Subject pronoun missing	*My mother been the first wife of our father. Always lead the other wives wherever they are invited.*
2. Misordered parts	
a. Verb before subject	*Escaped the professor from prison.*
b. Subject and object permuted	*English use many countries.*
B. *The Auxiliary System*	
1. *Do*	
a. Overuse in questions and negatives	*Never do you must spit like that.*
b. Underuse in questions	*Why we bow to each other?*
c. Overuse in affirmative sentences	*He does spend his holidays always at Benin.*
d. Underuse in negatives	*He writes not good books.*
2. *Have* and *Be*	
a. Misformation of perfect and progressive aspects	*We are stayed here already three weeks.*
b. Passive auxiliary misformation	*I have impressed with Plato.*
c. *Be* missing	*My mind always worried.*
d. *Do* misused with *be*	*Do they be happy?*
3. Modals	
a. Misformation of the next verbal word	*We should studying tonight.*
b. Misunderstanding of tense with modals	*You have could do it if you wanted to.*
4. Mismatching auxiliaries in tag questions	*She has been smoking less, isn't it?*
C. *Passive Sentences*	
1. Problems with formation of passive sentences	
a. Misformation of passive verb	*Each cushion given by our priest.*
b. Active order but passive form	*The traffic jam was held up by my brother.*
c. Absent or wrong preposition before agent	*She is not allowed to her parents to go.*
d. Passive order but active form	*Everything covered insurance against fire.*

151

TABLE 7-2   (continued)

Linguistic Category and Error Type	Example of Learner Error
2. Inappropriate use of passive	
a. Making intransitive verbs passive	*He was arrived early.*
b. Misusing passives in complex sentences	*Mark was hoped to become a football player.*
D. *Temporal Conjunctions*	
1. Limited and unlimited verbs	*Why don't you go and have a car?*
2. Misplacement of conjunctions	
a. Misplacement of *after*	*I got up after I brushed my teeth.*
b. Misplacement of *since*	*He broke his leg since he has thrown away his skis.*
c. Misplacement of *while*	*While you can't come in, I'm in here.*
3. Form of clauses after temporal conjunctions	
a. Non-finiteness of subordinate clauses	*After him goes, we will read a story.*
b. Superfluous *that*	*After that we walked, we felt very warm.*
4. Selection of predicate types	
a. Confusion in unlimited and limited verb selection	*I lost my wallet until Juan gave it back.*
b. Difficulties in changing limitedness of verb	*She kept her patience while the baby was repeatedly dropping his spoon.*
c. Misuse of negatives with temporal conjunctions	*We had to water the garden after it hadn't rained recently.*
d. Misuse of end-of-the-road predicates	*Life is complicated while you are old.*
5. Superficial tense agreement	
a. Failure to apply STAGR (Superficial Tense Agreement) with *before, after, until* and *while*	*After our last pennies have been spent we wanted to continue on our way home.*
b. Inconsistency in perfect use: *while*	*While you have worked, I make phone calls.*
c. STAGR misapplied: *since*	*They are studying in this school since they are six years old.*
d. Superfluous *will* and other future constructions	*Before you will leave you will kiss Grandma.*
E. *Sentential Complements*	
1. Subordinate constructions	
a. Misordering in subordinate constructions	*Rufus hopes that is going to U.S.A. soon.*

Linguistic Category and Error Type	Example of Learner Error

2. Problems with extraposition of fat subject*
   a. Omission of surrogate subject — *Is very hard for me to learn English right.*
   b. Wrong surrogate subject: *it* and *there* — *He is raining today.*
      It will be some club meetings on Tuesday.

3. Problems with infinitives and gerunds
   a. Leaving out the subject — *It astonishes me to be here; I thought you were in London.*
   b. Misformations with non-nominative subjects — *For me failing the exam would make Mother upset.*
   c. Misformations without subjects — *For to catch the bus, go to the next corner.*
   d. Special problems with *make, let, have* and *find* — *Taxes make people to be miserable.*
      You must have Cielo to bake some delicious bread.
   e. Snatched subject as subject for main clause — *Volkswagen buses are impossible to go too fast.*
   f. Snatched subject as object of main clause — *A girl was decided to play the piano.*
   g. Misformation of gerunds after prepositions — *You must not discourage him from write what he must.*

4. Choosing complement types of main verb meaning
   a. Forms taken by propositions and actions — *Mark thinks the beans needing fertilizer.*
   b. Difficulty with verbs which select infinitives — *We will offer carrying the furniture.*
   c. Difficulty with verbs which select gerunds — *Most of the pupils enjoy to have a holiday.*
   d. Wrong complement form after auxiliaries — *I will enjoy to swim.*

F. *Psychological Predicates*
1. Misordering of subject and object
   a. Misordering with reverse psychological verb — *The cat is on the dinner table, but my father doesn't bother that.*
   b. Misordering with straightforward psychological verb — *And physical geography prefer me more than anything else.*

2. Embedded sentence with reverse verbs
   a. Using the experiencer as subject — *I delight that you are so thin.*
   b. Wrong use of prepositions with *-ed* forms — *We were all bored about his teaching.*
   c. Free alternation of *-ed* and *-ing* forms of reverse verbs — *Tell me what you are disgusting by.*

TABLE 7-2   (*continued*)

Linguistic Category and Error Type	Example of Learner Error
d. Leaving out stimulus or experiencer	*When Americans excite, they talk too fast for me.*
e. Mismanaged extraposition	*Sarah annoys that the ice cream is so soft.*
3. Straightforward adjectives	
a. Misordering with straightforward adjectives	*The broken vase was furious to the shopkeeper.*
b. Misuse of adjectives as verbs	*It sads me in my heart to leave you.*
4. Reverse adjectives	
a. Misordering with reverse adjectives	*He is easy learning mechanical things.*
b. Misordering in embedded sentences	*He thinks you important to hurry up.*
c. Difficulty with causation	*She finds easy to make delicious the food.*

*fat subject—One that is a *clause*, rather than a simple noun phrase.

*From *The Gooficon: A Repair Manual for English* by M. Burt and C. Kiparsky, 1972. Courtesy of Newbury House Publishers, Rowley, MA 019769.

Omission

Omission errors are characterized by *the absence of an item that must appear in a well-formed utterance.* Although any morpheme or word in a sentence is a potential candidate for omission, some types of morphemes are omitted more than others.

Content morphemes carry the bulk of the referential meaning of a sentence: nouns, verbs, adjectives, adverbs. For example, in the sentence

Mary is the president of the new company.

the words, *Mary, president, new* and *company* are the content morphemes that carry the burden of meaning. If one heard

Mary president new company.

one could deduce a meaningful sentence, while if one heard

is the of the

one couldn't even begin to guess what the speaker might have had in mind.

Is, the, and *of* are **grammatical morphemes,** those little words that play a minor role in conveying the meaning of a sentence. They include noun and verb inflections (the *-s* in *birds,* the *-s* in *Mother's,* the *-ed* in *looked,* the *-ing* in *laughing,* etc.); articles (*a, the,* etc.); verb auxiliaries (*is, will, can,* etc.); (*is, was, am,* etc.); and prepositions (*in, on, under,* etc.). Languages that are more richly inflected than English use a greater variety of grammatical morphemes. For example, Pilipino uses verb infixes (e.g. the *-in* in *Kinain,* "ate"), reduplications (e.g., the *la* in *lalangoy,* "will swim"), and others.

Language learners omit grammatical morphemes much more frequently than content words. Within the set of grammatical morphemes, however, some are likely to be omitted for a much longer time than others. For example, it has been observed for child L_2 learners that the copula (*is, are*) and the *-ing* marker are used earlier in the English acquisition process than are simple past tense and third person markers (*looked, eats*). (See Chapter 8 for a full treatment of the acquisition order of grammatical morphemes.)

Omission errors are found in greater abundance and across a greater variety of morphemes during the *early* stages of L_2 acquisition. In intermediate stages, when learners have been exposed to more of the language, misformation, misordering, or overuse of grammatical morphemes are more likely to occur.

Omission of content words, although typical in the early stages of L_1 acquisition, is not as common in sequential L_2 acquisition where the learner is older and more cognitively mature. If content words are omitted in L_2 speech, it is usually occasioned by lack of vocabulary, and learners usually indicate their awareness of the missing constituent. Some use gestures to make their intended meaning clear; for example:

Researcher: *What's he doing?* (pointing to a boy eating)
Learner (child): *Him this* (gestures eating).

Unless circumstances require them to speak in the new language, many learners, however, will not produce such one- or two-word constructions, preferring to wait to speak until they have acquired more vocabulary items. Occasionally, the learner may use words and phrases from the first language or some other previously learned language in place of vocabulary still to be acquired.

Additions

Addition errors are the opposite of omissions. They are character-ized by *the presence of an item which must not appear in a well-formed utterance.*

Addition errors usually occur in the later stages of L$_2$ acquisition, when the learner has already acquired some target language rules. In fact, addition errors result from the all-too-faithful use of certain rules.

Three types of addition errors have been observed in the speech of both L$_1$ and L$_2$ learners: double markings, regularizations, and simple additions. These errors are good indicators that some basic rules have been acquired, but that the refinements have not yet been made.

Double Markings. Many addition errors are more accurately de-scribed as the failure to delete certain items which are required in some linguistic constructions, but not in others. For example, in most English sentences some semantic features such as tense may be marked syntactically only once. We say

> I didn't go.

although *go* takes a past tense marker when there is no auxiliary (such as *do*) on which to mark the tense, as in

> They went to lunch an hour ago.

The English rule for tense formation is: Place the tense marker on the first verb. In a simple affirmative declarative sentence, the main verb is the only verb, and thus takes the tense, as in the sentence above.

In a sentence where an auxiliary is required in addition to the main verb, the auxiliary, not the main verb, takes the tense. Learn-ers who have acquired the tensed form for both auxiliary and verb often place the marker on both, as in

> He doesn't knows my name.
> or
> We didn't went there.

Because two items rather than one are marked for the same fea-ture (tense, in these examples), this type of addition error has been called ***double marking.***

TABLE 7-3   Errors of Double Marking in L$_2$ Production

Semantic Feature	Error	Example of Error*
Past Tense	Past tense is marked in the auxiliary and the verb	She *didn't went/goed.*
Present Tense	Present tense is marked in the auxiliary and the verb	He *doesn't eats.*
Negation	Negation is marked in the auxiliary and the quantifier	She *didn't* give him *none.*†
		He *don't* got *no* wings.†
	Negation is marked in the auxiliary and the adverb	They *don't hardly* eat.
Equational Predicate	Equation is marked in two copula positions	*Is* this *is* a cow?
Object	The object is both topicalized and expressed in the object pronoun	That's *the man* who I saw *him.*
Past Tense	The auxiliary is produced twice	Why *didn't* mommy *don't* make dinner?

*These examples are taken from raw data collected by Dulay and Burt via the *Bilingual Syntax Measure* (lower and upper grade versions) and unstructured natural conversation, unless otherwise specified.

†These constructions are permissible in some varieties of English, and therefore must not be considered errors when analyzing the speech of persons who speak those varieties.

Table 7-3 presents the types of double marking errors commonly observed in L$_2$ performance.

Regularization[3]   A rule typically applies to a class of linguistic items, such as the class of main verbs or the class of nouns. In most languages, however, some members of a class are exceptions to the rule. For example, the verb *eat* does not become *eated,* but *ate;* the noun *sheep* is also *sheep* in the plural, not *sheeps.*

Whenever there are both regular and irregular forms and constructions in a language, learners apply the rules used to produce the regular ones to those that are irregular, resulting in errors of regularization.

Regularization errors that fall under the addition category are those in which a marker that is typically added to a linguistic item is erroneously added to exceptional items of the given class that do not take a marker. For example, *sheeps* and *putted* are both regularizations in which the regular plural and past tense markers -*s* and -*ed,* respectively, have been added to items which do not take mark-

3. "Regularization" is more narrowly defined than the more commonly used term "overgeneralization" which has been used to describe almost all developmental errors observed.

TABLE 7-4   Simple Addition Errors Observed in Child L₂ Production

Linguistic Item Added	Example*
3rd person singular -s	The fishes doesn't live in the water
Past tense (irregular)	The train is gonna *broke* it
Article *a*	*a* this
Preposition	*in* over here

*Taken from G. P. Venable (1974), *A Study of Second Language Learning in Chil-. dren.* Unpublished M.Sc. (Applied) Project, McGill University School of Human Communication Disorders. Reprinted by permission.

ers. Other such errors observed in learner performance include *deers*, *hitted* and *beated*. (Another set of regularization errors is found in the misformation category, which is presented in the following section.)

Simple Addition   errors are the "grab bag" subcategory of additions. If an addition error is not a double marking nor a regularization, it is called a simple addition. No particular features characterize simple additions other than those that characterize all addition errors—the use of an item which should not appear in a well-formed utterance. Simple addition errors observed in both L₁ and L₂ child speech include those listed in Table 7-4.

Misformation

Misformation errors are characterized by the use of *the wrong form of the morpheme or structure*. While in omission errors the item is not supplied at all, in misformation errors the learner supplies something, although it is incorrect. For example, in

The dog eated the chicken.

a past tense marker was supplied by the learner; it was just not the right one.

As in the case of additions, misformations are usually not random. Thus far, three types of misformations have been frequently reported in the literature: (1) regularizations; (2) archi-forms; and (3) alternating forms.

Regularization Errors   that fall under the misformation category are those in which a regular marker is used in place of an irregular one, as in runn*ed* for *ran* or goos*es* for *geese*. Table 7-5 lists the types

TABLE 7-5 Regularization Errors in the Misformation Category Observed in Child L₂
Production

Linguistic Item Misformed	Example*
Reflexive pronoun	*his*self (himself)
Regular past	I fall*ed* (fell)
Plural	*gooses* (geese)
	childs (children)

*These examples are taken from raw data collected by Dulay
and Burt via the *Bilingual Syntax Measure* (lower and upper
grade versions) and unstructured natural conversation, unless otherwise specified.

of overregularization errors observed in the verbal production of
child L₂ learners.

Learners also commonly make regularization errors in the *comprehension* of grammar. Chomsky (1969) for L₁ acquisition and d'Anglejan and Tucker (1975) for adult L₂ acquisition, both report that exceptional verbs like *promise* and *ask* cause miscomprehension when
they appear with reduced complements because they are treated as
though they were regular.

Table 7-6 below summarizes the sentence pairs which have sim-

TABLE 7-6 Irregular Predicates Causing Misinterpretation in L₁ and
Adult L₂ Comprehension

Sentence Pairs*		Interpretation
Regular: Don *allowed* Fred to stay.		
Irregular: Don *promised* Fred to stay.	*Erroneous:*	*Don promised Fred that *Fred* would stay.
	Correct:	Don promised Fred that *Don* would stay.
Regular: The girl *tells* the boy what to paint.		
Irregular: The girl *asks* the boy what to paint.	*Erroneous:*	*The girl asks the boy what *he* should paint.
	Correct:	The girl asks the boy what *she* should paint.
Regular: John is *eager* to see.		
Irregular: John is *easy* to see.	*Erroneous:*	*It is easy for *John* to see.
	Correct:	It is easy *to see John.*

*The sentence pairs are taken from A. d'Anglejan and G. R. Tucker (1975), following C. Chomsky
(1969), in *Language Learning, a Journal of Applied Linguistics 25,* pp. 281–296, "The Acquisition of
Complex English Structures by Adult Learners." Reprinted by permission.

ilar surface structures, but whose meaning (and deep structure) is different. The first sentence of each pair permits an interpretation which is typical for such a construction, but the second, because of the exceptional nature of the predicate, requires a different interpretation. The erroneous interpretation, given when students are still treating the exceptions as if they were regular, is given in the table beside the sentence which is misinterpreted.

Regularization errors abound in the verbal output of both first and second language learners, child and adult, in host and foreign language learning situations. The overextension of linguistic rules to exceptional items occurs even after some facility with the language has been acquired, since the pervasive principles governing the form and interpretation of more advanced and complex structures (complement types in English, for example) also have exceptions.

Archi-forms The selection of one member of a class of forms to represent others in the class is a common characteristic of all stages of second language acquisition. We have called the form selected by the learner an *archi-form*. For example, a learner may temporarily select just one of the English demonstrative adjectives *this*, *that*, *these*, and *those*, to do the work for several of them:

> that dog
> that dogs

For this learner, *that* is the archi-demonstrative adjective representing the entire class of demonstrative adjectives.

Learners may also select one member of the class of personal pronouns to function for several others in the class. For example,

> Give me that.
> Me hungry.

In the production of certain complex sentences, the use of the infinitive as an archi-form for the other complement types (e.g. gerunds and *that*-clauses) has also been observed:

> I finish to watch TV.
> She suggested him to go.

Madden et al. (1978) report that some learners substituted *does* for *are*, *do* and *is* in a sentence imitation task. For example,

How does [is] Mayor Beame getting the money New York City needs? (p. 113)

Finally, in the acquisition of French by English-speaking children, Ervin-Tripp (1974, p. 116) reports the use of *moi* for both *mon/ma* (my) and *moi* (me).

The particular form selected for such archi-use varies for different learners, but the use of archi-forms is a typical phenomenon in the acquisition of a new language. If a particular structure such as the nominative-accusative case distinction is acquired fairly early, the use of the accusative as an archi-form for both nominative and accusative constructions is observed early in the acquisition process. The past irregulars and past participles, on the other hand, are acquired relatively late, and thus archi-form usage for those structures (past irregular for both simple past and past participle) is observed during the later phases of L_2 acquisition.

Alternating Forms   As the learner's vocabulary and grammar grow, the use of archi-forms often gives way to the apparently fairly free alternation of various members of a class with each other. Thus, we see for demonstratives:

Those dog
This cats

In the case of pronouns, we see:

Masculine for feminine (or vice versa), as in:	*he* for *she*
Plural for singular (or vice versa), as in:	*they* for *it*
Accusative for nominative case (or vice versa), as in:	*her* for *she*

We have observed that in the production of verbs when the participle form (*-en*, as in *taken*) is being acquired, it may be alternated with the past irregular, as in:

I seen her yesterday.
He would have saw them.

In the acquisition of French, a common observation is the alternation of the articles, *le* and *la* (Ervin-Tripp, 1974, p. 117). Similar phenomena have been noted in Wode, Bahns, Bedey and Frank (1978). Although little direct research on the subject has been done, it seems that older language learners draw on a greater variety of forms than younger learners and thus tend to produce a wider variety of misformation errors. It has been noted, for example, that L_2 learners use *don't* as well as *no* and *not* to express negation in the first phase of learning English negation, whereas L_1 learners have been observed to use only *no* and *not*, producing *don't* only in the second stage (See Table 6-1). The more sophisticated mental apparatus of older learners probably allows them to process more information than younger learners in a given period of time. On the other hand, the observation that second language learners produce a wider variety of forms than first language learners may be an artifact: There have been more studies of second language acquisition than of first language acquisition in several domains, such as the acquisition of negation and questions. More first language data might reveal more variation.

Like addition errors, misformations indicate that some learning has transpired and that barring certain attitudes or environmental circumstances, the learner is on his or her way to target language proficiency.

Misordering

As the label suggests, misordering errors are characterized by the *incorrect placement of a morpheme or group of morphemes in an utterance*. For example, in the utterance

He is all the time late.

all the time is misordered.

Misordering errors occur systematically for both L_2 and L_1 learners in constructions that have already been acquired, specifically simple (direct) and embedded (indirect) questions. Learners, for example, have been observed to say

What Daddy is doing?

using the declarative sentence order that had been acquired. During a later phase of acquisition, when they have acquired the simple question order, they produce

I don't know what is that.

using a simple question order for *what is that?*. (See Chapter 6 for detailed discussion of the acquisition of interrogatives.)

In addition to these creative misordering errors, students have made written misordering errors that are word-for-word translations of native language surface structures. Examples include sentences like:

I met there some Germans. (Duskova, 1969),

and phrases such as:

another my friend (Duskova, 1969).

Similarly, English speakers occasionally produce similar misordering errors in second languages:

Hoffentlich du bist gesund.

(LoCoco, 1975; a literal rendering of *Hopefully you are healthy.* The correct form is *Hoffentlich bist du gesund*)

and

Ich bin glucklich sein hier.

(LoCoco, 1975; an exact translation of *I am happy to be here.* Correct German is *Ich bin glucklich hier zu sein.*)

English speaking children in French language immersion programs occasionally produce sentences such as:

Le chien a mangé les.

(Literally, *The dog ate some.* Correct French would be *Le chien les a mangé.*[4] See Selinker, Swain, and Dumas, 1975).

COMPARATIVE TAXONOMY

The classification of errors in a comparative taxonomy is based on *comparisons between the structure of L₂ errors and certain other types of constructions.* For example, if one were to use a comparative taxonomy to classify the errors of a Korean student learning English, one might compare the structure of the student's errors to that of errors reported for children acquiring English as a first language.

In the research literature, L_2 errors have most frequently been compared to errors made by children learning the target language as their first language and to equivalent phrases or sentences in the

---

4. This type of error is also found in the acquisition of French as a first language. Gregoire (1937) cites: *Il veut le; Je n'ai pas elle.*

learner's mother tongue. These comparisons have yielded the two major error categories in this taxonomy: developmental errors and interlingual errors. Two other categories that have been used in comparative analysis taxonomies are derived from the first two: ambiguous errors, which are classifiable as either developmental or interlingual; and, of course, the grab bag category, Other, which are neither.

Researchers have consistently found that, contrary to widespread opinion, the great majority of errors in the language output of L₂ learners is of the developmental type (see Chapter 5 for these findings). Although adults tend to exhibit more mother-tongue influence in their errors than do children, adult interlingual errors also occur in relatively small numbers, as long as language data are not elicited through timed translation tasks and ambiguous errors are taken into account. Figure 7-A illustrates the relationship and relative proportions of all four error types in a comparative taxonomy.

These findings have far-reaching implications for L₂ pedagogy, which has considered the contrastive analysis of students' L₁ and L₂ to be a major predictor of their errors. Instead, the research points to an emphasis away from contrastive analysis as a teaching tool, and towards a knowledge of developmental processes in L₂ acquisition.

FIGURE 7-A Illustration of the Relationship and Relative Proportions of the Four Error Types in a Comparative Taxonomy

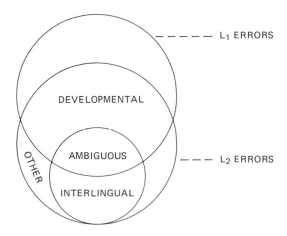

NOTE: The relative sizes of the circles and portions thereof represent an approximation of the relative proportions of the four error categories in a comparative taxonomy, although the precise proportions do vary depending on communication conditions and other factors. (See section on Research Findings, pp. 173–89 for discussion of the pertinent research.)

Developmental Errors

Developmental errors are *errors similar to those made by children learning the target language as their first language.* Take, for example, the following utterance made by a Spanish child learning English:

Dog eat it.

The omission of the article and the past tense marker may be classified as developmental because these are also found in the speech of children learning English as their first language.

Two considerations underlie the interest in comparing L_2 and L_1 acquisition errors. The first has to do with facilitating L_2 theoretical development. As we mentioned in Chapter 2, if characteristics common to both L_1 and L_2 acquisition could be identified, theoretical inferences that have been drawn from the large pool of L_1 research data may be applicable to L_2 acquisition theory as well.

The second consideration has to do with the role of the first language when learning a second. Since children acquiring a first language have not experienced learning a previous language, the errors they make cannot possibly be due to any interference from another language. When such errors are made by second language learners, it would be reasonable to hypothesize that mental mechanisms underlying general language development come into play, not the rules and structures of the learner's native language.

One of the difficulties inherent in comparing L_2 to L_1 errors is the required reliance on the *reported* findings in the L_1 acquisition literature. That an error is not reported in the literature is sometimes no guarantee that it is not produced by L_1 learners. Dulay and Burt remember such a discovery quite vividly. It was during their debut presentation of the results of a comparative analysis taxonomy of children's L_2 errors at the TESOL Convention in Puerto Rico in 1973. They reported having classified the omission of the head noun in an adjective phrase (*the skinny*) as an interlingual error (similar to the learner's native Spanish). Susan Ervin-Tripp, an L_1 researcher who happened to be in the audience, commented that her L_1 subject had produced such a construction, e.g. *the broken.* Fortunately, the new information enhanced the conclusions of the paper, but it certainly highlighted the methodological problem.

For the convenience of the reader, therefore, in addition to the above listing of the major developmental error types, we have included lists of English L_1 error types and examples and corresponding L_2 errors in Table 7-7.

TABLE 7-7 Equivalent L_1 and L_2 Errors Organized According to Surface Strategies*

CLASSIFICATION	L_1 EXAMPLES	L_1 SOURCE	L_2 EXAMPLES
OMISSIONS			
Omission of Major Constituents			
head noun	The broken ∧	Ervin-Tripp, quoted by Dulay & Burt (1973)	a dirty ∧ ; the skinny ∧ **
subject	∧ want it ∧ no going home	Menyuk (1963) Bloom (1970) p. 196	∧ play baseball ∧ no eating that
main verb: *has*	Kathryn ^has^ ∧ no shoe.	Bloom (1970) p. 196	Billy ^has^ ∧ no milk.
direct object	Don't throw ^it^ ∧ on my shoes.	Menyuk (1969)	Give ^it^ ∧ the little birds to eat. He like ^it^ ∧ .
Omission of Grammatical Morphemes			
preposition: *to, on, in*	I want to go ^to^ ∧ New York. Put the hat ^on^ ∧ .	Menyuk (1963)	Give ^to^ ∧ the little birds to eat. I fall down ^in^ ∧ the water. Go put your pajama ^on^ ∧ .
article: *the*	The ∧ giant wakes up. The ∧ book drop. The ∧ fire truck want a this. The ∧ man no go in there.	Menyuk (1963) Brown (1973) p. 317 Brown (1973) p. 393 Bloom (1970) p. 160	The ∧ car coming. The ∧ cat go there. The ∧ apple come down. The ∧ doggie eat it.
short plural: *-s*	more cookie^s^∧	Braine (1963) p. 412	It's got some flower^s^∧
long plural: *-es*	I have two necklace^/es/^∧	Menyuk (1963)	Those two house^/es/^∧

166

Grammatical form	Example	Source	Example	Source
auxiliary: *do, is/are*	How ^{do}∧ you take it out?		What ^{do}∧ you wanna eat?	Menyuk (1969)
	I ^{did}∧ not hurt him.		Do ∧ not go over there.	Klima & Bellugi (1966) p. 345
	Man ^{does}∧ no go in there.		I ^{do}∧ no have it.	Bloom (1970) p. 160
	is/are ∧ no going home.		is/are ∧ no eating that.	Bloom (1970) p. 196
auxiliary: *is, am*	Fish ^{is}∧ swim.		Car ^{is}∧ coming.	Brown (1973) p. 317
	I ^{am}∧ not crying.		How ^{am}∧ I gonna get there?	Klima & Bellugi (1966) p. 344
	∧ no going.		∧ no eating that.	Bloom (1970) p. 196
copula: *is, am*	This man ^{is}∧ not brother.		I ^{am}∧ sick.	Bloom (1970) p. 196
progressive: *-ing*	Fish swim^{ming}∧.		A father is come^{ing}∧.	Brown (1973) p. 317
	I'm play^{ing}∧ with it. }		Cat go^{ing}∧ there.	Cazden (1972) p. 38
	Dey are stand^{ing}∧ up. }			
regular past tense: *-ed*	Book drop^{ped}∧.		He close^d∧ it.**	Brown (1973) p. 317
irregular past tense: *fell, came, ate*	Good Beech fall down^{fell}∧		I fall down the water.^{fell}∧	Foulke & Stinchfield (1929) in Kahane, Kahane & Saporta (1971)
			Apple come down.^{came}∧	
			Doggie eat it.^{ate}∧	
third person singular	It don't fit in here.^{es}∧		He don't swim.^{es}∧	Bloom (1970) p. 212

TABLE 7-7 (continued)

CLASSIFICATION	L₁ EXAMPLES	L₁ SOURCE	L₂ EXAMPLES
OMISSIONS *Omission of Grammatical Morphemes (continued)*			
infinitive marker: *to*	I like ^^{to} do it. I want ^^{to} draw it.	Menyuk (1969)	He don't like ^^{to} eat.
ADDITION *Double Marking*			
present indicative	Joe doesn't like(s) it.	Ervin-Tripp (1964) p. 403	Bill doesn't like(s) it carrots.
regular past	I didn't spill (ed) it.	Cazden (1972) p. 46	Why didn't you came to school?
irregular past	Did I caught it? He(s) was in trouble	Klima and Bellugi (1966) p. 350 Harrison (1974)	Did I did it? The bird stoled it
direct object	We took it away (the hat) another (one)	Menyuk (1963) Brown, Cazden & Bellugi (1968) p. 314	Put it down (card). You don't get it (the coffee). another (one) hat
Simple Addition			
third person singular	I do(es)n't know how. They do(es)n't cut my finger.	Slobin (1971) p. 13	The fishes do(es)n't live in the water.

break

168

		Source	
article: *a*	Fire truck want (a) this.	Brown (1973) p. 393	(a) this (a) that
preposition: *in*	You shop (in) over there.	Menyuk (1963)	(in) over here outside (from)

MISFORMATIONS
Overregularization

reflexive pronoun	himself He's licking (hisself)	Menyuk (1963)	himself (hisself)
regular past	fell (falled)	Cazden (1972) p. 45	fell I (falled).
third person singular	got(s)	Cazden (1972) p. 44	He got(s) a flower.

Archi/Alternating Forms

auxiliary: *does/is*	is What (does) he putting on the top?	Harrison (1974)	is He (don't) looking.
prepositions: *at/to, on/in*	to Daddy took me (at) the train.	Menyuk (1963)	on (in) the feet.
subject pronoun: *he/she*	she Mommy was so mad so (he) spanked Blackey.	Menyuk (1963)	She (He) was not looking. The mother's over there and (he's) nervous. she's
possessive pronoun: *she, she's/her; him's/his*	her (she's) his (him's) her	Cazden (1972) p. 44	her That's (she's) house. his (him's) Her
	(She) school	Menyuk (1969)	(She) name is Maria.**

TABLE 7-7 (continued)

CLASSIFICATION	L₁ EXAMPLES	L₁ SOURCE	L₂ EXAMPLES

MISFORMATIONS
Archi/Alternating Forms (continued)

CLASSIFICATION	L₁ EXAMPLES	L₁ SOURCE	L₂ EXAMPLES
negative: *no/not*	*not* Man (no) go in there. *not* (no) going home.	Bloom (1970) p. 160 Bloom (1970) p. 196	*not* I (no) have it. *not* (no) eating that.
quantifiers	*some* Put (a) gas in. *some* I hadda have (a) caps on my teeth. *some* I see (a) teeth. *some* Have (a) pants.	Slobin (1971) p. 8 Harrison (1974) Menyuk (1963) Miller & Ervin-Tripp (1964) p. 363	*some* *some* (a) water; (two) milk *some* (a) carrots *some* He got (a) toys.**

MISORDERING

CLASSIFICATION	L₁ EXAMPLES	L₁ SOURCE	L₂ EXAMPLES
aux in simple question	What this (is)?	Menyuk (1963)	What this (is)?
aux in embedded question	I know what (is) that.	Menyuk (1969)	I know what (is) that.
adverb	I eat (sometimes) candy.	Menyuk (1969)	Is (there) happy; is (there) not happy.

*See pp. 151–163 for discussion of surface strategies taxonomy. All data are taken from Venable (1974) except where marked with **, which are taken from Dulay and Burt's raw data.

Interlingual Errors

As mentioned earlier, interlingual errors are similar in structure to a semantically equivalent phrase or sentence in the learner's native language. For example,

the man skinny

produced by a Spanish speaker reflects the word order of Spanish adjectival phrases (e.g. *el hombre flaco*).

To identify an interlingual error, researchers usually translate the grammatical form of the learner's phrase or sentence into the learner's first language to see if similarities exist. For example, if the learner produced

Dog eat it

the researcher would translate the grammatical form

The dog ate it.

into Spanish

El perro lo comió.

then compare both sentences to see if the learner's L_1 structure is discernible in the L_2 sentence. In this case it is not.

The term "interlingual" was chosen instead of the equally common labels "interference" or "transfer" because "interlingual" seemed to be the least explanatory in connotation. As the discussion in Chapter 5 pointed out, terms such as "interference" and "transfer" imply, at least to some, certain *explanations* of these errors; for example, that the learner's native language somehow automatically "interferes" with the learning of the L_2, or automatically "transfers" to the learner's developing L_2 system. Such inferences must be justified before they are made, and should not be confused with a simple description of the error.

Interlingual errors, as defined here, simply refer to L_2 errors that reflect native language structure, regardless of the internal processes or external conditions that spawned them. A full discussion of the multiple sources of interlingual errors would necessarily cover external environmental conditions as well as internal processing factors. These have been taken up in Chapters 2 and 3, after which the role of the first language in second language acquisition was discussed (Chapter 5).

Ambiguous Errors

Ambiguous errors are those that could be classified equally well as developmental or interlingual. That is because these errors reflect the learner's native language structure, and at the same time, they are of the type found in the speech of children acquiring a first language. For example, in the utterance

> I no have a car

the negative construction reflects the learner's native Spanish and is also characteristic of the speech of children learning English as their first language.

The ambiguous category is particularly important in a comparative taxonomy. Assigning such errors to a separate category ensures the clarity of the findings resulting from a comparative error analysis and enables researchers to draw clear theoretical inferences from the rest of the data.

Other Errors

Few taxonomies are complete without a grab bag for items that don't fit into any other category. For example, in the utterance

> She do hungry

the speaker used neither her native Spanish structure (the use of *have* for *is* as in *She have hungry*), nor an L_2 developmental form such as *She hungry* where the auxiliary is omitted altogether. Such an error would go into the Other category.[5]

 In this particular type of taxonomy, the grab bag errors should be of more than passing interest. Since they are not similar to those children make during first language development, they must be unique to second language learners; and further, since they are not interlingual, at least some must be unique reflections of creative construction. A study of such errors could provide useful insights into the specific differences between older and younger minds with respect to the organization of linguistic input. It seems that these differences should be reflected in systematic L_2-specific errors, which for now, given the fledgling state of the art, are classified as "Other." We expect, however, that future research will uncover a set of L_2 developmental errors, creative errors unique to L_2 learners.

5. In Dulay and Burt's 1974 comparative analysis of children's errors, they called these errors "unique," referring to their being unique to L_2 learners.

Research Findings

Investigations of the incidence of developmental and interlingual errors date back to the error analysis movement in the late sixties. At that time, the prevailing view was that second language learners' errors were largely interlingual. It was still believed that the differences between languages was the primary source of difficulty in second language learning.

The advent of generative linguistics in the sixties, however, brought with it a focus on the systematic, developing constructions apparent in all children's speech as they learn their first language. In particular, researchers pointed to the systematic omissions of certain nearly meaningless items in the sentences and phrases children produced. The omissions of these grammatical morphemes, together with the regularization of morphological rules and other de-. velopmental errors, were held up as evidence of a universal mental structure responsible for language acquisition.

The change in the perceived role of the first language in second language acquisition began with the observation that the number of errors in second language performance that could be attributed to first language influence was far smaller than had previously been imagined. In the first empirical study undertaken in which the grammatical errors made by children were actually counted and classified, less than 5% were found to reflect the children's first language (Dulay and Burt, 1974a). Since this initial finding, numerous studies have been conducted to determine the incidence of interlingual and developmental errors in the speech and writing of children and adults who are learning English as a second language in both host and foreign language environments. These studies include the acquisition not only of English as a second language, but also of Welsh, French, Spanish, German, and Urdu. Likewise, the subjects learning English represent a variety of first-language backgrounds, including Spanish, Japanese, Norwegian, Greek, and French. Both child and adult language learners have come under researchers' scrutiny in host and in foreign language environments. Finally, a variety of language elicitation tasks have been used across a number of language modes, including comprehension, production, composition and reading.

Although precise proportions differ from study to study, all the investigations conducted to date have reached the same general conclusion: *the majority of errors made by second language learners are not interlingual, but developmental.*

Three sorts of studies are available in the literature:

1. *Proportion studies* in which errors in an entire body of speech or writing are classified and counted, enabling the researcher to state in quantitative terms the relative proportion of each error type;

2. *Quasi-proportion studies* in which the errors are analyzed and classified but not counted, permitting qualitative estimates, but not quantitative statements about the proportions of interlingual and developmental errors; and

3. *Occurrence studies* in which the occurrence of particular developmental or interlingual errors is reported, but no attempt is made to address proportion.

We have chosen to present proportion studies in some detail because they speak most directly and precisely to the issue of proportion of error types. The quasi-proportion studies are discussed in terms of their contribution to the available pool of empirical evidence bearing on the issue. The briefly summarized occurrence studies are not directly relevant, but they may be considered exploratory with respect to the delineation of particular characteristics of each error type.

As we mentioned earlier, the development of research methodology for error analysis research is still in its infancy. Comparison across studies is therefore difficult because of differences in definitions of error categories and language elicitation techniques. Enough has been done, however, to provide general direction for teaching and future research.

Child Studies   A survey of the available empirical evidence strongly indicates that developmental errors comprise the great majority of the errors children make while acquiring a second language.

The first published study that investigated the proportion of interlingual and developmental errors for L₂ learners included three groups of Spanish-speaking children who were learning English in different parts of the United States. One group was in a New York City school, and two were in California schools. Some 179 children, aged 5–8, were included in the sample.

The children's speech was collected using a structured communication technique (the *Bilingual Syntax Measure* research version) which yields natural speech. The *Bilingual Syntax Measure* consists of a natural conversation between the child and the examiner about concrete things and events, guided by cartoon-type pictures and questions designed to elicit a range of target structures. (The instruments are described in detail in Chapter 8, pp. 203–9 and 250–58.

The data analysis consists of several steps:

1. Utterances containing errors were extracted from the children's speech.
2. The grammatical version of each of the extracted utterances and its corresponding native language equivalent was supplied.
3. Utterances that did not contain opportunities for the commission of both interlingual and developmental errors were eliminated.
4. Each error was *provisionally* classified into the Developmental, Interlingual, and Other categories without considering the ambiguous classification. For example, the omission of the auxiliary and the misformation of the negator in *No eat* (*He doesn't eat*/(*El) no come*) were provisionally classified as both Developmental and Interlingual.
5. All errors classified as both developmental and interlingual were subsequently removed from those categories and reclassified as ambiguous.[6]
6. The errors in each category were counted and percentages were determined.

The number and proportion of Developmental, Interlingual and Other errors were reported for 513 unambiguous erros (See Table 7-8) and for each of the six syntactic structures represented in the data (Tables 7-9 to 7-14).

As Table 7-8 shows, 87.1% (447 out of 513) of the errors were Developmental, reflecting the same error types as those made by children learning English as a first language. On the other hand,

TABLE 7-8   Summary of Error Count*

| | Number of Errors | | |
Age	Developmental	Interlingual†	Other†
5 years (33 children)	98	5	2
6 years (51 children)	113	6	16
7 years (52 children)	123	7	13
8 years (43 children)	113	6	11
TOTAL	447	24	42

*Copyright © 1974. Teachers of English to Speakers of Other Languages. Reprinted with permission of the authors and publisher.

Tables 7-8–7-14 are adapted from H. Dulay and M. Burt, "Errors and Strategies in Child Second Language Acquisition." *TESOL Quarterly, 8*, p. 2.

†Called "Interference" and "Unique," respectively, in Dulay and Burt (1974a).

6. Since the purpose of this study was to resolve certain theoretical issues revolving around proportions of developmental and interlingual errors, the ambiguous errors were excluded from further analysis and thus not reflected in the final counts.

TABLE 7-9   Error Count for Structure 1: NP-V-Pron*

Example of Structure: The dog ate it.
Example of Developmental Error: (The) dog eat it.
Example of Interlingual Error: (The) dog it ate. (*El perro se lo comió*)

	Number of Errors		
Age	Developmental	Interlingual†	Other†
5 years	18	0	1
6 years	21	0	0
7 years	27	0	2
8 years	27	0	1
TOTAL	93	0	4

*Copyright © 1974, Teachers of English to Speakers of Other Languages. Reprinted with permission of the authors and publisher.
†Called "Interference" and "Unique," respectively, in Dulay and Burt (1974a).

TABLE 7-10   Error Count for Structure 2: Det-Adj-N*

Example of Structure: the skinny man
Example of Developmental Error: skinny; skinny man
Example of Interlingual Error: (the) man skinny (*el hombre flaco*)

	Number of Errors		
Age	Developmental	Interlingual†	Other†
5 years	14	0	0
6 years	30	1	0
7 years	15	0	0
8 years	15	0	0
TOTAL	74	1[1]	0

*Copyright © 1974. Teachers of English to Speakers of Other Languages. Reprinted with permission of the authors and publisher.
†Called "Interference" and "Unique," respectively, in Dulay and Burt (1974a).
[1]When this paper was presented at the 1973 TESOL Convention, L_2 Interlingual errors of the type Det-N ("the skinny," "the fat") were reported. However, Susan Ervin-Tripp, who was present, reported that she had found the same error type in her English first data, e.g., "the broken." Thus we eliminated those errors from our count, as they are ambiguous.

4.7% (24 out of 513) of the errors were interlingual, reflecting the structure of Spanish. Finally, 8.2% (42 out of 513) were Other, being neither of the types found in the published L_1 literature nor reflective of the students' first language.

For children learning English in a host environment then, we see that the great majority of error types are developmental; an insignificant proportion are interlingual.

The confidence with which this statement is made derives from

TABLE 7-11   Error Count for Structure 3: Pron-(Aux)-(Neg)-VP*

Example of Structure: He doesn't eat.
Example of Developmental Error: He not eat.
Example of Interlingual Error: Doesn't eat (No come)

Age	Number of Errors		
	Developmental	Interlingual†	Other†
5 years	58	4	1
6 years	49	5	13
7 years	70	7	9
8 years	55	6	10
TOTAL	232	22	33

*Copyright © 1974, Teachers of English to Speakers of Other Languages. Reprinted with permission of the authors and publisher.
†Called "Interference" and "Unique," respectively, in Dulay and Burt (1974a).

TABLE 7-12   Error Count for Structure 4: Det-N-Poss-N*

Example of Structure: the king's food
Example of Developmental Error: king food
Example of Interlingual Error: the food (of the) king (la comida del rey)

Age	Number of Errors		
	Developmental	Interlingual†	Other†
5 years	2	1	0
6 years	2	0	0
7 years	2	0	0
8 years	8	0	0
TOTAL	14	1	0

*Copyright © 1974. Teachers of English to Speakers of Other Languages. Reprinted with permission of the authors and publisher.
†Called "Interference" and "Unique," respectively, in Dulay and Burt (1974a).

the pool of empirical data provided by nine other studies which reaffirm this finding. The studies are of the quasi-proportion sort—those whose conclusions include statements on the proportion of developmental and interlingual errors found, but whose analysis do not provide actual frequency counts and percentages. For example, after discussing the structures analyzed, the authors conclude with statements such as the following:

Although the English equivalents of the syntactic structures examined were well established, neither word for word translation nor L_1 interference was found in the new language.

(Hansen-Bede, 1975, p. 123)

TABLE 7-13   Error Count for Structure 5: NP-be-Adj*

Example of Structure: They are hungry.
Example of Developmental Error: They hungry.
Example of Interlingual Error: They have hunger. (*Ellos tienen hambre*)

Age	Number of Errors		
	Developmental	*Interlingual†*	*Other†*
5 years	1	0	0
6 years	2	0	2
6 years	4	0	0
8 years	4	0	0
TOTAL	11	0	2

*Copyright © 1974. Teachers of English to Speakers of Other Languages. Reprinted with permission of the authors and publisher.
†Called "Interference" and "Unique," respectively, in Dulay and Burt (1974a).

TABLE 7-14   Error Count for Structure 6:

$$(NP - Aux) - V + ing - (Infin) - \begin{cases} NP\text{-}Prep\text{-}NP^* \\ NP\text{-}NP \end{cases}$$

Example of Structure: The mother is giving food to the birdie.
Example of Developmental Error: The mother give food to birdie.
Example of Interlingual Error: The mother him give food to the birdie.
                    (*La mamá le dió la comida al pajarito*)

Age	Number of Errors		
	Developmental	*Interlingual†*	*Other†*
5 years	5	0	0
6 years	9	0	1
7 years	5	0	2
8 years	4	0	0
TOTAL	23	0	3

*Copyright © 1974. Teachers of English to Speakers of Other Languages. Reprinted with permission of the authors and publisher.
†Called "Interference" and "Unique," respectively, in Dulay and Burt (1974a).

No deviation could be attributed to the children's mother tongue.

(Gillis and Weber, 1976, p. 92)

For interpretation tasks and translations both, direct word-for-word translations did not account for the evidence as well as did learner strategies quite like those mother tongue learners employ.

(Ervin-Tripp, 1974, p. 126)

Similar comments are made in the other studies. Characteristics of these studies are summarized in Table 7-15, which displays available child comparative error analysis research.

All of the studies refer to second language acquisition in a *host environment*, such as English in the United States or Great Britain, French in Switzerland, Urdu in Pakistan, and Welsh in Wales.

Some of the studies are longitudinal case studies involving one or two children, while others are cross-sectional studies involving larger groups of students. All of the studies used some form of natural communication, either structured or unstructured, to elicit speech (see Chapter 10 for discussion); two used additional translation tasks; and one an additional imitation task. Several studies analyzed a wide range of syntactic structures (designated "General" in the table) while others focused on a selected few. All investigated *oral production* rather than writing.

Data analyses are similar to that described in the Dulay and Burt study above, with the exception of Step 6 (the frequency counts). For example, Ravem reports that his son Rune did not produce the Norwegian structure $N + V + (N) + Neg$, as in:

Han arbeider ikke.	(He works not.)
Vi tok det ikke.	(He took it not.)

Instead, he produced the English first language acquisition structure $N + Neg + VP$, as in:

I not like that.
I not looking for edge.

(Ravem, 1968, p. 180)

Similarly, Price offers a comparison of typical Welsh utterances of his subjects to their English equivalents, reporting that they reflected Welsh rather than the native-English word order. These are summarized in Table 7–16.

As we mentioned earlier, many of the analyses include observations of children making errors which would *not* have occurred had the L_1 structure been followed. For example, Ervin-Tripp (1974) reports that her English-speaking subjects misinterpreted French passives as actives even though the word order of French passives mirrors the English equivalents.

The scattered incidence of interlingual errors is also reported in some proportion studies. Ravem, for example, mentions some instances of interlingual errors in *Yes/No* questions;

Like you me not, Reidun?

TABLE 7-15 Summary of Child Comparative Error Analysis Research

STUDY	L_1/L_2	SAMPLE SIZE	ENVIRON-MENT	ELICITATION METHOD	MODE	STRUCTURES STUDIED
Proportion Studies						
Dulay & Burt, 1974	Spanish/English	179	Host	SNC[a]: Bilingual Syntax Measure	Oral	General (See Tables 7-9 to 7-14)
Quasi-Proportion Studies						
Ervin-Tripp, 1974	English/French	31	Host	1. SNC: Comprehension tasks	Comprehension	General
				2. UNC[b]: a) Diary Records	Oral	General
				b) Child-child interaction		
				3. LM[c]: a) Limitation	Oral	General
				b) Translation		
Gillis & Weber, 1976	Japanese/English	2	Host	UNC: Free conversation	Oral	Negatives, Interrogatives, Imperatives
Hansen-Bede, 1975	English/Urdu	1	Host	UNC: Free conversation	Oral	General
Hernández-Chávez, 1972	Spanish/English	1	Host	UNC: Interaction with classmates and school staff	Oral	General
Milon, 1974	Japanese/English	1	Host	UNC: Interaction with classmates	Oral	Negatives
Politzer & Ramírez, 1973	Spanish/English	120	Host	UNC: Storytelling	Oral	General

	Language	N	Host/Foreign	Data	Oral	Word Order in Adjective and Possessive Constructions (See Table 7-16)
Price, 1968	English/Welsh	21	Host	UNC: Classroom speech	Oral	Oral
Ravem, 1968	Norwegian/English	2	Host	1. SNC: Conversation 2. LM: Translation	Oral Oral	Negatives, Interrogatives Negatives, Interrogatives
Venable, 1974	Greek } French } /English	5 Greek 4 French	Host	1. SNC: a) Bilingual Syntax Measure b) Conversation 2. UNC: a) Picture description b) Teach game to experimenter c) Free conversation	Oral Oral	General (See Table 7-7) General (See Table 7-7)
Wode, 1976	English/German	1	Host	1. UNC Free conversation 2. Experimental sessions (undefined)	Oral Oral	Negatives Negatives
Occurrence Studies						
Boyd, 1975	English/Spanish	12	Foreign	1. SNC: a) Modified Kernan Blount b) Bilingual Syntax Measure 2. UNC: a) Storytelling b) Free conversation 3. LM: a) Limitation b) Reflexive elicitation	Oral Oral Oral	General General General
Selinker et al., 1975	English/French	20	Foreign	UNC: Free conversation	Oral	General

[a] Structured natural communication [b] Unstructured natural communication [c] Linguistic manipulation (see Chapter 10)

TABLE 7-16   English/Welsh Comparative Analysis of Word Order in Adjective and Possessive NP Constructions*

Construction	Actual Utterance	English Equivalent
	Welsh (L$_2$)	
N + Adj	blodyn coch	flower red
N + Adj + Adj	cyw bach melyn	chick little yellow
Poss'd + Poss'r	esgidiau Dadi	shoes Daddy
Poss'd + Adj + Poss'r	blodyn gwyn Karen	flower white Karen
Poss'd + Det + Poss'r	cadair y babi	chair the baby

Construction		Example
	English (L$_1$)	
Adj + N		a red flower
Adj + Adj + N		a little, yellow chick
Poss'r + Poss'd		Daddy's shoes
Poss'r + Adj + Poss'd		Karen's white flower
Det + Poss'r + Poss'd		the baby's chair

*With acknowledgments to Eurwen Price, "Early Bilingualism," in C. J. Dodson, E. Price and I. T. Williams (eds.), Towrds Bilingualism. Cardiff: University of Wales Press, 1968. Reprinted by permission.

where his son uses Norwegian word order. Venable (1974) lists a few possible Greek- and French-influenced errors, and Dulay and Burt (1974a) report twenty-four instances of interlingual errors in their data. It is clear, however, that when a comprehensive view is taken of the errors compiled in the available proportion studies, the data pool comprises a powerful empirical demonstration of the prevalence of developmental errors in child L$_2$ speech.[7] Occurrence studies merely present instances or analyses of one or more error categories and do not speak directly to the proportion issue.

All these studies focused on the speech children produced. One study (Gonzalez and Elijah, 1979) investigated reading. The researchers studied the developmental reading behavior of seventy-five second to ninth grade Hispanic bilingual students, to deter-

7. We must point out here that Politzer and Ramirez (1973) concluded from their study that "the intrusion of Spanish, though certainly not the only cause of error, plays a considerable role" (p. 59). This conclusion, however, is based in part on the classification of the omission of the regular past tense markers as interlingual, presumably due to phonological factors. If this analysis is correct, this error type should not be included in a proportion analysis of grammatical errors, as physiological factors involved in the pronunciation would be confounded with cognitive factors responsible for syntax development. If on the other hand, the phonological explanation is set aside, it must be noted that the absence of the past tense marker is also typical of first language learners, suggesting that the errors may be more accurately classified as ambiguous. Past tense errors, including the omission errors at issue, comprised 51% of the total errors analyzed.

mine the kinds of language difficulties the children encountered when learning to read English. Children were tested with a cloze procedure (McLeod, 1970), and their errors were categorized into four types: illogical, logical, interference and other. After counting the error types in each category, Gonzalez and Elijah report that 11.7% of all errors made (across five reading levels) could possibly be classified as interference (interlingual). They write that ". . . in reading, as in oral speech production, children tend to separate the knowledge they have of their first language from language strategies used in reading material written in the second" (p. 23).

Adult Studies Studies conducted on the speech and writing of adults learning second languages have also found that the majority of non-phonological errors adult language learners make do not reflect their mother tongues. The proportion of interlingual errors that have been observed, however, is larger than that observed for children. The studies that state actual proportions (White, 1977; and LoCoco, 1975) report an 8-23% incidence of interlingual errors in various samples.[8] LoCoco (1976) and Bertkau (1974) noted that only a few individuals were responsible for most of the interlingual errors in their data. This observation indicates that characteristics unique to certain individuals may be closely related to the incidence of interlingual errors. This and other explanations are discussed in Chapter 5.

The two quasi-proportion studies available (one on oral production, the other on comprehension) report that virtually no interlingual errors were observed:

> There was no evidence of marked first language interference in the learner's English sentence constructions.
>
> (Hanania and Gradman, 1977, p. 88)

> Contrary to expectation, the second language learners . . . even those in the beginning group, appeared not to process the target sentences by relating them to similar structures in their native language . . . they do not attempt to apply language-specific rules appropriate to their mother tongue to the interpretation of sentence in the target language.
>
> (d'Anglejan and Tucker, 1975, p. 293)

---

8. As mentioned previously, error studies that suffer from serious methodological weaknesses are not considered here, as their results cannot be interpreted meaningfully. Two criteria were used to identify such studies: (a) the failure to classify ambiguous errors separately; and (b) the use of tasks that have a high probability of introducing bias (timed translation and the linguistic manipulation task of filling in blanks). See Chapter 10. Both Taylor's (1975) and Olsson's (1974) proportion studies suffer from these two weaknesses.

TABLE 7-17 Summary of Adult Comparative Error Analysis Research

STUDY	L₁/L₂	SAMPLE SIZE	ENVIRON-MENT	ELICITATION METHOD	MODE	STRUCTURES STUDIED
Proportion Studies LoCoco, 1975, 1976	English/{ German / Spanish }	28–48	Foreign	1) UNCᵃ: a) Picture description b) Composition	Written	General
				2) LMᵇ: Translation	Written	General
Olsson, 1974	Swedish/English	424	Foreign	LM: Fill-in-the-blanks	Written	Passive verb forms
Taylor, 1975	Spanish/English	20	Host	LM: Timed translation	Written	General
White, 1976	Spanish/English	12	Host	SNCᶜ: Bilingual Syntax Measure	Oral	General
Quasi-Proportion Studies d'Anglejan & Tucker, 1975	French/English	40	Foreign	SNC: C. Chomsky's tasks	Comprehension	Verb complements of *ask, tell, promise, easy, eager*
Hanania & Gradman, 1977	Arabic/English	1	Host	UNC: a) Social conversational questions b) Recall English expressions c) Picture descriptions	Oral	General

Occurrence Studies

Bertkau, 1974	Japanese⎫ Spanish⎬ /English	30			Oral	Relative clause
Duskova, 1969	Czech/English	50	Foreign	UNC: Composition	Written	General
Jain, 1974	Hindi/English	*	*	UNC: Written scripts	Written	General
Richards, 1971	**	*	*	*	*	General
Scott & Tucker, 1974	Arabic/English	22	Foreign	UNC: Picture description	1) Oral 2) Written	General
Valdman, 1975	English/French	16	Foreign	Quasi LM: Request for question referring to imagined situation	Oral	Interrogatives

[a] Unstructured natural communication
[b] Linguistic manipulation
[c] Structured natural communication
* Not specified
** Japanese, Chinese, Burmese, French, Czech, Polish, Tagalog, Maori, Maltese and major Indian and West African languages/English

Unlike the child studies, which have fairly uniform characteristics, the available adult studies differ in a number of critical features such as elicitation task, language mode investigated, language environment, and error categories used. The studies are displayed in Table 7–17.

The subjects for White's study were twelve Spanish-speaking adults from Venezuela who were studying intensive English at Concordia University in Montreal, having had some formal English instruction in their native country. The students had been exposed to eight months of study in Canada at the time the experiment was undertaken and fell into intermediate and advanced levels of proficiency.

Oral production data were elicited using the *Bilingual Syntax Measure*. Following the Dulay and Burt (1974a) method, White classified and tallied Developmental, Interlingual[9] and Other errors, excluding Ambiguous errors from the developmental and interlingual counts. A total of 541 errors were classified and grouped into 12 grammatical categories. The results appear in Table 7–18 below.

As Table 7–18 shows, 60.3% (272 out of 451) of the errors were classified as Developmental; 20.6% (93 out of 451) were classified as Interlingual (but see below); and 19% (86 out of 451) were classified as other (including 37 Ambiguous errors).

It is interesting to note that the bulk of the interlingual errors are in two categories: *It-be-X* and *Possessive*. White notes that nearly all (37 out of 43) of the *It-be-X* errors were of the sort *is X*, where *it* was apparently omitted. In that regard, she mentions that Cancino et al. (1975) noticed the same phenomenon and have persuasively argued that the *is X* error may be one of pronunciation rather than of grammar. Cancino et al. suggest that the pronunciation of *it's* and *is* by Spanish speakers learning English may not be distinguishable to the listener, i.e. it may be an unanalyzed chunk. An imitation experiment they conducted shows that their Spanish speakers did not make the distinction in their speech. If the *is X* error is indeed a phonological error, as the data suggest, the proportion of grammatical interlingual errors in White's study drops from 20.6% to 12.4%.

LoCoco made two investigations of adult second language acquisition in a *foreign* language environment. In her 1975 study, she examined the errors of native English-speaking students enrolled in Spanish and German classes at a university in Northern California.

The language data were collected by asking the students to write

9. Referred to in White's study as "interference errors."

TABLE 7-18 Comparative Error Types by Grammatical Category*

| Grammatical Category | Number of Errors | | | Number of Correct Forms |
	Developmental	Interlingual*	Other	
Possessives	21	19	8	48
NP-be-predicate	15	3	0	155
Tense	85	0	0	a
Word Order	0	9	5	a
Articles	25	0	6	a
It-be-X	0	37	0	15
NP V-ing	20	1	0	69
Omission of plural	37	0	0	51
Omission 3rd singular /s/	36	0	0	33
Verb + infinitive	7	0	7	30
Prepositions	5	9	5	26
Agreement	7	2	19	30
TOTAL	272	93	86	457

*Adapted from L. White (1977), "Error Analysis and Error Correction in Adult Learners of English as a Second Language." In *Working Papers in Bilingualism, 13*, 42–58. Reprinted with permission of the author.

a Number not given by White.

a composition on a topic of their choice. Four written samples were obtained in this manner for the two groups of students (one studying German, the other Spanish) at different points during the quarter of language instruction they were receiving. Between 28 and 48 students were included for each language at each sampling. The first sample was taken three weeks after the beginning of the quarter, the last at the end of the quarter. At the first sample, of course, the students could write scarcely anything in the new language.

LoCoco used error categories which were essentially subcategories of those used by the other proportion studies,[10] (e.g. White, 1977; Dulay and Burt, 1974a). In order to allow comparability across studies, the subcategories are collapsed as follows: (a) Lack of transfer, intralingual and communicative collapse into *Developmental;* (b)

10. The following definitions are quoted from LoCoco, 1976, pp. 98–100: "*Lack of transfer errors* take place when L_1 and L_2 have the same rule, and the rule is not applied in L_2; or when both languages do not have a rule which the learner applies in L_2. *Intralingual errors* occur when L_1 does not have a rule which L_2 has; the learner applies an L_2 rule which produces an error. Errors were termed *communicative* when the learner attempted to use a structure or word whose lexical, semantic and functional characteristics had not been taught in the classroom. Errors were labelled *interlingual* errors when L_1 has a rule which L_2 does not have and the L_1 rule is applied to L_2. *Dual errors* are evidenced when L_1 does not have a rule which L_2 has, and no rule is applied in L_2. *Overlap errors* . . . are those which could derive from two or more sources."

TABLE 7-19   Percent of Comparative Error Types in Spanish and German for English-Speaking University Students*

	Developmental		Interlingual		Ambiguous	
	% Spanish	% German	% Spanish	% German	% Spanish	% German
Sample 1 (earliest)	63.4	70.6	11.5	23.0	25.0	6.2
Sample 2	63.6	76.1	14.7	12.4	21.5	11.4
Sample 3	67.8	71.6	11.7	18.6	20.4	9.8
Sample 4 (latest)	62.3	74.3	14.9	16.4	22.8	9.2
Mean	68.7%		15.4%		15.8%	

*Adapted from V. LoCoco (1975), "An Analysis of Spanish and German Learners' Errors." In *Working Papers in Bilingualism, 7,* 96–124. Reprinted with permission of the author.

Interlingual remains as is; and (c) Dual and Overlap collapse into *Ambiguous.*

The developmental category thus derived probably includes errors that would have been classified as Other according to our working definition; and some errors in the derived ambiguous category would probably have been developmental. These would not be serious misclassifications, however, since they do not affect the proportion of interlingual errors. The proportion of incidence of each error category is displayed in Table 7–19 separately for the Spanish and German samples and for each sampling over time.

As the table shows, interlingual errors comprise, on the average, only 15.4% of the total errors, whereas developmental errors comprise 68.7%.

LoCoco also noted that only 25% of the German subjects contributed to the higher values obtained for interlingual errors. Similarly, Bertkau (1974) reports that only 3 of his 15 Japanese-speaking students were responsible for nearly all of the interlingual errors he observed.

In her second study, LoCoco (1976) again examined the errors of adults learning a second language in a foreign language environment. Her subjects were 28 English-speaking students taking an elementary Spanish course in a California university. The purpose of this study was to compare the effects on errors of three tasks used to elicit speech in the written mode: translation, picture description and composition.

Again, in over a hundred errors classified, the incidence of interlingual errors was low, even lower than in the first study across all three tasks: 13.2% for translation, 13.0% for composition, and 8.3% for picture description.

COMMUNICATIVE EFFECT TAXONOMY

While the surface strategy and comparative taxonomies focus on aspects of the errors themselves, the communicative effect classification deals with errors from the perspective of their effect on the listener or reader. It focuses on distinguishing between errors that seem to cause miscommunication and those that don't. Underlying this type of error analysis is the question: which types of errors render a phrase or sentence incomprehensible to the listener or reader?

Research has shown that certain types of errors make a critical difference as to whether or not the listener or reader comprehends the speaker's intended message. Errors that affect the overall organization of the sentence hinder successful communication, while errors that affect a single element of the sentence usually do not hinder communication.

The number of systematic studies on the communicative effect of errors are relatively few. They represent an important beginning, however, and the results obtained thus far provide a sound basis for continued error analysis from the perspective of communicative effect. The results of such analyses have important implications for second language curriculum design as well as for psycholinguistic research on the processes of language comprehension.

The first communicative effect taxonomy was worked out by Burt and Kiparsky (1972) and Burt (1975). Burt and Kiparsky collected several thousand English sentences containing errors made by adult EFL learners from all over the world—Germany, Japan, France, Turkey, Ethiopia, Korea, Thailand, and Latin America, as well as by foreign students in the United States. The errors were taken from tape recordings of spontaneous conversations and from written compositions and letters, many of which were gathered by Peace Corps Volunteers and EFL teachers.

In order to determine the relative importance of various error types to the communicative effect of a sentence, they selected from their collection of ungrammatical sentences those containing *two or more* errors. They then asked native speakers of English (the company janitor, the car mechanic and shopkeepers) to make judgments about the relative comprehensibility of a sentence as each error was corrected, one at a time or several at a time. For example, the sentence

English language use much people.

contains three errors: the article *the* is missing in front of *English language, much* is used instead of *many,* and the subject and object are inverted. Burt and Kiparsky asked their native English-speaking judges to tell them which of the following partially corrected versions of the original sentence was easiest to comprehend:

1. The English language use much people.   (*the* inserted)
2. English language use many people.   (*much* corrected)
3. Much people use English language.   (word order corrected)

The unanimous verdict was that version 3 was the most comprehensible, whereas 1 and 2 hardly improved the original sentence. Moreover, the correction of both *the* and *much* in version 4:

4. The English language use many people.

was still considered much less intelligible than the single word order correction in version 3.

In another example:

Not take this bus we late for school.

correcting each of the errors results in five versions:

1. We not take this bus we late for school.   (*we* inserted)
2. Do not take this bus we late for school.   (*do* inserted)
3. Not take this bus we will late for school.   (*will* inserted)
4. Not take this bus we be late for school.   (*be* inserted)
5. If not take this bus we late for school.   (*if* inserted)

The first four versions of the sentence were judged as not having much effect on the comprehensibility of the sentence. In fact, three out of four judges pointed out that, though unlikely, the speaker could have meant to say "We shouldn't take this bus. If we do, we'll be late for school." In version 5, the insertion of the connector *if* makes the speaker's original intentions immediately clear, and prevents any misunderstanding. The single insertion of *if* did more to convey the speaker's intended meaning than the four other corrections combined in version 6 below.

6. We do not take this bus we will be late for school.

Version 6 is still ambiguous, whereas

5. If not take this bus we late for school.

clearly communicates the speaker's intention.

This procedure was followed for some 300 sentences containing more than one error. Burt and Kiparsky discovered that errors which significantly hinder communication (in the sense that they cause the listener or reader to misunderstand the message or to consider the sentence incomprehensible) are of a certain type, while those that do not hinder communication are of another type.

Global Errors   Errors that affect *overall sentence organization* significantly hinder communication. Because of the wide syntactic scope of such errors, Burt and Kiparsky labeled this category "global." The most systematic global errors include:

Wrong order of major constituents

e.g. English language use many people.

Missing, wrong, or misplaced sentence connectors

e.g. (If) not take this bus, we late for school.
He will be rich until he marry.
　　　　　(when)
He started to go to school since he studied very hard.

Missing cues to signal obligatory exceptions to pervasive syntactic rules

e.g. The student's proposal (was) looked into (by) the principal.

Regularization of pervasive syntactic rules to exceptions
(in transformational terms, not observing selectional restrictions on certain lexical items)

e.g. We amused that movie very much.
　　(That movie amused us very much.)

Local Errors   Errors that affect *single elements (constituents) in a sentence* do not usually hinder communication significantly. These include errors in noun and verb inflections, articles, auxiliaries and the formation of quantifiers. Since these errors are limited to a single part of the sentence, Burt and Kiparsky labeled them "local." Local errors are clearly illustrated in the examples discussed above. The global/local distinction can be extended to the classification of errors in terms of those that sound more "un-English" to a listener or reader than others. For example, compare:

> Why like we each other?
>   and
> Why we like each other?

Both of these can be understood without too much trouble, but Burt and Kiparsky's judges found the first more "un-English" than the second. The most compelling explanation for this difference seems to be that the first version violates the typical Subject-Verb-Object order in English, while the second does not. The English language, especially American English, takes great pains to maintain the Subject-Verb-Object (SVO) order (Bever, 1971; Greenberg, 1961). For example, in most questions, rather than inverting the main verb and subject to signal an interrogative (as many languages do), English inverts the auxiliary if there is one. If there is no auxiliary, the participle *do* is used as a question cue. In this way, English preserves the SVO order.[11] For example:

> Is *he sleeping?*
> Why does *she wear those clothes?*

The lone exception of this general rule occurs when *be* is used as a main verb:

> Is *she* here?

It is interesting to note that children learning English as their first or second language typically make errors where SVO is maintained but *do* is omitted: *Why we like each other?* But errors where the verb is inverted are rarely heard (see Brown, 1973).

Based on this kind of analysis, Burt and Kiparsky were led to suggest that the global/local distinction seems to be a most pervasive criterion for determining the communicative importance of errors. In other words, students must control *global grammar* in order

---

11. When the SVO order is violated, English provides cues to signal the violation, as in the passive construction where the OVS order is signalled by *be* + past participle (+*by*): The proposal *was* looked into by the principal.

to be easily understood while it is possible to communicate successfully without controlling *local grammar.* Local grammar, of course, must be learned if the speaker is to approximate native fluency, but if successful communication is the learner's primary purpose, global grammar must receive top priority.

In addition to basic word order and sentence connectors, Burt and Kiparsky mentioned two other aspects of English grammar that often yield global errors: **psychological predicate constructions** and **selectional restrictions on certain types of verbs in sentential complements.** Both of these share an important and by now familiar characteristic: they are exceptions to pervasive principles of English.

Psychological Predicates   Many predicates (both verbs and adjectives) describe how a person feels about something or someone. They describe psychological states or reactions.

> She loves that dish.
> We're glad you're here.

Psychological verbs always require (1) the animate being who experiences the feeling, called the *experiencer,* and (2) the thing or person that causes the feeling to come about, called the *stimulus.* Most verbs that can relate an animate noun (one that can do or experience things, a living being) and an inanimate noun require that the animate noun be the subject and the inanimate noun be the object. For example:

> He broke the window.
> She bought two boxes of pencils.

Many psychological verbs also follow this rule:

> They dislike latecomers.
> We prefer Dutch chocolate.

Some psychological verbs, however, require the order of experiencer and stimulus to be reversed, as in:

> This lesson bores me.
> The performance amused everyone.

This reverse order of experiencer and stimulus (animate and inanimate nouns, respectively) is an exception to the pervasive English order. Students who have learned the general rule unsuspectingly apply it to the exceptional verbs (reverse psychological verbs), producing sentences such as:

He doesn't bother the cat.
(The cat doesn't bother him.)

I don't amuse that.
(That doesn't amuse me.)

Sometimes reverse psychological verbs are misused with animate stimuli:

Call your mother—she worries you.
(You worry her.)

He doesn't interest that group.
(That group doesn't interest him.)

Here the sentence meaning is entirely obscured or changed.

Students, especially older ones, frequently attempt to use these verbs before learning their exceptional character. The result is miscommunication, as the examples above illustrate.[12]

Similar difficulties arise with a group of reverse adjectives that behave in the same peculiar fashion. That is, after students have learned to use regular adjectives,

He's happy to see you.
We're glad you came.

where the experiencer is in first position, they use reverse adjectives the same way, producing sentences such as:

She is hard to get anything done.
I'm wonderful to see you.

Misorderings with reverse psychological predicates affect overall organization and seriously hinder communication.[13]

Choosing Complement Types A second global area of English syntax is the complement system. Complements, or subordinate

12. Reverse psychological verbs include: *delight, elate, interest, overwhelm, worry, confuse, frighten, thrill, impress, fascinate, flatter, disappoint, mislead, horrify, charm, please, satisfy, bother, depress, shock, insult, excite, surprise, relieve, disgust, bore, scare, offend.*
13. The following is a partial list of reverse adjectives: *good, possible, terrible, wonderful, probable, awful, important, fantastic, painful, necessary, strange, simple, easy, great, stupid, okay, difficult, bad.*

clauses, usually take one of three forms in English: *that*-clauses (*No one believes that we will survive this*); infinitives (*I want to sleep*); and gerunds (*He avoids working late*). The improper selection of these complement types can lead to errors that seriously impede communication.

Infinitives and gerunds are often used in English when their implied subjects may be omitted because they are a repetition of a noun in the main clause anyway. For example:

We plan to go to New York next week.
We avoid sleeping past seven.

English speakers know that the implied subject of *to go* and *sleeping* is the preceding noun in the main clause, *we*.

Infinitives are used when their implied subject is the *same* as the **subject of the main clause,** as in *we plan to go*, where the subject of *to go* is *we*. Otherwise, the infinitival subject must be included, as in:

We want him to go to New York next week.

From time to time, beginning students will omit the subject of an infinitive when the implied subject is *not* the same as the subject of the main clause. This results in sentences like:

I couldn't walk yet after the baby was born so the doctor didn't want to go home. (Intended . . . didn't want me to go home)

Mother has a lot of work. Daddy expects to stay at her office late. (Intended . . . Daddy expects her to stay at her office late)

Although the student's sentences sound normal, they clearly do not convey the intended message because English speakers interpret subject-less infinitives to refer to the subject of the preceding main clause.

After students have learned this pervasive quality of infinitives in English—that the implicit infinitival subject is the preceding noun—their troubles are not yet over. There are exceptions to this principle. The exceptional verbs require the subject to be mentioned in both the main clause and in the subordinate clause even though it is the same in both. Not realizing this, students sometimes produce sentences like:

Anna told the priest to have six children.
          (that she had six children).

The verb *tell* requires the subject of the subordinate clause to be repeated, even if that subject is the same. English usually requires that these verbs have *that*-clause as subordinate clauses, since *that*-clauses always require a subject to be present. For example:

	He found out that he was healthy.
Not:	He found out to be healthy.
But:	He wants to be healthy.

The following small, but well-used, group of verbs in English behaves in this way:

think	know	find out	report
tell	notice	say	assume
ignore	doubt	acknowledge	

Another error analysis study also found that errors in the English verb complement had negative communication effects. Following Burt and Kiparsky (1972), Johansson (1975) conducted a communicative error analysis, calling the effect of the error its degree of "irritability." Johansson constructed his own set of sentences containing errors, including errors he felt might have been made by Swedish learners of English: errors in verb complementation (*My doctor suggests me to take a holiday*); error in agreement (concord) (*John says that the visitors has probably left*); and certain word order errors (*Not a single mistake they have ever made*). Using university students as well as elementary and secondary students to judge the sentences through direct and indirect tasks, he found that errors of verb complementation attained the highest irritability index.

Hendrickson (1976), who used Burt and Kiparsky's (1972) global/local distinction in his research on the effectiveness of error correction, proposed an interesting and potentially useful extension of the global/local error classification—a technique to help distinguish a student's *linguistic* and *communicative* proficiency level.

To define communicative proficiency, one takes the proportion of global errors to total errors. The resulting figure (a percentage) reflects the degree to which global grammar has not been acquired; that is, the degree to which a learner's total errors are global errors is the degree to which global grammar has *not* been acquired. Since global grammar is necessary for effective communication, the global-to-total error ratio could reflect a student's *communicative proficiency index.* The lower the relative number of global errors, the higher the student's communicative proficiency index. Likewise, the local-to-total errors proportion might be used to determine a *linguistic proficiency index;* that is, the degree to which the student controls linguistic aspects of language that are not crucial for communication. The higher the proportion of local-to-global errors, the lower the student's linguistic proficiency index.

This extension of the global/local error classification promises to be a very useful technique to distinguish between a student's ability to communicate *effectively* and a student's ability to speak *grammatically.*

SUMMARY

Error analysis was inspired by the generative linguistics movement of the sixties which focused on the creative aspects of language learning. This focus has helped to raise the status of errors from unwanted forms to the relatively important status of indicators of learning and guides to teaching.

The use of error classifications or taxonomies to propose sources of errors has taken up a good portion of the error analysis research literature. The explanation of error types, however, is not simply a matter of assigning a single source to each error that occurs. To the extent that language learning is an interaction of internal and external factors, explanations of errors will have to be multidimensional and include factors beyond the observable characteristics of the errors. Since taxonomies were intended to classify concrete observable phenomena, their use as explanatory frameworks for L_2 errors is questionable.

The explanation of errors is left, therefore, to those sections in the book dealing with the learner's environment and internal processing mechanisms, the interaction of which results in language acquisition. In this chapter, we have limited our discussion to the descriptive aspects of error taxonomies, on the assumption that the accurate description of errors is a separate activity from the task of inferring the sources of those errors.

Different definitions of error categories and error types in the published literature have prevented meaningful cross-study comparisons or validation of results. We have attempted to address this problem by stating the purposes and defining the categories included in the taxonomies researchers have used. Four major types of descriptive taxonomies are presented: linguistic category, surface strategy, comparative, and communicative effect taxonomies.

Finally, in an effort to bring the latest research to bear on the presentation of the descriptive aspects of error analysis, the literature has been comprehensively surveyed and research findings presented for each major taxonomy. The highlights are recapitulated below.

1. L_2 learners manipulate (subconsciously) surface elements of the language they are learning in systematic ways, including:
   a. The omission of grammatical morphemes—items that do not contribute much to the meaning of sentences;
   b. The marking of a given semantic feature on two or more items in an utterance when only one marker is required;
   c. The regularization of rules;
   d. The use of archi-forms, one form for the several required;
   e. The alternating use of two forms, whose conditions for use are still being internalized;
   f. The misordering of items in constructions that require the reversal of word-order rules that had been previously acquired, or when word order may vary in certain linguistic environments; and
   g. The addition of grammatical morphemes where none is required.

2. The great majority of the grammatical errors found in the language output of L_2 learners is similar to those made by L_1 learners of the target language rather than to the structure of the L_2 learner's mother tongue. Although adults tend to exhibit more mother tongue influence in their errors than do children, adult errors that reflect L_1 structure also occur in small proportions.

3. Errors that significantly hinder communication exhibit certain characteristics that are distinguishable from those whose effects on communication are negligible; that is, they affect those parts of grammar that refer to overall sentence organization, such as word order and connectors.

Errors comprise a significant portion of a learner's language performance. Together with transitional constructions, acquisition orders and other performance aspects, errors provide important insights into the processes of second language acquisition and instruction.

STUDY QUESTIONS

1. a. For each of the following utterances, do you see a logic behind the errors that appear? If yes, indicate what the logic (or strategy) seems to be.
   1. *She runned fast to get away.*
   2. *He doesn't wants to go.*
   3. *He fat man.*
   4. *Hat the is there.*
   5. *That dogs are mines.*

   b. Which error would you least expect an L_2 learner to make?

2. Imagine you are an ESL teacher. Your students expect you to correct their work, yet many of them feel embarrassed when they make errors. Imagine they produced the following:

1. *Him have car. He easy to go there.*
2. *She break leg since she throw away skis.*
3. *Everything covered insurance against fire.*
4. *They offer carry book to car.*
5. *I amuse the movie.*

   a. What approach would you use in correcting the sentences? Justify your selection.
   b. Correct the sentences according to the approach you selected.

3. Consider the following utterance produced by a Spanish speaker:

He no have bicycle.
(El no tiene bicicleta.)

   a. What errors are there in the utterance?
   b. Would you classify them as interlingual?
   c. Explain your answer.

4. Suppose someone suggested setting up a taxonomy that classified errors into the following categories: (1) environmental (2) filtering errors (3) organizer errors (4) monitor errors (5) age-related errors.
   a. Would you encourage the person to use such a taxonomy?
   b. If yes, what rationale underlies your endorsement? If no, what arguments would you use to dissuade the person from going ahead with the taxonomy?

5.a. Tape record and transcribe the speech of a second language learner, or ask the learner to write a composition. The speech corpus or the composition should have at least fifty utterances or sentences that are not repetitions or imitations.
   b. Select a taxonomy (or combination of taxonomies) and indicate your rationale for the selection.
   c. Perform an error analysis of your data based on the taxonomy you selected.
   d. Write up your findings in terms of proportion of each error type. Discuss the implications of your findings in terms of L_2 learning processes or teaching practices.

8

Acquisition Order

Language acquisition is a gradual process that can take anywhere from several months to several years. During this time, the learner acquires the different structures that make up a language: tense endings, plural markers, negative sentences, complements, and so forth. Learners acquire some of these structures almost immediately. The ordering of the subject, verb, and object in a simple sentence, for example, is learned very early, as is the *-ing* ending on English verbs (*She's working*). Other structures, such as simple verb tenses, are acquired later, and still others only after much natural exposure to the language. Studies of acquisition order seek to determine the order in which learners acquire language structure.

For a long time people believed that students learned structures in the order in which they were taught. Teachers have noticed, however, that no matter how much they drill or correct certain errors, students keep making them. Recently, for example, English teachers in Panama corroborated what many other teachers have told us: getting students to add the third person *-s* to a verb (as in *She likes papayas*), or to use *has* instead of *have* (*Mary has a cold*) is a losing battle when teachers attempt it early in an English as a Second Language course. Students may use these items correctly in a drill or a memorized dialogue, but they invariably fail to do so in spontaneous conversation.

Researchers have finally discovered the major reason behind such apparently intractable errors: the third person *-s* and *has* appear relatively late in the order in which learners naturally acquire English structures. If such structures are presented early in a course, students will have an inordinately difficult time learning them and will not learn them until they have acquired enough of the English rule system. Students may be able to learn some structures *consciously*, but true subconscious acquisition will come only when the students are ready (as we saw in Chapter 2).

In current practice, major aspects of language teaching often involve the ordering of structures: sequencing lessons, organizing language textbooks, developing reading material, and selecting items for language tests. Even teachers' reactions to students' errors are influenced by what they think a student should know at a certain point in the learning process. If teachers knew the order in which students naturally tend to learn language structures, they could work with the process rather than against it.

L_2 researchers have been particularly inspired by Roger Brown's now classic longitudinal study of the acquisition of English as a first language. Brown studied three unacquainted children to whom he gave the research aliases of Adam, Eve and Sarah. Analyses of their speech collected at weekly intervals over a four-year period revealed that these three now famous children learned fourteen English grammatical morphemes in a similar order. Brown's finding was subsequently corroborated in a cross-sectional study of twenty-four children (de Villiers and de Villiers, 1973).

The absence of direct correspondence between the order found and certain environmental characteristics added particular strength to Brown's findings. Brown found that the structures that were most frequently produced in the children's linguistic environment were not necessarily learned earlier; nor was positive reinforcement (in the Skinnerian sense) effective for language acquisition.

These results led Brown to suggest that "we presently do not have evidence that there are selective social [environmental] pressures of any kind operating on children to impel them to bring their speech into line with adult models" (1973, p. 105). Indeed, Brown suggested that ". . . children work out rules for the speech they hear, passing from levels of lesser to greater complexity, simply because the human species is programmed at a certain period in its life to operate in this fashion on linguistic input" (1973, pp. 105–106).

This intriguing picture of the language learning process, together with its far-reaching implications for second language teaching, led to the initial studies of L_2 learning sequences. Might there also be a common order of acquisition for certain L_2 structures? Would it be the same or different from the sequence found for first language learners? All the studies performed to date revolve around one major question in one way or another: Is there an acquisition order for certain English structures which is characteristic of L₂ learners?

Nearly every well-designed study has answered this question in the affirmative. Researchers have discovered an L₂ acquisition order which is characteristic of both children and adults, and which, for as yet unknown reasons, is similar for both speaking and writing, provided that the data studied are natural conversations or compositions. This general conclusion is one of the most exciting and significant outcomes of the last decade of second language acquisition research.

The L₂ acquisition order is somewhat different from the L₁ order (Dulay and Burt, 1974 and 1977), although not enough work has been done yet to determine the specific reasons underlying the differences. Such a determination would comprise a major contribution to cognitive developmental psychology. In general, as we have said before, the mental age differences between first and second language learners probably play a major role.

The existence of an ordered set of L₂ structures does not mean that there is no variation at all in the acquisition orders that have been observed. Naturally, individual learners show idiosyncratic behavior in certain aspects of language acquisition, as they do in all other behavior. Certain structures in English, such as articles, are particularly susceptible to variation across subjects.

As we shall see later, differences in observed L₂ acquisition orders are more commonly brought on, however, by shortcomings in researchers' methods or designs than by real ordering differences among learners. The use of inappropriate or insufficient data, treating close but unordered relationships as ordered, and other research problems that will be discussed later, have served to cause unnecessary confusion. Perhaps such confusion is inevitable in a new field such as this, but the importance of the development of a body of data that can be compared across different studies cannot be overstressed. We have thus devoted the second half of this chapter to some of the commonly used methods in acquisition order research. (The first part of the chapter focuses on the findings of researchers so as not to distract readers with detailed reference to technicalities of design and analysis.)

Most of the L₂ sequence studies have investigated grammatical morphemes: noun and verb inflections, articles, auxiliaries, copulas, and prepositions. These almost trivial items of language have been a popular subject of study because grammatical morphemes are easily elicited—almost any verbal utterance contains several—

and it is fairly easy to determine whether they are used correctly. Moreover, Brown's methodological insights into grammatical morpheme analysis facilitated the development of analytical methods for L_2 research. More recent acquisition order studies have, however, also included structures such as word order in various constructions.

CHILD STUDIES

The first published study that investigated acquisition order for L_2 learners was a pilot study of eight English grammatical morphemes in the speech of three groups of six-to-eight-year-old Spanish-speaking children. The sample consisted of ninety-five Chicano[1] children from Sacramento, California; twenty-six Mexican children studying in San Ysidro, California, a town five miles away from Tijuana, Mexico where the children lived; and thirty Puerto Rican children from the East Harlem district in New York City.

These three groups of children differed in their amount of exposure to English. Most of the East Harlem children had not lived in the United States more than a year and were exposed to English in school through a bilingual program where subject matter was taught in both Spanish and English with no formal instruction in ESL. The children in San Ysidro were exposed to English only in school, as they returned every afternoon to their homes in Tijuana; however, English was the sole medium of instruction in the school. Most of the Sacramento children were born in the United States and were attending a bilingual program which included formal ESL instruction.

The speech of the children was collected using a **structured conversation** technique, the *Bilingual Syntax Measure* questions. This elicitation method consists of a natural conversation between the child and the researcher about concrete things and events, guided by questions designed to elicit a range of target structures. For example, pointing to a cartoon picture of a very fat boy and one of a very thin man, the researcher asks, *Why do you think he's so fat?* Children spontaneously respond with suggestions such as: *He eats too much; He eats all day; He eats junk; He drinks too much beer*, and other sundry comments on the proposed eating and drinking habits of the fat boy. The use of a structured conversation technique ensures that the speech produced is natural—the child focuses on

1. "Chicano" usually refers to persons of Mexican descent who live in the United States. It is often used synonymously with "Mexican American." (See also Reyes, 1978.)

communicating something, be it an opinion, idea or some other form—while at the same time guaranteeing the elicitation of a specific range of desired structures.

After the speech samples had been tape recorded, transcribed and checked, they were scored to determine the degree to which the children controlled the structures they themselves had offered in conversation. For example, if the child said *He eat all day,* the omitted third person singular *-s* could be scored as could the form of the nominative masculine pronoun which was correctly formed in this case. Each structure that was attempted and scored eventually ended up with a possible score ranging from 0% to 100%, representing the degree of control or correct use the learner had displayed. The scores were then averaged across the children in each group and the average score for each structure was ranked in descending order. The three rank orders obtained were then compared to determine their degree of similarity.

The Study Summary (Figure 8-A) captures the essence of the findings: *The acquisition sequences obtained from the three groups of children were strikingly similar.* This was so even though each group on the whole was at a different level of English proficiency.

These preliminary results suggested that there might indeed be a universal or natural order in which L₂ learners acquire certain syntactic and morphological structures. Encouraged by the findings of their pilot investigation, Dulay and Burt undertook a second more extensive study. This time they compared Chinese- and Spanish-speaking children's acquisition sequences for eleven English grammatical morphemes, adding three to the eight in the first study.

As in the original study, all the children were administered an expanded version of the *Bilingual Syntax Measure* in order to elicit speech samples. The structured conversations were tape recorded, transcribed, checked and submitted to various analyses. Different statistical methods of computation and analysis were used in order to test the stability of the results obtained.

As Figure 8-B illustrates, contours of the Spanish and Chinese children's acquisition orders for these structures are very similar, for both methods of computation used.

The studies presented so far tend to give the impression that the grammatical structures of English are acquired one at a time in a clear, linear order. This additive and oversimplified picture of the learning process results in part from the statistical methods used to analyze and present the data: namely, linear rank orders.

Groups of structures typically cluster together with very close scores. For example, one group may exhibit scores of 81, 82, and

FIGURE 8-A   Study Summary: Dulay & Burt (1973)
Comparison of Acquisition Sequences for 8 English Grammatical Morphemes for 3 Groups of Spanish-Speaking Children

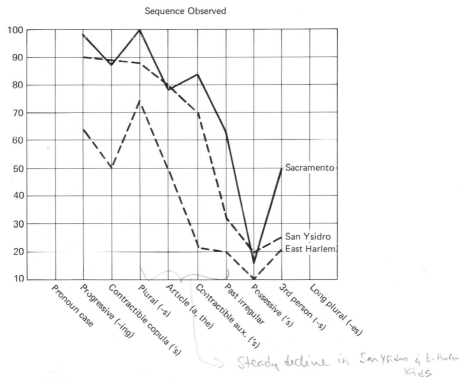

SAMPLE:			
N:	151	Research Design:	Cross-sectional
Age:	6–8 years old		
L₁:	Spanish	Elicitation Technique:	Structured conversation
L₂:	English	L₂ Environment:	Host

Sequence Observed

Sacramento

San Ysidro
East Harlem

Pronoun case · Progressive (-ing) · Contractible copula ('s) · Plural (-s) · Article (a, the) · Contractible aux. ('s) · Past irregular · Possessive ('s) · 3rd person (-s) · Long plural (-es)

Steady decline in San Ysidro & E. Harlem Kids

84, while another may cluster at 96, 98, and 99. If all six of these items are ranked in descending order, the simple ranking of 1st, 2nd, 3rd, 4th, 5th, and 6th will give the impression that the items are equally distant from each other. In fact, however, it is more likely that the items in the lower 80's form a group and are learned more or less together, and that the items in the upper 90's form

order is not the same

obligatory content for the use of a morpheme

FIGURE 8-B Study Summary: Dulay & Burt (1974b)
Comparison of Acquisition Sequences for 11 English Grammatical Morphemes for Spanish- and Cantonese-Speaking Children Using 2 Methods of Analysis

SAMPLE:

N:	115	Research Design:	Cross-sectional
Age:	6–8 years old		
L₁:	55 Chinese	Elicitation Technique:	Structured conversation
	60 Spanish		
L₂:	English	L₂ Environment:	Host

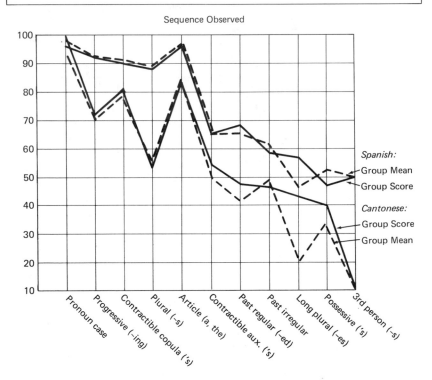

Sequence Observed

Spanish:
Group Mean
Group Score

Cantonese:
Group Score
Group Mean

Pronoun case / Progressive (-ing) / Contractible copula ('s) / Plural (-s) / Article (a, the) / Contractible aux. ('s) / Past regular (-ed) / Past irregular / Long plural (-es) / Possessive ('s) / 3rd person (-s)

Correlation Coefficients (Spearman) and Significance Levels: (p < .001) for all correlations

	Spanish Group Score	Cantonese Group Mean	Cantonese Group Score
Spanish Group Mean	.96	.96	– – –
Spanish Group Score	– – –	– – –	.95
Cantonese Group Mean	– – –	– – –	.98

another such group. Items within each group may well be unordered with respect to each other.

The concept that *groups* of structures are acquired, rather than one structure at a time, is by now shared by most language acquisition researchers. One can easily see clustered scores for the structures in nearly every carefully conducted "rank order" study, often with distinct "breaks" between groups, such as those in the example above.

To bring quantitative methods of analysis into line with learners' behavior, Dulay and Burt introduced a new procedure for data analysis that yielded acquisition *hierarchies* (ordered groups of structures) rather than sequences. (See pp. 222–25 for description.) They applied the new method, the "Ordering-Theoretic Method" (Bart and Krus, 1973), to new speech data collected from 421 children in 10 states in the United States. Three groups were analyzed separately: the Chinese group from the 1974 study; the Spanish group from the same study; and the new Spanish group from the national study. As expected, given the results of the sequence studies, the resulting hierarchies were extremely similar. The items that were identical for all three groups are summarized in Figure 8-C.

The hierarchy shows that the items in Group I are acquired before all the items in the Groups below it. Items in Group II are acquired after those in Group I, but before those in Groups III and IV, etc. The reverse is also true. Namely, the acquisition of the items in Group IV implies the acquisition of the items in Groups I to III.

That children acquire certain grammatical morphemes in a predictable order is a finding that has been replicated in two other studies: Fathman, 1975; Kessler and Idar, 1979. These studies used a variety of research methods and different elicitation techniques, and include children from four language backgrounds (Korean, Spanish, Vietnamese and Japanese). Makino's (1979) study of 777 Japanese adolescents learning English in Japan also showed a learning order similar to that found by Dulay and Burt (1974) and the other studies. These supporting studies lend special strength to natural sequences findings because they used different methods of natural speech elicitation than that used in the initial Dulay and Burt studies and they include longitudinal data as well. One study of one Japanese child learning English in the United States [Hakuta (1974)], reported a low correlation between the order obtained for the child and Dulay and Burt's findings. In light of Makino's study of almost 800 Japanese speakers, however, it is likely that Hakuta's subject was idiosyncratic.)

It is thus highly probable that *children of different language back-*

FIGURE 8-C Study Summary: Dulay & Burt (1975)
Acquisition Hierarchy for 13 English Grammatical Morphemes for Spanish-Speaking and Cantonese-Speaking Children

SAMPLE:

N:	536	Research Design:	Cross-sectional
Age:	5-9 years old		
L₁:	461 Spanish	Elicitation Technique:	Structured conversation
	55 Chinese		
L₂:	English	L₂ Environment:	Host

Acquisition Hierarchy Observed

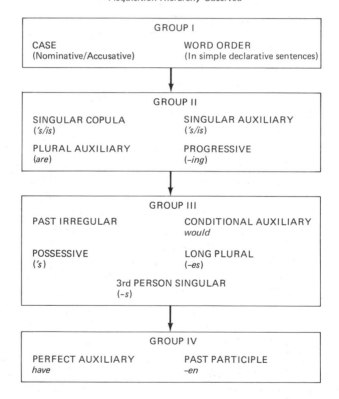

GROUP I

CASE
(Nominative/Accusative)

WORD ORDER
(In simple declarative sentences)

GROUP II

SINGULAR COPULA
('s/is)

SINGULAR AUXILIARY
('s/is)

PLURAL AUXILIARY
(are)

PROGRESSIVE
(-ing)

GROUP III

PAST IRREGULAR

CONDITIONAL AUXILIARY
would

POSSESSIVE
('s)

LONG PLURAL
(-es)

3rd PERSON SINGULAR
(-s)

GROUP IV

PERFECT AUXILIARY
have

PAST PARTICIPLE
-en

NOTE: Please see Table 8-2 for the precise definition of the structures in this hierarchy.

grounds learning English in a variety of host country environments ✓
acquire eleven grammatical morphemes in a similar order. Although
some idiosyncratic variations occur, the trend of acquisition in natural host country environments is clearly discernible.

BMK (1974)

ADULT STUDIES

The first published adult study of acquisition order (Bailey, Madden
and Krashen, 1974; Figure 8-D) investigated the possibility that
adults might show an acquisition sequence similar to that found for
children for the eight structures initially studied by Dulay and Burt
(1973). The sample consisted of seventy-three adults representing
twelve language backgrounds, all of whom were enrolled in English
as a Second Language classes at Queens College in New York.

As in Dulay and Burt's 1973 study, these researchers administered the *Bilingual Syntax Measure* to elicit the speech samples for
study. And, as in previous studies, the structured conversations were
tape recorded, transcribed and checked. Scoring and analysis for
sequences à la Dulay and Burt (1973) followed.

In this investigation, nearly half the sample were Spanish speaking. To ensure that the acquisition sequences for this subgroup and
the other subjects would not be lumped together unjustifiably, Bailey et al. first compared the sequence obtained from the Spanish
speakers as a group to that of the group representing the other
eleven languages. Since they found a similar sequence for both
groups, Bailey et al. compared the sequence for the total sample to
the sequence Dulay and Burt had reported in their pilot (1973) study
and in their 1974 study.

Both comparisons showed that *the contours for the acquisition* ✓
sequences of the children and adults studied are very similar. This
initial sequence study of adult morpheme acquisition permits us to
suggest that whatever internal factors are interacting with language
input in children to produce the results we see, they seem to be
operating in adults as well. Furthermore, the first language of the
L_2 learner, whether child or adult, does not appear to affect the result of this interaction: the sequences observed for all groups are
similar.

Several other studies have investigated acquisition sequences for
adults from different language backgrounds (Larsen-Freeman, 1975;
Krashen, Houck, Giunchi, Bode, Birnbaum and Strei, 1977; Fuller,
1978; Christison, 1978; and Kessler and Idar, 1979). Using a variety
of research methods and elicitation tasks, researchers drew on subjects representing over twenty-two language backgrounds. These

FIGURE 8-D Study Summary: Bailey, Madden & Krashen (1974)
Comparison of Adult and Child Acquisition Sequences for 8 Grammatical
Morphemes

SAMPLE:			
N:	73	Research Design:	Cross-sectional
Age:	17–55 years old		
L₁:	Greek, Persian, Italian, Turkish, Japanese, Chinese, Thai, Afghani, Hebrew, Arabic, Vietnamese	Elicitation Technique:	Structured conversion
L₂:	English	L₂ Environment:	Host

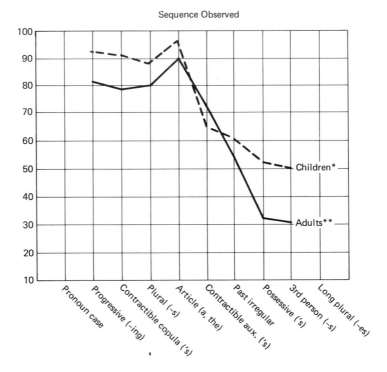

Sequence Observed

Correlation Coefficients and Significance Levels:

	Adults (Spanish Ss)
Children	rho = .976 (p < .01) (Spearman)

*Dulay & Burt (1974).
**Bailey, Madden & Krashen (1974).

210

studies confirmed Bailey, Madden and Krashen's finding that adults
and children acquire certain grammatical morphemes in a similar
order.

WRITING VS. SPEAKING

One of the first studies to examine acquisition sequences in written
work was conducted by Krashen, Butler, Birnbaum, and Robertson
(1978) at the University of Southern California. Their sample consisted of seventy university students from four different language
backgrounds who were learning English. Krashen et al. obtained
their data by asking their ESL students to write descriptions of car-
toons. The researchers encouraged the students to write as much as
they could in the time available. For the seven structures they examined, Krashen et al. obtained an acquisition sequence very similar to that obtained by other studies that had focused on speech.
Figure 8-E compares the written sequence Krashen et al. obtained
for adults to the oral sequence obtained by Bailey, Madden and
Krashen (1974) for adults.

To date, three other studies have investigated acquisition sequences in the written work of university and high school students:
Andersen's (1976), Fuller's (1978), and Makino's (1979). Over twenty
structures were investigated, including those that Dulay and Burt
had studied. The studies represented learners from over fifteen languages, and in two cases, learners were in a foreign language environment.

The results of all these studies indicate that *the acquisition sequences and hierarchies of certain structures elicited in natural writing are virtually identical to those observed in oral production.*

COMPARISON WITH L₁ ACQUISITION

Many people have asked us whether the L_2 order is the same as that
obtained for L_1 learners. We find that there are some similarities
and some differences.

Nine English grammatical morphemes were included in both L_1
and L_2 acquisition order research. Dulay and Burt (1974) compared
the order in which their L_2 subjects and Brown's first language
learners acquired these morphemes. They found that the L_1 and L_2
orders differ in certain aspects. Figure 8-F illustrates the differences
and Table 8-1 displays the Spearman rank order correlation coefficients obtained.

The irregular past tense, the article, the copula and the auxiliary

FIGURE 8-E   Comparison of Acquisition Sequences of 7 English Grammatical Morphemes Produced in the Oral and Written Modes

SAMPLE:

N: 70
Age: Adult (not further specified)
L₁: Arabic, Persian, Japanese,
              Spanish
L₂: English

Research
Design: Cross-sectional

Elicitation   Unstructured communication
Technique: (Writing)

L₂
Environment: Host

Sequence Observed

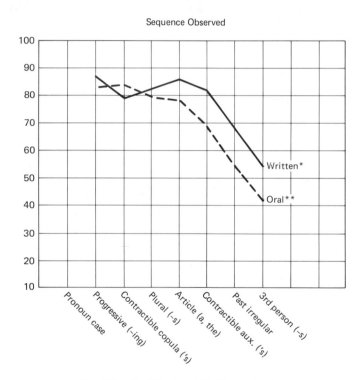

Correlation Coefficients and Significance Levels:

	Written
Oral	$rho = .723$ (p < .05) (Spearman)

*Sequence obtained by Krashen, Butler, Birnbaum & Robertson (1977).
**Sequence obtained by Bailey, Madden & Krashen (1974).

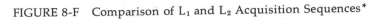

FIGURE 8-F   Comparison of L₁ and L₂ Acquisition Sequences*

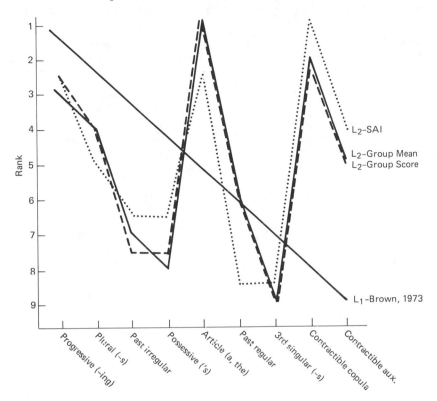

*From *Language Learning, a Journal of Applied Linguistics*, Dec. 1974, 24, 2, p. 258. Reprinted by permission.

TABLE 8-1   Spearman Rank Order Correlation Coefficients*

| | L₁ | | | L₂ | | |
	Brown	de Villiers Method I	de Villiers Method II	Group Score	Group Means	SAI
Brown		.84	.78	.43	.42	.39
de Villiers Method I			.87			
Group score					.98	.89
Group means						.91

*From *Language Learning, a Journal of Applied Linguistics*, Dec. 1974, 24, 2, p. 257. Reprinted by permission.

show the greatest amount of difference.[2] Except for the irregular past tense, these grammatical morphemes are acquired *earlier* in L_2 than in L_1.

Krashen et al. (1978) point out that the acquisition order for just the five bound morphemes (the ones attached to content words, e.g. the *-s* in *eats* or the *-ing* in *smiling*) are similarly ordered for L_2 and L_1 learners. Rank order correlations range from .8 to .9.

Not enough research has been done to explain the similarities or differences between L_2 and L_1 acquisition orders. In fact, we still have not discovered the principles underlying the L_2 order by itself nor the L_1 order by itself.[3]

SIMPLE AND EMBEDDED *Wh*-QUESTIONS

The findings described thus far focus primarily on the acquisition order for grammatical morphemes. Although sparse, there is some data on higher level structures. Using both structured and unstructured conversation techniques, Dulay and Burt (1977) studied the order in which Spanish- and Keres-speaking children acquired *wh*-questions. The hierarchical method of analysis revealed the following order of acquisition for the two language groups:

> What's that/this?
> ↓
> What are those/these?
> ↓
> I don't know what those/these are.
> ↓
> I don't know what that/this is.

"↓" indicates that the acquisition of the structure at the top of the arrow precedes the acquisition of the one at the bottom.

As the acquisition order illustrates, the correct form of simple questions precedes their correct form in embedded contexts, in which the simple questions must take on an uninverted form. It is interesting that although *What's that?* is the first learned of this group of related structures, its correct form in the embedded context is the last to be learned. It is likely that *What's that?* is learned as one vocabulary word at first (as opposed to *What are those?*), making it

---

2. When these morphemes were rank ordered, there were approximately four ranks between L_2 and L_1.

3. As mentioned in Chapter 3, Brown (1973) explored grammatical and semantic complexity to find the principles underlying the L_1 order he discovered. He found that neither by itself could completely explain the order. He concluded that a combination of linguistic and semantic complexity must underlie the L_1 order.

difficult for the learner to segment it appropriately when required to do so. (For further discussion of structures learned as unanalyzed wholes, see Chapter 9.)

REFLEXIVE PRONOUNS

Dulay and Burt (1977) studied the acquisition of a subset of reflexive pronouns for the Spanish-speaking group. (See Chapter 7 for a discussion of transitional forms in the acquisition of reflexive pronouns. We focus here on the order of acquisition of the mature forms.) Since all the children were learning Standard English, it was possible to include forms such as *himself* and *themselves* in the study. The order observed for the reflexive pronouns studied is as follows:

he, self[4]
↓
him, her, them
↓
herself
↓
himself
↓
themselves

This acquisition order demonstrates the learner's creative learning of reflexive structures. Children learn *himself* later than *herself* because they treat the reflexives as possessive contructions, i.e. as *his-self* at first, since they already use possessive structures at first. *Her* is the possessive form but *him* and *them* are not. So we get *herself*, *hisself*, and *theirself* at the same point in development, together with basic possessive constructions such as *his basket* and *their food*. Because the feminine form of the reflexive pronoun uses the possessive form, the feminine reflexive form is acquired early, obscuring its temporary misclassification into the possessive structure. The late acquisition of *themselves* results from failure to pluralize the -*self*, rather than from any characteristic of the formation of reflexives.

VARIABILITY

So far, all the findings presented in this section have focused on the similarity of the sequences and hierarchies of acquisition observed.

4. Although there were not enough occasions for these forms to be included in the analysis, both were observed being used by beginning speakers. Had the sample included more beginning speakers, more of these forms might have been observed. It is possible that forms such as these, if they appear in a learner's speech, precede the others presented in the above.

It would be misleading, however, to give the impression that the learning orders have been identical. Although outweighed by the similarities, differences have also been observed.

Two structures—the article and the short plural—have shown some variability in the acquisition sequence. In studies conducted by Dulay and Burt (1975), Fathman (1975), and Kessler and Idar (1977), both structures have shown less systematic development than the other structures studied, the article showing more variation than the plural. In Dulay and Burt (1975), for example, some hierarchical ordering relationships for these two structures differed for Spanish- and Cantonese-speaking children. In Kessler and Idar (1977), the relative ordering relationships for these two structures appeared to be unsteady during the course of their acquisition. In Fathman's (1975) study, a difference appeared in the ordering of the article for the Korean and Spanish groups. And in Hakuta's (1974) study of a Japanese girl's acquisition of English, the plural and the article appeared later than in any of the other sequence studies. Unfortunately, no explanations have been forthcoming for this variability. Future research should cast some light on these findings.

Some of the variability reported in the research literature has, however, been induced by faulty research methods. Since L_2 acquisition order research began only in the mid-1970's, research techniques are relatively new and still evolving. For this reason, we have devoted the rest of this chapter to describing the new techniques in some detail and to discussing some methodological pitfalls which plagued some of the early research and which future researchers can avoid.

RESEARCH METHODOLOGY

Readers who are not interested in the details of research methodology may skip the rest of this chapter. In this section no additional substantive findings will be discussed.

We wrote this section to help interested readers conduct sound acquisition order research. To date, this information is available only in scattered journal articles and anthologies. We will describe analytical techniques that were developed specifically for L_2 acquisition order research, along with statistical procedures that are needed to compare sequences. We also discuss procedures which yield misleading findings and which future researchers can easily avoid. Discussion of more general research methods (e.g. comparison of longitudinal and cross-sectional designs that are applicable beyond acquisition order research) is postponed until Chapter 11.

Definition and Context of Structures

A precise definition of the structures being studied and the specification of the contexts in which they occur are critical to the valid investigation of acquisition order. The English plural, for example, may be short (the -s attached to nouns) or long (the syllabic -es attached to nouns ending in s or z). Research has shown that the short plural is acquired before the long plural, and therefore, it occupies a different place in a rank order than does the long plural. If, for instance, a researcher unwittingly combined the two plural forms into a single plural structure, the placement of the combined plural in a sequence might be different from the placement of short or long plural separately. If another researcher studied only the short plural, a valid comparison could not be made. If the comparison were made inadvertently, the apparent difference in rank order would be a false difference. Special efforts in this area before analysis begins are, therefore, a good investment.

A similar example involves word order. Although it has been shown that basic word order is one of the first rules acquired by learners acquiring English, this has been observed for simple declarative sentences only. It is well known that word order in questions (where an auxiliary inversion rule is required) is not controlled until later in the acquisition process, well after the basic word order of simple declarative sentences has been established.

Similarly, children learn pronoun case early, but this is so only for simple subjects or objects. In coordinate noun phrases, especially those appearing in subject position, pronoun case is not used correctly until much later by many learners. *Me and him* or *him and me* often persist long after the correct use of pronoun case in simple noun phrases has been acquired.

Different findings resulting from differing definitions can easily be avoided if researchers take care in defining the linguistic contexts in which their structures appear. Other researchers can then replicate the studies properly. Or, if a researcher is planning to replicate the findings of an existing study, every effort must be made to define the structures exactly as specified in the earlier study. Otherwise, the results will not be comparable.

Descriptions of the structures that have been studied most frequently are presented in Table 8-2.

Obligatory Occasions   The concept of "obligatory occasion" introduced by Roger Brown (1973) for L_1 research is also central to computing L_2 acquisition orders. Most verbal utterances that consist of

TABLE 8-2   Definitions of Structures Used in the Dulay and Burt Studies (1973, 1974 b&c, 1975)

Word Order	The order of constituents in simple and compound declarative sentences. (Interrogatives and complex sentences are not included, nor are temporal adverbs.)
Pronoun Case	Nominative and accusative case in simple pronoun subjects or objects, *excluding* coordinate noun phrases such as *he and I*. Regularly elicited were the pairs *he-him, they-them,* and less frequently *she-her*.
Plural	Only the short plural is included in this category (both the /s/ and /z/ allomorphs), e.g. doors and windows. All cases of back to back *s's* were excluded, as one cannot normally tell where the *s* belongs, e.g. *the windows seem big,* where one cannot readily tell if the plural marker is present or not.
Singular Copula	Third person singular of *be,* as in *She is/'s a girl*. All cases of back-to-back *s's* were excluded, e.g. *He's so fat.*
Progressive	*-ing* in any progressive tense, whether present, past, or future, as in *He is/was/will be feeding the birds.* (Gerunds not included.)
Singular/Plural Auxiliary	The third person singular and plural of *be,* is in *She is/'s dancing; They are/'re sleeping.* In the case of the singular, back-to-back *s's* were excluded (e.g. *She's singing*).
Article	Both *a* and *the* were combined under the general category of article.
Past Regular	The /t/ and /d/ allomorphs of the past regular were scored. The /ɨd/allomorph was not elicited. Cases of back to back stops were omitted (e.g. *He walked today*), as one cannot tell if the past marker was supplied.
Past Irregular	The irregular past form of main verbs, such as *ate, stole,* and *fell*. Auxiliaries (*was, were,* etc.) are not included here nor are past participles such as *gone*. When a child offered a verb such as *eated*, past irregular was scored as a misformation.
Conditional Auxiliary	The auxiliary *would* in simple conditional and perfect conditional constructions, e.g. *If she turned around she would/'d see them; He would/'d have stolen it.*
Possessive	The possessive marker *'s* on nouns, e.g. *the girl's flower*. This was scored separately from the possessive pronouns. Examples with back-to-back *s's* were omitted.
Present Indicative	This was scored whenever a third person singular noun or pronoun appeared in subject position immediately followed by a main

218

verb. (*Does* and *has* used as main verbs were not included in this category.) Cases of back-to-back *s's* were omitted, e.g. *She eats so much*.

Long Plural	All cases where the /ɨz/ allomorph is required for plural formation, as in *houses* and *noses*.
Perfect Auxiliary	The auxiliary *have* in perfect conditional constructions, e.g. *She would have/'ve eaten it; They should have/'ve taken it with them*.
Past Participle	The marker *-en* on the main verb in a perfect construction, e.g. *They have taken the basket; She would have fallen down too*.

more than one morpheme create occasions where certain morphemes are required. For example, in the utterance *She is dancing* a mature native speaker of English would never omit the ending *-ing*, because it is obligatory that *-ing* be attached to any verb in English when expressing a present progressive action. When learners speak a language still being acquired, they will create obligatory occasions for morphemes in their utterances, but they may not furnish the required forms. They may omit them, as in *He like hamburgers*, or they may misform them, as in *They do hungry*, where something was supplied for the copula, but it wasn't quite the right thing.

The concept of obligatory occasion helps the researcher quantify precisely the degree of acquisition of specific structures using the natural utterances learners offer. As Brown put it:

> . . . one can set an acquisition criterion not simply in terms of output but in terms of output-where-required. Each obligatory context can be regarded as a kind of test item which the child passes by supplying the required morpheme or fails by supplying none or one that is not correct. This performance measure, the percentage of morphemes supplied in obligatory contexts, should not be dependent on the topic of conversation or the character of the interaction.
>
> (Brown, 1973, p. 255)

Treating each obligatory occasion for a morpheme as a "test item," Dulay and Burt scored each item as follows:

no morpheme supplied	= 0 points ("Two child")
misformed morpheme supplied	= 1 point ("Two childs")[5]
correct morpheme supplied	= 2 points ("Two children")

5. No partial credit was allowed in L₁ studies, while such credit was allowed in Dulay and Burt's studies and, subsequently, in most other L₂ acquisition studies.

This scoring process resulted in two scores for each structure in each subject's total speech corpus: the subject's *actual score* for each structure, which varied according to the subject's performance on that structure; and the *expected score* for each structure, which was always two points for each occasion of a structure in the subject's protocol. The expected score for a given structure depends on the number of obligatory occasions for a structure in a subject's total corpus.

When a researcher has scored all obligatory occasions of the structures under investigation, at least two computational methods are available: the *Group Score Method* and the *Group Means Method* (Dulay and Burt, 1974b). When Dulay and Burt undertook their initial acquisition order studies, there had been no previous cross-sectional investigations of L_2 sequences. Although they were able to adopt some basic scoring procedures from Brown's L_1 research, Dulay and Burt had to develop some new methods of analysis appropriate both for a cross-sectional design and for L_2 acquisition. The two methods described below are the two most frequently used in L_2 cross-sectional research.

Group Score Method

The method bears this label because the group of subjects for whom an acquisition sequence is to be determined (e.g. the fifty-five Chinese children of Dulay and Burt's [1974b] sample) receives a single score for each grammatical morpheme. The group score for a particular morpheme is obtained as follows: Add the expected scores (where each occasion is worth two points) for that morpheme across all the children in the group, and add the actual scores for each obligatory occasion of that morpheme across all children. Then divide the total actual score by the total expected score, and multiply the result by 100. This will yield the group's percentage of accuracy in producing that structure.

To illustrate the method, let us take five utterances produced by three children and compute the group score for the Past Irregular. (See table on following page.)

Using the scores thus obtained, the structures are then ranked according to *decreasing group score*, from which their acquisition sequence may be inferred. (See Figure 8-B, page 206 for sequences thus obtained in Dulay and Burt's [1974b] study.)

The advantage of this method is that even a subject who has just one obligatory occasion for a morpheme in her or his speech corpus is admitted into "the group." The assumption made is that the error introduced in using only one obligatory occasion from a subject

	Past Irregular	
	Raw Score	Occasion
Child 1: He *eated* it.	1	2
This man *taked* it away.	1	2
Child 2: He *bite* it.	0	2
Child 3: He *stole* it.	2	2
The dog *took* it.	2	2
	6	10

$$\text{Group Score} = \frac{\text{actual score}}{\text{expected score}} = \frac{6}{10}$$

$$.6 \times 100 = 60$$

whose performance may be variable will be minimized by the size of the sample. For example, a subject may have one occasion for a morpheme and miss it, but another subject might only have one occasion and provide it. In both cases, the subjects might be in the process of acquiring the morpheme in question, meaning that they sometimes supply it, and sometimes not. However, their scores should tend to "even out" when the sample is large enough.

The potential weakness of the method is that when a morpheme is not yet fully acquired, the learner sometimes supplies it and sometimes not. Thus the contribution of only one obligatory occasion by a subject to the group may not accurately reflect that subject's degree of acquisition, and the statistical assumption that a large sample would in the end iron out that inaccuracy may still be a real risk. The Group Means Method was designed to correct for that weakness.

Group Means Method

To reduce the effect of variability, Dulay and Burt eliminated from their sample all learners who had fewer than three obligatory occasions for a morpheme on which a score was computed. For example, if a child had two obligatory occasions for the long plural, but three or more for the other ten morphemes, that child would be excluded from the long plural computation, but not from the others. For each child who had three or more obligatory occasions of a morpheme, a structure score was computed.

Each subject's structure score, like the group structure score, is obtained by computing a ratio whose denominator is the sum of the child's expected scores for each obligatory occasion and whose numerator is the sum of the actual scores. The resulting quotient is multiplied by 100 to yield a whole number. For example, if a subject has six occasions for the copula and correctly supplies the copula three times, misforms it twice and omits it once, the structure score for that morpheme could be computed as follows:

$$\text{Structure Score}_{cop} = \frac{2+2+2+1+1+0}{12} = .67 \times 100 = 67$$

Mean structure scores for the group are then computed. An acquisition sequence is obtained by ranking the morphemes according to *decreasing mean structure scores.* The sequences obtained by both methods for each group may be compared by computing Spearman rank order correlation coefficients. The Spearman coefficient may be used to compare any two sequences. Three or more sequences may be compared by computing the Kendall coefficient of concordance. The computation of these coefficients is described in *Appendix A* for the convenience of readers interested in trying out the procedures. Since these correlation procedures are standard statistical techniques, they may be found in any statistics text that includes correlation (e.g. Marascuilo and McSweeney, 1977, Chapter 16).

Hierarchical Analysis: The Ordering-Theoretic Method

The Ordering-Theoretic Method (Bart and Krus, 1973) was used by Dulay and Burt to remedy the weaknesses of rank orders in determining L_2 acquisition orders. It is also known as the "tree method" (following its origin in mathematical tree theory) or the "hierarchical method."

The hierarchical method permits one to identify groups of structures which are acquired at roughly the same time and to determine the order in which each group is acquired. The resulting order is an *acquisition hierarchy,* as opposed to an *acquisition sequence* which is the result of rank order analysis.

The hierarchical method is based on a Boolean algebraic model and requires that each structure have only two possible values, 0 or 1. For each subject, a structure is assigned a value of 1 if it has been acquired, and 0 if it has not been acquired. In Dulay and Burt's studies, a structure was considered to be acquired if it was used 90% correctly, given at least three obligatory occasions per subject for a given structure. A score of 89 or lower would receive a 0 for that structure.

The pattern of responses for each child is then determined for every ordered pair of structures. The possible response pattern for each pair of structures is:

1,1 Both structures have been acquired.

1,0 The first named structure has been acquired; the second has not.

0,1 The first named structure has not been acquired; the second structure has been acquired.

0,0 Neither structure has been acquired.

In order to form the hierarchy, one has to determine which pairs of structures consistently exhibit the 1,0 pattern across subjects (denoting that the first structure had been acquired but not the second). The occurrence of the opposite pattern (0,1) is called a *disconfirming case*. In the Ordering-Theoretic Method, the percentage of disconfirming cases is determined for all possible ordered pairs of structures. When the percentage of disconfirming cases is sufficiently small, it can be inferred that the first structure of the pair precedes the second.

The percentage of disconfirming cases for all pairs of structures may be presented in a confirmation matrix, as illustrated below:

TABLE 8-3   Sample Disconfirmation Matrix for Hierarchical Analysis

Structure	1	2	3	4	5	•	•	•
1 Word Order	—	0	0	0	1			
2 Pronoun Case	1	—	1	2	1			
3 Progressive-*ing*	13	13	—	6	6			
4 Auxiliary Singular	25	25	17	—	12			
5 Auxiliary Plural	21	21	17	16	—			
•								
•								
•								

In reading the table, the first structure is given in the row and the second structure in the column. In our example, for the pair Progressive-*ing* precedes Auxiliary Singular, there were 6% disconfirming cases, and for the pair Auxiliary Plural precedes Pronoun Case there were 21% disconfirming cases.

In constructing the hierarchies, one structure is said to precede another if five percent or fewer disconfirming cases were found, although occasionally 6 or 7% may be accepted.

In determining the percentage of disconfirming cases, one will sometimes find that the reverse order of the pair whose order is being determined also has a very small percentage of disconfirming cases. For example, in our sample matrix, we see that for the pair pronoun case and word order, there are one percent disconfirming cases, suggesting that pronoun case precedes word order. However, in the reverse relationship, word order and pronoun case, there are 0% disconfirming cases, suggesting that word order precedes pronoun case. Clearly they cannot both precede each other.

Structures that exhibit a small percentage (7% or less) of disconfirming cases in *both* directions are considered to be an unordered pair. In addition, any numerical relationship in which one pair was 7% or less, and in which the reverse was not at least twice as large, was also considered to be an unordered pair. (Burt, Dulay and Hernández-Chávez, 1980.)

After constructing a disconfirmation matrix, the next step is to construct a "stair matrix" which displays the ordering relationships obtained. Table 8-4 is a stair matrix constructed from the disconfirmation matrix in Table 8-3. Finally, from the stair matrix, a simple succession of structure groups can be drawn to display the hierarchy. Group I structures are acquired before the structures in both Groups II and III, while the Group II structure is acquired before the Group III structures only.

One can also state the hierarchical findings in an implied fashion: The acquisition of Group III structures implies that Group I and II structures have been acquired and the acquisition of the Group II structures implies that the Group I structures have been acquired.

The hierarchical method enables researchers to uncover relationships among groups of structures that had been obscured by previous rank order methodology. To the extent that language acquisition is a process of acquiring groups of structures rather than one structure at a time, this method seems to be the most appropriate method of analysis available for cross-sectional research.

Some Pitfalls in Acquisition Order Research

Some procedures used for data collection or analysis may seriously distort the results of a study. In acquisition order research, such methodological pitfalls have been most evident in studies that have reported variation from commonly found orders or lack of systematicity in the order in which structures are acquired. We discuss three sources of data distortion specific to acquisition order research in order to help researchers avoid similar pitfalls. Other potentially

TABLE 8-4 Sample Stair Matrix and Sample Acquisition Hierarchy

Sample Stair Matrix

	Word Order	Pronoun Case	Progressive -ing	Auxiliary Singular	Auxiliary Plural
Word Order			+	+	+
Pronoun Case				+	+
Progressive -ing				(6)	(6)
Auxiliary Singular					
Auxiliary Plural					

NOTE: "+" 's indicate 5% or fewer disconfirming cases; "6" indicates 6% disconfirming cases.

Sample Acquisition Hierarchy

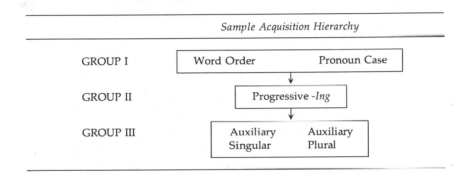

misleading procedures that also affect other areas of L₂ research are discussed in Chapter 10.

Failure to Distinguish between Purposes of Linguistic Manipulation Tasks and Natural Communication Tasks As discussed earlier (Chapters 2 and 3), linguistic manipulation tasks tap different linguistic skills than do natural communication tasks. All of the acquisition orders found by the studies described in this chapter have been based on data elicited through some kind of natural communication task. In this kind of task, the subject's focus is on the message, idea, or opinion being offered via speech or writing, so that the task may be said to approximate natural conversation or writing.

In two available sequence studies, however, subjects were asked to perform linguistic manipulation tasks. Linguistic manipulation tasks are so designed that the learner must focus on the linguistic form of what is being produced, with no aim to communicate. (See Chapter 10, pp. 248–49 for further discussion of the tasks.)

The distinction between natural communication and linguistic manipulation tasks is important for many reasons, but in acquisition research it takes on special importance. Whether the learner's focus is on communication or linguistic manipulation may affect the grammaticality of the language produced and thereby may affect the acquisition orders one observes.

To date, writing is the only mode in which both linguistic manipulation tasks and communication tasks have been given. Andersen (1976), Fuller (1978), Krashen, Butler, Birnbaum and Robertson (1977), all used the written mode to administer communication tasks. Larsen-Freeman (1975) administered a written linguistic manipulation task.[6]

Larsen-Freeman gave her subjects a copy of a story in which every sentence or sentence fragment had a missing morpheme. The subjects were asked to fill in the blank with a morpheme, or to draw a line through the blank if they thought none was required. When a bound morpheme was required, the stem to which it was to be attached was provided in parentheses preceding the blank. Clearly, the choices to be made were grammatical only, and indeed, the subjects' conscious attention had to be concentrated on grammatical form to produce the proper response.

This task focus is quite different from that where subjects write or speak about topics of interest to them, making choices about the content of what they produce. For example, Andersen (1976) asked his eighty-nine subjects to write freely on several topics, as did Krashen et al. (1977) with their seventy subjects. Fuller (1978) used a written form of a "wug-type" test (e.g. *This is a wug. These are two* _____.) in which the students could also respond with a focus on content rather than on grammar.

In Figure 8-G, we compare the order obtained by Larsen-Freeman's written linguistic manipulation task given to Arabic and Persian speakers to that obtained by Krashen et al. (1977) via natural communication tasks.

As we see from this comparison, there is little similarity between the order obtained through the linguistic manipulation tasks and that obtained through communication tasks, even though in both studies the language mode was the same—writing. As the correlation coefficients under the graph indicate, the Japanese and Spanish groups in Larsen-Freeman's study also showed little relationship to the order obtained by Krashen et al.

6. In the speaking mode, only communication tasks have been administered, and all the acquisition sequences observed have been similar, including that in Larsen-Freeman's (1975) study.

FIGURE 8-G Comparison of Natural Communication and Linguistic Manipulation Sequences for 7 English Grammatical Morphemes

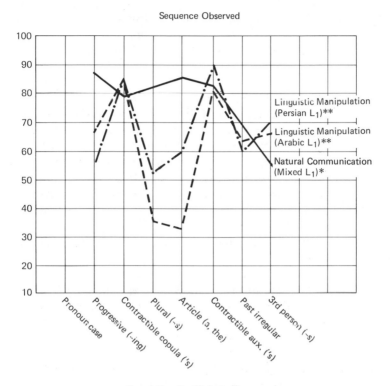

Sequence Observed

Correlation Coefficients (Spearman):

Natural Communication	Linguistic Manipulation			
	Japanese Ss	Arabic Ss	Persian Ss	Spanish Ss
	rho = .06	rho = −.17	rho = −.30	rho = .23

*Krashen et al. (1977).
**Larsen-Freeman (1975).

In a recent follow-up study, Houck et al. (1978) replicated Larsen-Freeman's results for the written linguistic manipulation task. They administered the same task to a group of some twenty-seven adult students from six language backgrounds, all of whom were learning English at the University of Southern California. The order obtained for the written linguistic manipulation task was very similar to the one Larsen-Freeman initially obtained. This "linguistic manipulation" order was *not* the same as the acquisition order observed for the natural communication tasks that Krashen et al. (1977) and many others used.

It seems then, that one source of *pseudo* but systematic variability is the elicitation task. Such variability is not the result of a factor in the acquisition process, but has been induced by the data collection method.

Insufficient Data For All Subjects   From time to time, lack of appropriate data has interfered with the accuracy of what might otherwise have been a valid study. For example, such a lack led Cancino, Rosansky and Schumann (1975) in a study of the acquisition of the English auxiliary to draw conclusions that were not warranted. Cancino et al. reported that "there is a great deal of variability in terms of order of appearance" for the eighteen auxiliaries that they had studied in their five subjects. Such a statement assumes, of course, that all subjects had at least an example of each structure studied in their protocol. This was not the case in the Cancino et al. study.

The order of eighteen auxiliaries was discussed for five subjects; however, only two auxiliaries, *is* and *can*, appeared in the data of all five subjects (p. 427). (These were also two of the auxiliaries that appeared earliest for all five subjects.) For the rest, comparable structures appeared in only some subjects' data. For example, only three of the same auxiliaries appeared in four subjects, five appeared in three subjects, and eight structures appeared in only one or two subjects. Needless to say, it is not justified to state that structure X is ordered eighth for one subject and third for another, when the latter has only two comparable structures in the data. It is probable that if the other five structures had been present in the second subject in our example, structure X would have been ordered eighth as well.

Pseudovariability of this sort disappears when precautions for dealing with insufficient data are taken (see Krashen, 1977a for further discussion).

Close Rank Order Scores   As we discussed earlier, structures with scores of, for example, 82 and 84; or 90 and 91 may not be meaningfully ordered with respect to each other. Using rank ordering techniques, however, one would have to rank the scores just mentioned as ranks 4, 3, 2, and 1, respectively. If in another study the ranks of the first two and the last two were reversed, one would obtain a radically different ranking of these four (hypothetical) structures, namely, ranks 3, 4, 1, and 2. This problem is resolved in large measure by hierarchical analysis or by determining confidence intervals for scores in a rank order (see Fuller, 1978).

Acquisition order research findings have far-reaching applications. Not only can they provide a basis for the development of L_2 learning theory, they can profoundly affect L_2 curriculum, teaching, and testing practices.

SUMMARY

In this chapter we have presented a variety of key acquisition order studies together with the methodology used to conduct them. In one way or another, all the studies revolve around one major question: *Is there an acquisition order for certain English structures which is characteristic of L_2 learners?*

As we have seen, nearly every soundly designed study has answered this question in the affirmative. An L_2 acquisition order has been discovered which is characteristic of both children and adults, and which, for as yet unknown reasons, holds for both oral and written modes, provided natural communication tasks are used to elicit the language data. This general conclusion is surely one of the most exciting and significant outcomes of the last decade of second language acquisition research.

There is general agreement that second language learning proceeds by the acquisition of *groups* of structures in a certain order. Figure 8-C illustrates the order characteristic of most second language learners.

While it has been shown that L_2 development is characterized by the orderly acquisition of structures, variability is also a factor in the L_2 process. We have seen that certain structures in English are particularly susceptible to variation across subjects. We also know that individual learners will show idiosyncratic behavior in certain aspects of language acquisition, as in all other behavior. However, pseudo variability, brought on by shortcomings in researchers' methods, is a more common phenomenon in the literature than real variability. Use of inappropriate or insufficient data, treating close but unordered relationships as ordered, and other problems discussed in this chapter, have served to cause unnecessary confusion which may have impeded progress. But perhaps this is inevitable in a new field such as this. Theories and methodologies are still being developed, training of researchers has hardly begun, and a comprehensive set of methodological guidelines does not yet exist. Thus some of the commonly used methods to determine acquisition order are described in this chapter, including the Group Score and Group Means Methods to determine acquisition sequences and the Ordering-Theoretic Method to determine acquisition hierarchies.

STUDY QUESTIONS

1. A researcher regularly taped the verbal interaction between teacher and students in an ESL class over 3 months, and found that the teacher used the third person singular -s and the copula *is* very often in her speech. On the other hand, she used the long plural -*es* very seldom. The students included beginning, intermediate, and advanced levels. At the end of the 3-month period:
   a. Would you expect most of the students to have acquired the third person-*s*? Explain.
   b. Would you expect most of the students to have acquired the copula? Explain.
   c. Do you think anyone acquired the long plural? Explain.

2. a. Compute the acquisition sequence for *Past Irregular, Pronoun Case,* and *Short Plural* -*s* based on the following speech proto-col: "Yesterday we go to a tea. Many womans from Peru was there. They all good friends for many years. They bringed many good things new for us for eat. We talk about reforma educativa in Panama. Our friends take us home."
   b. Would you expect a similar order from a composition written by the same person?
   c. The person from whom the speech data was collected had been taking an English grammar course for a year and was very good at learning grammatical rules. She was given a test on the Past Irregular, Pronoun Case, and Short Plural.

Items were of the following sort:

Fill in the blanks with the correct morpheme:

Yesterday the women ___(go)___ to a party.

Make the following plural:

One boy: **Two** _____   One table: **Two** _____

Would you expect to obtain the same acquisition order from the test data? Explain your prediction.

3. Consider the following results of a cross-sectional study on the acquisition of grammatical morphemes:

	Structure Score
Progressive -*ing*	.99
Pronoun Case	.98
Short Plural	.97
Article	.95
Copula	.93
Auxiliary	.92
3rd person	.90
Long plural	.90

a. Do you think the sample for this cross-sectional study was well chosen? Explain.
b. From these data, could you say that:
   1. Pronoun case was acquired before Short Plural?
   2. Progressive -*ing* was acquired before Short Plural?
   3. Auxiliary was acquired before third person?
c. Do you think it would be useful to compute rank order correlation to compare this sequence to those obtained in other studies? Explain.

9

Special Constructions

Certain kinds of utterances that language learners produce have unique characteristics that require special consideration and analysis. These include what have been called in the literature "routines" and "patterns."

A number of case studies from the neurological literature suggest that automatic speech, such as *you know* or *How are you?*, is distinct from rule-governed aspects of language. Such routines seem to be available in both the left and right brain hemispheres, while creative language appears to be localized in the left. Subjects with left hemispheric damage have been observed to lose rule-governed aspects of language while maintaining control over whole chunks of unanalyzed speech.

From the L_1 acquisition research, we have seen that young children have been observed by some researchers to produce unanalyzed stretches of speech which are far beyond their developing L_2 rule system. These include whole utterances such as *It's my turn*, or parts of utterances such as *That's a* _____. Often the unanalyzed pieces are those of extraordinarily high frequency in the environment. The acquisition of such constructions seems to be comparable to learning long vocabulary words.

Routines are whole utterances that are unusually error-free and show no transitional stages of development or systematic order of acquisition. They are learned as unanalyzed wholes, much as one learns a single word. Routines are produced on certain occasions, such as *How are you?* as a greeting, or *It's my turn!* in a game. The learner usually needs routines to participate in games or social events, and therefore, even if their syntactic structure is far beyond the second language maturity of the organizer, they can be learned through rote memorization.

Patterns are utterances that are only partially unanalyzed. They include an open slot for a word or phrase such as *That's* _____. or *Do you want* _____? The unanalyzed portions of patterns are, like routines, often beyond the second language maturity of the organizer and usually shows no stages of development or acquisition order. It has been suggested that learners use them because they are heard with unusually high frequency, sometimes resulting in problems of segmentation. For example, if one constantly hears *That's* _____ and rarely hears *that* (without the *'s*), one might reasonably assume that *that's* is a single word. It is not uncommon to hear utterances like *That's is mine* from learners.

Both first and second language learners use routines and patterns, but second language learners appear to be more prone to using them as communicative devices. Second language learners not only have a greater capacity for learning routines and patterns (due to longer memory spans and greater cognitive maturity), but they may have a greater need for them because they must function in real-life situations that demand early use of the target language.

The major question regarding routines and patterns is how their learning and use relate to the subconscious acquisition of the rule-governed aspects of the structure of the language. Although it is too early to state firm conclusions, the available findings are consistent and suggestive.

NEUROLOGICAL STATUS OF ROUTINES AND PATTERNS

The neurolinguistic evidence points to the fact that automatic speech is neurologically different from rule-governed language in that in adult monolinguals it is localized on both sides of the brain. In contrast, rule-governed language is localized in the left hemisphere. Furthermore, automatic speech can be preserved in cases of aphasia (loss or impairment of speaking ability).

Van Lancker (1975) defines automatic speech as "conventional greetings; overused and overlearned expressions, (such as *Be careful* and *First things first*), pause fillers such as *you know* and *well*, certain idioms, swearing, and other emotional language, perhaps stereotyped questions and answers, commands, . . ." (p. 25). Automatic speech thus appears to share some of the characteristics of routines and patterns. If automatic speech is related to routines and patterns, as it seems to be, then routines and patterns may have a fundamentally different representation in the brain than other kinds of language.

The primary evidence that automatic speech may be represented in both sides of the brain is the fact that routines and patterns are often preserved in cases of nonfluent (syntactic) aphasia and after left hemispherectomy. Patients who have suffered left brain damage, who have lost the ability to speak, can often use automatic speech, as can those who have undergone removal of the left hemisphere during adulthood. A. Smith (1966) describes a case of a man who underwent left hemispherectomy at age 48. The surgery left him nearly totally speechless:

> E.C.'s attempts to reply to questions immediately after operation were totally unsuccessful. He would open his mouth and utter isolated words, and after apparently struggling to organize words for meaningful speech, recognize his inability and would utter expletives or short emotional phrases (e.g. *Goddamit*). Expletives and curses were well articulated and clearly understandable. However, he could not repeat single words on command or communicate in "propositional" speech until 10 weeks post-operatively.

Expressive speech showed some development in E.C., but Smith reported that his rule-governed language was still "severely impaired" 8 months after the operation.

Whitaker (1971) studied a patient who was suffering from nonfluent aphasia and who exhibited an interesting sort of automatic speech behavior: He responded to nearly every question or attempt at conversation with the utterance *What'cha gonna do right now? yea yea*. Whitaker points out to the student of neurolinguistics that one cannot use such utterances as data in determining a patient's true linguistic competence: ". . . on the basis of [this one] utterance, it would be rather farfetched to assume that L.S. [the patient] had retained the *wh*-question transformation and correct pronominal reference . . ." (pp. 145–146).

Thought to be related to automatic speech are "ictal speech automatisms," words or utterances spoken by psychomotor epileptics during, before, or immediately after seizures. Ictal speech automatisms consist of stereotyped expressions (*I beg your pardon*) and emotional utterances which are spoken out of context. As with automatic speech, these seem to be associated with the right side of the brain as well as the left. Serafatinides and Falconer (1963), in agreement with other studies, found that "of 15 patients with truly ictal speech automatisms 4 were operated on the left side and 11 on the right or recessive side" (p. 345).

ROUTINES AND PATTERNS IN FIRST LANGUAGE ACQUISITION

As we mentioned in Chapter 2, Brown (1973), in his first language acquisition study, noted that some of his subjects' sentences were memorized wholes and patterns. He suggested that prefabricated routines in child speech were the result of the child's frequently hearing a structure that was, at the time of production, beyond the child's level of linguistic maturity. Brown and Hanlon's description of this phenomenon is most instructive:

> The parents of Adam, Eve, and Sarah did produce certain *wh*-questions at a very high rate in a period when children did not understand the structure of *wh*-questions. What happened then? The children learned to produce the two most frequently repeated *wh*-questions, *What's that?* and *What doing?* on roughly appropriate occasions. Their performance had the kind of rigidity that we have learned to recognize as a sign of incomprehension of structure: they did not produce, as their parents of course did, such structurally close variants as *What are these?* and *Who's that?* and *What is he doing?* When, much later, the children began to produce all manner of *wh*-questions in the pre-posed form (such as *What he wants?*) it was interesting to note that *What's that?* and *What are you doing?* were not at first reconstructed in terms of the new analysis. If the children had generated the sentences in terms of their new rules they ought to have said *What that is?* and *What you are doing?* but instead, they, at first, persisted with the old forms . . . We suggested that any form that is produced with very high frequency by parents will be somehow represented in the child's performance even if its structure is far beyond him [or her]. He [or she] will find a way to render a version of it and will also form a notion of the circumstances in which it is used. The construction will become lodged in his [or her] speech as an unassimilated fragment. Extensive use of such a fragment probably protects it, for a time, from reanalysis when the structure relevant to it is finally learned.
>
> (Brown and Hanlon, 1970, pp. 50–51.
> See also Cazden, 1972, p. 110.)

Thus, routines appear to be immune to rules at first. This clearly demonstrates that routines are part of a system that is separate from the process generating rule-governed, propositional language. It is also evidence that such constructions do not become creative constructions. Rather, the subconscious acquisition of the rule system appears to evolve independently.

Another indication that routines and patterns are the result of a different process than those related to the development of a productive rule system is the fact that Brown's subject Adam correctly produced many patterns (such as *It's a* _____, and *That's* _____.) very early on. Brown notes, however, that related propositional forms show a learning curve, with a gradual increase in accuracy over time. The patterns and routines used by the children, on the other hand, do not show such a learning curve or developmental sequence. They were correctly produced from the first.

Thus, many patterns and routines develop in advance of rule-governed linguistic maturity and independently of other more creative constructions. In time, however, some patterns and routines may be re-analyzed by the learner and dissolve into the L_2 rule system.

R. Clark (1974) espoused a somewhat different view in a paper appropriately entitled, "Performing without Competence." She argues that children's speech becomes creative through "the gradual analysis of the internal structure of sequences which begin as prepackaged routines" (p. 9). Clark's conclusions are based on her analysis of her son, Adam (not to be confused with Brown's subject of the same name), who was about three years old at the time of the study. Adam, according to Clark, would often use his own or another's previous utterances as constituents for his own utterances. For example:

ADAM	R. C.
Mummy you go.	
	Where?
Mummy you go swings.	

In addition, Adam tended to use routines, trying to use a phrase in situations close to where he heard it. For example, he would say *I carry you* when he wanted to be carried, having heard his father say this sentence on numerous occasions.

This use of routines and patterns may not be atypical. R. Clark, however, suggests that for Adam routines seemed to evolve into patterns, for example, when a hot meal was brought to the table, *Wait for it to cool* was frequently said, and it became a routine for Adam. After several weeks of hearing this, Adam was heard to say *Wait for it to dry* when hanging up a washcloth. Also, many of

Adam's long sentences were the result of juxtaposing existing routines. For example, *I want* **you get a biscuit for me** consists of the pattern *I want* _____ plus the boldfaced portion, which existed as an independent routine for Adam.

While acknowledging the existence of a separate creative process, Clark suggests that the use of routines and patterns was the central means for language development for Adam. This conclusion is quite different from that reached by Brown after his five-year study.

The work of Peters (1977) helps to resolve this apparent conflict. Peters distinguishes "analytic" and "gestalt" styles of first language development. The **analytic style,** which is used for referential and labeling functions, is the rule development described in most studies of child language acquisition, including those by Brown and his co-workers. The **gestalt style** is the attempt to use whole utterances in a socially appropriate situation; it is thus used in more conversationally defined contexts.

Peters suggests that there is individual variation among children as to which style will predominate. One of the factors that may determine which style a child will prefer appears to be what the child hears. She suggests that the analytic child may have received clear caretaker speech, while the gestalt child may have received more rapid, conversational input.

More importantly, any given child may use one style for one situation and the other for another situation. Peters's subject Minh appeared to speak analytically when naming, and used the gestalt style for social functions. Other investigators (Dore, 1974; Nelson, 1975) have also noted this kind of variation. Nelson, for example, distinguishes a "referential" style used by children who are more oriented to things, objects, and actions on objects, from an "expressive" style, used by children who are more person or socially oriented. Perhaps the latter is related to Peters's gestalt style and the former to the analytic style.

Peters's analysis is strengthened by Dore's (1974) analysis of two child L_1 learners, M (female) and J (male). While M produced isolated words during the period her speech was studied, J tended to make more use of language for communication, often using intonation alone. J's language use also tended to involve other people more than M's did; he used language more instrumentally than M, who was more prone to "label, imitate, and practice words" (p. 628). What the children heard was different to some extent. M's mother "set up routines in which she would pick up an item, label it, and encourage her daughter to imitate it" (p. 627). "J and his mother did not participate in word-learning routines." (p. 628). Dore suggests that "there may be two partly separate lines of development—word development versus prosodic development" (p. 628).

Peters suggests that gestalt users may "have to convert slowly and painfully to a more analytic approach to language" (p. 13), holding that rule-governed (analytic) language eventually predominates. Thus, gestalt language, which involves the heavy use of routines and patterns, may be a temporary strategy for learners who need to go beyond their analytic competence to solve certain communication problems that their rule-governed language system cannot yet handle.

ROUTINES AND PATTERNS IN SECOND LANGUAGE ACQUISITION

While there has been no direct comparison, the impression one gets from the literature on child second language acquisition is that the second language learner relies more on routines and patterns than does the first language learner. A number of different L_2 researchers have provided evidence for this phenomenon.

Hatch (1972) describes the case history of Paul, a four-year-old Chinese speaker learning English in the United States (see also Huang, 1971; Huang and Hatch, 1978). Paul was exposed to English in an informal environment, interacting with American children in school and on the playground. He made early use of the gestalt style. During the first month, "it seemed as if Paul were learning by imitation. He might repeat the sentence immediately after the other person said it, or he might remember it and use it later in the appropriate situation" (p. 31). "Propositional" speech appeared in the second month and looked quite similar to the analytic speech one generally sees in descriptions of child first language acquisition. Some typically analytic sentences included

This kite.
Ball no.
Paper this.
Wash hand?

At the same time, Paul was using complex routines such as

Get out of here.
It's time to eat and drink.

which he had learned by imitation. Hatch summarizes the situation: "Quite clearly two separate and very distinct strategies were running side by side. After *Week 12* it became increasingly difficult to separate out imitations since Paul's rule stages moved so fast that he quickly caught up with the language as it was spoken by the other children in the playground" (p.31).

The picture Hatch describes for Paul resembles, in reverse, what one may see in recovery patterns in aphasia. Alajouanine (1956) notes that when propositional speech returns, "fixed phrases" may disappear. The memorized routines are immune to the ungrammaticality of the aphasic's developing language.

Apparently, the routines and patterns for the L_2 learner serve primarily as a short-cut, a pragmatic tool to allow social interaction with a minimum of linguistic competence. A longer memory span and higher level of cognitive development apparently permits L_2 learners who are "still at the two word stage in rule formation . . . to recall and use longer imitated sentences" (p. 33).

In another case history, Hakuta (1974) reported on the linguistic development of Uguisu, a Japanese speaking five-year-old acquiring English in informal situations in the United States. Hakuta reports that he found evidence for "learning through rote memorization of segments of speech without knowledge of the internal structure of those speech segments" (p. 287).

Hakuta's study is mostly concerned with patterns. The evidence he provides for the existence of patterns in Uguisu's speech is quite similar to that Brown (1973) provided in his discussion of Adam. For example, copula forms in certain linguistic contexts are judged to be patterns due to the lack of a learning curve. Uguisu produced forms like *This is* _____ accurately from the outset, while learning curves from other items (like the progressive and auxiliary morphemes, including *is* in other contexts) were gradual.

From these studies one may conclude that the child L_2 learner has both an increased need and the mental capacity to use routines and patterns. The L_2 child is placed in peer and school situations that demand linguistic interaction before competence is attained the slow way, and the older child's more developed short term memory allows him or her to pick up and retain the necessary formulas to permit interaction.

In another study of routines and patterns in child second language acquisition, Wagner-Gough (1975) noted that her child subject Homer relied heavily on routines and patterns to communicate and often incorporated them into his speech. Although this is similar to R. Clark's findings, Wagner-Gough hypothesizes that patterns do not directly evolve into rule-governed language: "It is quite clear that there is no transfer between some imitations and subsequent free speech patterns. For example, a learner may say "*My name is Homer* in one breath and *He Fred* in another, the former being a memorized pattern and the latter the learner's own rule" (p. 71). Thus, this researcher, too, suggests basic differences between memorized and rule-generated language.

Fillmore (1976) studied the speech produced by five Spanish-speaking children in an American kindergarten and observed that the children used routines and patterns very early and very heavily. She calculated that their use ranged from about half to nearly all of the total number of utterances at the early stages in the school setting. As the children progressed, reliance on routines and patterns dropped to a low of 37% in the most advanced child at the end of the year.

Fillmore suggested that the linguistic environment of the classroom and playground was conducive to the learning of routines and patterns. The daily classroom routine, for example, allowed the children to easily figure out what was being said since all teachers followed, to a large extent, predictable patterns of behavior. The children thus rapidly acquired classroom expressions which were used daily (*It's time to clean up; Finish your milk*). Playground games also have predictable language components that can be picked up rapidly.

Fillmore suggests that "formulaic speech" is learned first in order to permit social interaction. The desire to participate in activities with target language speakers appears to underlie the L_2 learner's tuning in to socially useful but non-creative speech. (Fillmore, however, like R. Clark, also believes that early memorization of routines and patterns is central to the acquisition of rule-governed language. This position is the opposite of that suggested by the neurolinguistic literature and held by Brown, 1973 and Cazden, 1972 for L_1 acquisition; Krashen and Scarcella, 1978 and Wagner-Gough, 1975 for L_2 acquisition.)

The use of routines and patterns is reported in only one adult study, to our knowledge. Hanania and Gradman (1977) studied the English development of Fatmah, a nineteen-year-old Arabic speaker living in the United States. Fatmah had little formal schooling in Arabic and encountered English "primarily in natural communicative settings" (p. 76). Hanania and Gradman report that at the start of their study Fatmah's English output "consisted mainly of memorized items that are commonly used in social contexts with children." They also noted that "the use of these expressions, however, does not imply that she recognized the individual words within them, or that she was able to use the words in new combinations.

They were merely strings of sounds that she used appropriately in particular situations" (p. 78). In other words, she knew routines. For instance, *See you* meant "I'll be seeing you," used on occasions when her friends were parting. Attempts to lead her to combine it with *I can* to form *I can see you* were not only unsuccessful but confusing. Fatmah also used patterns in the early stages, such as *Thank you, I can't . . . ,* and *Do you like?*

Hanania and Gradman's summary statement concerning Fatmah's syntactic development describes their subject's subsequent acquisition of the L_2 rule system:

> The adult in the present study proceeded to learn the language creatively. She did not simply imitate models of the language but acquired elements selectively and built them into syntactic units which became progressively more complex. The pattern of her linguistic development was similar to that of first language learners. Early constructions were constrained to two-term utterances, and the growth of sentence complexity occured along the same lines (pp. 87–88).

This study suggests that there may be a general similarity between adult and child use of routines and patterns as a facilitator of social interaction when productive rules have not yet been acquired.

Although adult data on routines and patterns are sparse, it is quite obvious that adults, too, rely on them, perhaps even more than do children. Anyone who has traveled in a foreign country is aware of the usefulness of survival phrases such as *How much is this?* Straining to remember what natives say when they bid one good-bye at the end of a visit, when they order meals, when they buy train tickets or engage in other social exchanges are all part of learning patterns and routines that will ease one's stay in a foreign country. And often, unfortunately, these constructions are all an adult learns during a short visit abroad.

Although much more research must be conducted on this very interesting aspect of second language acquisition, we do know that routines and patterns are constructions whose internal structure appears to be beyond the level of learners' productive rule-governed system. They provide L_2 learners with a means of communicating in the second language long before they have acquired the rules of that language.

SUMMARY

Our review of the available literature describing unanalyzed or partially analyzed constructions in the language development of L_1 and L_2 learners makes it clear that these special constructions, *routines* and *patterns*, comprise a complex phenomenon whose precise role in the acquisition process is still not entirely clear.

From the neurological literature, we have reviewed a number of case studies suggesting that "automatic speech" appears to be distinct from rule-governed aspects of language. For example, routines seem to be available in both the left and right brain hemispheres, while creative language appears to be localized in the left. Subjects with left hemispheric damage have been observed to lose rule-governed aspects of language, while at the same time maintaining control over whole chunks of unanalyzed speech.

From the L_1 acquisition research it appears that young children have been observed by some researchers to produce unanalyzed stretches of speech which are far beyond their developing L_2 rule system. These include whole utterances, known as **routines,** e.g. *It's my turn;* or parts of utterances of **patterns,** such as *That's a* _____. Often the unanalyzed pieces are those of extraordinarily high frequency in the environment. The acquisition of such constructions seems to be comparable to learning long vocabulary words.

For L_2 acquisition, both routines and patterns have been observed. The incidence of such utterances appears to be a function of the social situations in which L_2 learners wish to participate. The need to interact with other members of a group (especially at school) and the frequent and predictable social and concomitant linguistic environments in which L_2 students find themselves, appear to be the primary reason for the early acquisition of these aspects of language in such situations.

Findings such as these point to an interesting and important aspect of language learning—the use of partially or totally unanalyzed constructions—whose internal structure appears to be beyond the level of the learner's rule-governed system. Of major importance in the study of these constructions is the specification of their relation to the acquisition of the rule-governed aspects of the L_2. The nature of the interaction among these phenomena is an important question which remains to be answered.

STUDY QUESTIONS

1. Would you expect all of the following utterances from one student on the same day? Explain.

He fly kite.	You going to movie?
This is my mother.	Pass the ball. It's my turn.
We no like candy.	Why she crying?

2. Memorizing dialogues is a common activity in second language courses. Given the selection of topics below, pick the dialogues you think would be most beneficial to the students.

Greetings
Asking *yes/no* questions
Using negative sentences
Expressing apologies
Expressing gratitude
Expressing plurality
Making introductions

Justify your choices.

3. If you heard a child say

That's is a house

how would you explain the double copula (*'s is*) error?

4. What role (if any) do you think memorizing phrases and sentences has in second language learning?

10

Aspects of L₂ Research Methodology

Second language acquisition professionals have traditionally been more interested in developing teaching methodologies than in doing basic research on second language learning. Consequently, L_2 research techniques are still evolving, gradually becoming more precise and rigorous.

This chapter is not intended to be a comprehensive treatment of L_2 research methodology; another book would be required to accomplish that. Rather, we would like to give readers a picture of some of the methodological issues researchers think about as they attempt to answer questions about the nature of second language acquisition. The preceding chapters have already described research methods specific to particular areas of investigation (e.g. acquisition order; errors). In this chapter we discuss topics that are basic to almost any L_2 research study.

We also hope to stimulate further development of L_2 research techniques since the study of L_2 acquisition often requires procedures of data collection and analysis that are different from those appropriate for L_1 acquisition or other linguistic research. Finally, we hope this chapter contributes towards generating sound research data on L_2 acquisition.

Three areas of L_2 research methodology are discussed: (1) selection of research design; (2) language elicitation techniques; and (3) determination of the learner's overall level of L_2 development. In addition, we note two problem spots that researchers tend to overlook but which may influence results: back-to-back phonemes and memorized wholes.

SELECTION OF THE RESEARCH DESIGN

As in any study, one of the first steps in a language development study is the selection of one's basic research design. The study of a few learners over an extended period of time is called a **longitudinal design.** The study of a large group at one point in time is called a **cross-sectional design.** Both have been used productively in the history of psychological research. Each design makes different demands on the researcher, and these must be carefully weighed before a choice is made.

Longitudinal Design

Roger Brown, who legitimized the use of very small samples in longitudinal designs, argued that the collection of rich speech samples from a small number of subjects would reveal as much, if not more, about universal trends in language acquisition as the use of relatively sparse speech corpora from large numbers of subjects. The use of three children in his sample set the scene for other longitudinal studies which have ranged in sample size from one to six.

Length of study in longitudinal L_2 acquisition research has ranged from four to eighteen months, although Brown's L_1 study spanned four years. Frequency of data collection has also varied, from once a week to once a month. No specific minimum guidelines have been set for sample size, frequency of data collection, length of the language elicitation sessions, or length of study. Obviously, the larger the sample, the more frequent the data collection, the longer the elicitation sessions; and the more extended the period of study, the larger one's data base will be. The decisions regarding these parameters of study are usually controlled not by deep scientific criteria, but by the inevitable constraints on the researcher's resources.

The criteria for selection of subjects for study will depend on the researcher's interest, although again, it is often the availability of certain subjects that dictate the focus of study. For example, if one happens to have friends who are willing to turn over their children or themselves for, say, an hour every week for a year, then a researcher might very well decide to make use of the opportunity. If one's research priorities are not flexible, however, much time must be spent selecting appropriate subjects, so that one's time investment is worthwhile. Longitudinal studies require a long-term commitment on the part of researcher and subject(s).

The strength of a longitudinal study lies in the fact that the data collected represent the speech of the learner actually developing over some period of time. The order obtained should thus reflect the true acquisition order of the subjects, provided, of course, that the data collection and analysis are conducted properly.

One drawback of a longitudinal study is that the small sample could produce atypical results. (For example, the acquisition order Hakuta [1975] obtained from his single Japanese-speaking subject turned out to be atypical when compared with other studies including other Japanese-speaking children learning English.) When the results of a longitudinal study are taken together with the findings from other longitudinal or cross-sectional studies, however, such research becomes an invaluable part of the data base used in formulating principles of language learning. Readers who are interested in techniques for longitudinal data analysis techniques may find Brown (1973) and Cazden (1972) helpful.

Cross-Sectional Design

A cross-sectional design is one where language data are collected from a relatively large sample of learners at one point in their language development. Such a design simulates actual development over time by including many learners who are at different stages of L_2 development. If the sample is adequate and if appropriate analytical requirements are met, then the language data collected may be analyzed to obtain acquisition orders which reflect the characteristics of language systems developing over a period of time.

Sample sizes used in the language development literature range from 24 to over 1200. Typically, an instrument of some kind is developed and administered to the group of subjects in order to facilitate efficient collection of comparable data. Data collection may take from a few days to several weeks, depending on the number of subjects and the availability of assistants to help administer an instrument or conduct interviews. (Analytical methods for cross-sectional designs in L_2 acquisition order research were presented in detail in Chapter 8 and those used in error research were described in Chapter 7.)

LANGUAGE ELICITATION TECHNIQUES

At about the same time that the research design is being contemplated, the researcher must decide on the kinds of elicitation tasks to use in gathering the language data. Elicitation tasks refer to the manner in which the language is elicited from the subjects by the researcher. At least two dimensions are involved: the **task mode** and the **task focus.** The task mode refers to the language mode tapped: speaking, writing, comprehension or reading. The task focus, on the other hand, refers to the kind of focus required of the subjects when performing the task, namely, whether the focus is on content—the message, idea, or opinion being offered—or on the linguistic forms or rules of the language used in the task.

As mentioned in earlier chapters, most tasks researchers use to elicit speech samples or verbal responses may be grouped according to the presence or absence of a communicative focus. Accordingly, we label them "natural communication tasks" and "linguistic manipulation tasks," respectively.

A **natural communication task** is one where the focus of the student is on communicating an idea or opinion to someone rather than on the language forms themselves. In such situations the speaker subconsciously uses the grammar rules acquired to convey the message. For example, a question such as *Why do you think he's so fat?* (asked by a researcher while pointing to a fat character) elicits an opinion or idea from the student which is directed towards that specific situation. The student typically responds with little, if any, conscious focus on linguistic form (with little appeal to the monitor).

A **linguistic manipulation task** focuses the student's attention on performing the conscious linguistic manipulation required by the task. For example, asking a speaker to transform *No one was here* into a *yes/no* question requires manipulation of the elements in the sentence. The activity in itself does not serve any communicative function for the subject. Rather, the subject is consciously focusing on the linguistic rules required to perform the operation requested, an activity which is rarely a part of natural communication.

Data generated by natural communication tasks permit one to make statements concerning the subject's normally developing (and subconscious) grammar, while linguistic manipulation tasks permit one to make statements concerning the student's meta-linguistic awareness, that is, the conscious knowledge and manipulation of the rules and forms of a language. Unfortunately, these two kinds of linguistic knowledge do not seem to be directly related. The tasks tapping each provide quite different results. For example, as we saw in Chapter 8, orders of acquisition obtained using manipulation tasks are different from those obtained using communication tasks.[1] Similarly, many adults are consciously aware of linguistic rules and can correct their errors when asked to do so, but when conversing naturally, they do not apply those rules.

1. Whether *all* linguistic manipulation tasks result in a similar order to each other remains to be seen.

TABLE 10-1 Comparison of Natural Communication and Linguistic Manipulation Tasks*

	Natural Communication	Linguistic Manipulation
Definition	1. Taps subject's unconscious use of grammatical rules to produce utterances in a conversation. 2. Uses natural speech where subject's focus is on communicating something.	1. Taps subject's conscious application of linguistic rules to perform a noncommunicative task. 2. Uses artificial "speech" where student's focus is on a given rule.
Some Types	1. Structured communication, unstructured communication, etc.	1. Translation, morpheme completion, transformation, substitution, etc.
Advantages	1. The language sample obtained represents natural communication of the skill that is ultimately being assessed. 2. The task is virtually free of confounding task biases.	1. Target structures seem to be readily obtained.
Disadvantages	1. Certain structures are extremely difficult to elicit naturally, e.g. perfect tenses (had seen).	1. Confounds conscious knowledge and use of grammar rules with ability to use the language for communication.

*Copyright © 1978. Teachers of English to Speakers of Other Languages. Reprinted with permission of the authors and publisher. 12, 2, p. 186.

Table 10-1 provides a summary of communication and manipulation tasks in terms of their definitions, advantages and disadvantages regarding their appropriateness and efficacy as indicators of language development.

Natural communication tasks may be subdivided into two types: structured and unstructured tasks. Table 10-2 illustrates this breakdown. Both structured and unstructured tasks represent natural language use, but the choice of task depends on the focus of the researchers.

If the goal is to elicit a specified range of structures naturally, yet within a limited time span, say five to ten minutes, a **structured** communication task is more appropriate. If one is interested in language produced in an unplanned fashion (as far as the elicitation of

TABLE 10-2 Comparison of Structured and Unstructured Communication Tasks*

	Structured Communication	Unstructured Communication
Definition	1. Natural conversation between subject and researcher where researcher asks subject specific questions designed to elicit target structures naturally and systematically.	1. Natural conversation between subject and researcher, interviewer or other person where there is no intent to elicit specific structures.
Advantages	1. Target structures may be elicited, e.g. *Wh*-questions. quickly; more efficient than unstructured communication.	1. Structures that are difficult to elicit with specific questions may be offered by subjects spontaneously.
Disadvantages	1. Not all structures are easily elicited, e.g. *Wh*-questions.	1. A great deal of speech must usually be collected before a sufficient range of structures is used by the subject to permit assessment of level of language development.
		2. One cannot make any statements about the subject's control over structures *not* offered during the collection periods (since one cannot be certain why a structure was not offered, i.e. whether the situations did not require it or whether the subject did not know how to use it).

specific structures is concerned), as in free conversation, and if one is able to collect enough spontaneous language to obtain a large enough range of structures, a ***non-structured*** communication task would be used.

In cross-sectional studies, the structured communication task is typically used because it is fairly short and can be administered to a large sample within a reasonable time period. In longitudinal studies, the unstructured tasks have been commonly used, often in combination with some structured communication task.

CONSIDERATIONS IN DETERMINING
OVERALL LEVEL OF L₂ DEVELOPMENT

In describing learners' developing speech, researchers often refer to "stages," "levels," or "steps" of language development. They speak of a learner being at an early, intermediate, or advanced level of language development. Implicit in such terms is the notion that certain characteristics of each level are unique and irreversible.

The last decade of L_2 research activity has resulted in various attempts to address characteristics of different points along the L_2 developmental continuum. We have some notion of acquisition order (Dulay and Burt, 1974, 1978; Bailey, Madden and Krashen, 1974; Krashen, Madden and Bailey, 1975; Kessler and Idar, 1977; Andersen, 1976; Fuller, 1978; Makino, 1979), and information on transitional constructions learners use during the process of acquiring complex structures such as negation and interrogatives (Ravem, 1974; Milon, 1974; Gillis and Weber, 1976; Wode, 1976; Hanania and Gradman, 1977; Cazden et al., 1975; Hakuta, 1975). However, there is as yet no consensus on an overall index or metric that can be used to define stages of L_2 development independently of characteristics of the stages.

First language acquisition stages are defined in terms of "mean length of utterance" (MLU). The stages range in average morpheme length from 1.75 morphemes to 4.0 (Brown, 1973). To determine the L_1 stage, one simply computes the average number of morphemes per utterance in a sample of 100 utterances. Such a metric allows researchers to study the linguistic characteristics of learner speech in each stage to identify its unique characteristics and thereby piece together the developmental process.

MLU does not work for L_2 development. Brown, who developed MLU, noted that the metric works well for learners whose MLU's are between 1.75 and 4 but "By the time the child reaches Stage V . . . [defined as the point where children exhibit an average MLU of 4.0], he is able to make constructions of such great variety that *what* he happens to say and the MLU of a sample begin to depend more on the character of the interaction than on what the child knows, and so the index loses its value as an indicator of grammatical knowledge" (Brown, 1973, p. 54).

Most of the L_2 learner speech studied by researchers is four MLU's or longer. The MLU is, thus, no longer appropriate, as has been pointed out by Cazden (1972) and Dulay and Burt (1974).

The lack of clear guidance in this area has led to a host of criteria used by different researchers, including:

1. **Mean sentence length** (e.g. Larsen-Freeman, 1978);
2. **Quantity of speech** (e.g. *Ilyin Oral Interview, Moreno Oral English Proficiency Test*);
3. **Number of errors** (e.g. Larsen-Freeman, 1978);
4. **Number of T-units** (Hunt, 1970);
5. **Number of descriptors** (e.g. *Bilingual Inventory of Natural Languages*, 1976);
6. **Degree of grammatical correctness** (e.g. Dulay and Burt, 1974; *Bilingual Syntax Measure*, 1975);
7. **Use of certain transitional constructions** (e.g. Dulay and Burt, 1978);
8. **Acquisition of certain structures** (Dulay and Burt, 1974; *Bilingual Syntax Measure*, 1975 and 1978).

The first two measures of development listed depend on some aspect of quantity. While quantity is a workable metric for short utterances, Roger Brown noted that when longer utterances are involved, length becomes unreliable as an index of language development. Since the speech of L₂ learners is usually more than four morphemes long, these two criteria have serious drawbacks as overall measures of L₂ development. For example, longer sentences are not always more advanced than shorter ones. Compare:

She is giving the babies food.
She is feeding them.

The first example has six words, the second, four. Yet most native English-speakers agree that the second reflects more advanced knowledge of English than the first. *Feed* appears to be a more sophisticated vocabulary item than the synonymous *give food to*. Children in the elementary grades rarely used *feed* while older children did so frequently to describe a picture of a mother bird feeding her babies. (This was noted in California field test data of the *Bilingual Syntax Measure,* [Burt et al., 1976]).

Similarly, speech samples with the same number of errors do not always indicate a comparable level of development. Compare:

She couldn't have saw it.
We seed it go up in there.

Each sentence has one error (*saw* for *seen* in the first example; *seed* for *saw* in the second). Yet most native English-speakers would agree that the first example reflects more advanced knowledge than the second. The difference is that the second speaker does not know enough of the language to make the error the first speaker made.[2]

Criteria 4, 5, and 6 above single out some linguistic items (e.g. descriptors, subordinate clauses) and use their frequency to determine developmental level. While such frequencies may predict level for some learners, it may introduce bias against others who for reasons of style do not choose to use the items in the particular speech sample elicited. For example, a child who sees a picture of a cat in a tree may pick the action in the picture to talk about rather than the characteristics of the items in the picture. The child might say:

The cat ran up the tree and waited for the dog to go by.

Such a sentence, which contains no adjectives or adverbs, is nevertheless a proficient English utterance including structures that are acquired relatively late.

It appears that variables related to quantity are only indicators of language development under certain conditions, such as for very young children learning their first language and still developing their memory capacities; or to distinguish learners at the very beginning of language acquisition who have only learned a few words. Quantity fails to predict development in most other cases, however.

The last two criteria listed above describe the kind of linguistic knowledge the learner is said to have at some level of proficiency. Certain steps in the L_2 acquisition process have been characterized by the occurrence of transitional constructions, as discussed in Chapter 6 or the acquisition of certain structures as discussed in Chapter 8.

While transitional constructions and acquisition order do not suffer from the weaknesses of measures based on quantity, they rely on particular items of syntax and do not fulfill the need for an overall metric of L_2 development which can be used to independently validate the steps or stages indicated by acquisition order or transitional constructions. The weakness of measures relying on particular items is that we do not know whether the interval between, for instance, one transitional construction and another is equivalent to another sequence of transitional constructions or to groups of morphemes in a hierarchy. For example, is a learner who is at Step 2 in the acquisition of negation also at Step 2 in the acquisition of *wh*-questions or at Group 2 in the acquisition of grammatical morphemes?

Degree of grammatical correctness (Criterion 6 above) is one measure that does not suffer the shortcomings just described. It tempers

---

2. The first error reflects the erroneous use of the irregular past form *saw* for the past participle *seen*; the second error shows that the irregular past form *saw* has not yet been acquired.

quantity by superimposing a value for correctness and it takes into account all the morphemes and structures produced, not just a select few.

The *"Syntax Acquisition Index"* (SAI) (Burt et al., 1975) is, to our knowledge, the only such index currently available.[3] We thus describe it here in some detail. SAI reflects the degree of grammaticality of the subject's total speech corpus or of a randomly selected sample of utterances.

SAI is computed as follows: (1) Correct all the utterances in the subject's speech corpus that are ungrammatical; (2) Assign points to the grammatical version of each of the learner's utterances (*Developed Form Value*); (3) Subtract points from the grammatical form to reflect those parts of the learner's utterances that are still developing (*Response Value*); and (4) Compute a ratio whose numerator is the sum of the Response Values for all utterances and whose denominator is the sum of all the corresponding Developed Form Values. The quotient is multiplied by 100 to yield the SAI score.

A system of weighted morphemes outlined in Table 10-3 was used to assign point values to both the learner's utterances and the corresponding grammatical forms of those utterances. For example, if a subject's response value is 80, and the developed form value is 160, the SAI would be 50, computed as follows:

$$SAI = \frac{80 \text{ (Sum of Response Values)}}{160 \text{ (Sum of Developed Form Values)}} \times 100 = 50$$

A variety of examples whose SAI's are computed appear in Table 10-4, below. The SAI reflects the degree of grammaticality of the entire language corpus obtained from a learner at a given point in time.

The SAI was developed for speech corpora resulting from a structured conversation where all subjects give one-utterance responses to a certain number of questions (25–40) designed to elicit a wide range of structures (the *Bilingual Syntax Measure* [BSM]).

An examination of BSM English L_2 data collected from more than 1200 children in ten states revealed that the most meaningful oral proficiency groupings were obtained with the following SAI ranges:

95–100
85–94
45[4]–84

3. Hendrickson (1978) is working on another index based on degree of grammaticality. He is using ratios of global to local errors and vice versa.
4. Children who produced enough speech to be scored did not score under 45. Children who did not produce enough speech to be scored (See Burt et al., 1975 and 1980 for criteria) were placed in two lower "non-speaking" levels of proficiency.

TABLE 10-3   General Rules for Assigning Points to the Developed Form in Computing the SAI*†

1 POINT MORPHEMES

A. All plain words are worth one point. A plain word is one that has no grammatical ending attached to it, and is in its regular form. Examples are given below.

verbs; give, want, like, eat, have
nouns; worm, man, guy, fatso, king, thing
articles: a, an, the
prepositions: in, on, to, into
conjunctions: and, because, 'cause, then, but
negatives: not/n't, no, nothing, none
adverbs: there, hardly, only, never, ever, so, as, still, maybe
demonstratives: this, that
modals: will/'ll, can, must
plain auxiliaries: have/'ve, be
quantifiers: some, much, more, lot, lots

B. Grammatical endings on verbs, nouns, and adjectives are also worth one point. Ending types are given below.

VERBS

progressive-ing: giving, mopping, having
perfect-en: eaten, been
regular past-ed: dropped
regular third person-s: eats, wants, lives
irregular third person: has, does

NOUNS

plural-s: windows, sandwiches, houses, flowers
possessive's: king's, man's

ADJECTIVES

comparatives: bigger, fatter
superlatives: biggest, fattest

NOTES: (1) Disregard any "back-to-back" *s*'s because it is nearly impossible to tell where the *s* belongs. Structures affected include:

   (a) singular copulas and auxiliaries (e.g. He's so fat, she's smiling),
   (b) third person singular indicative (e.g. He eats so much), (c) short plural (e.g. He has windows so he can see) and (d) possessive pronoun (e.g. his sandwich).

(2) Disregard past regular *-d* when it is followed by a word beginning with *th* or *d* because it is difficult to tell where the "stop" belongs (e.g. She looke*d d*own, He droppe*d th*e apple).

(3) Do not score *ain't*.

2 POINT MORPHEMES

All words (nouns, verbs, and auxiliaries) that are not in their regular (plain) form, because they convey an extra bit of meaning, are worth two points. These are often called "irregular" forms. For example, *took, ate, was, are* changed in form because they convey the past tense; or *those* and *these* are changed in form to convey the plural. In addition, pronouns are worth two points. They express case, number, and gender.

Other examples are given below.

irregular auxiliaries; are/'re, has/'s, was, is/'s
modals tensed: would/'d, might, should, could
irregular plurals: children

irregular quantifiers: any, anything
all pronouns except it: I, me, you, she, her, he, him, they, them
plural demonstratives: those, these
irregular verb forms: took, bit, fell, ate, had/'d

3 POINT MORPHEMES
All the possessive pronouns are worth three points. Examples are *hers, his, theirs.*

---

*See Table 10-4 for examples of actual computations.
†M. Burt, H. Dulay and E. Hernández-Chávez. Reproduced by permission from the *Bilingual Syntax Measure Technical Handbook.* Copyright © 1976 by Harcourt Brace Jovanovich, Inc., New York. All rights reserved.

At least 75% of the children in the lowest level had acquired two structures; at least 75% of the children in the middle level had acquired nine structures including the first two, while at least 75% of the children in the highest level had acquired 14 structures including the first nine (see Table 10-5). The grouping of structures acquired at each proficiency level is similar to that reported in other basic research on English acquisition order (Dulay and Burt, 1974; Fathman, 1975; Kessler and Idar, 1977; Makino, 1979; Bailey, Madden and Krashen, 1974; Krashen, Madden and Bailey, 1975; Fuller, 1978; Andersen, 1976).

Burt, Dulay and McKeon (1980) have adapted the SAI for use with speech data collected via **un-structured** communication. They used the same computational procedures and cutting points for levels, but specified certain conditions that had to be met before an SAI score could be computed validly. They used SAI levels to study the kinds of errors learners make at different levels of English L₂ development.[5]

Problem Spots

Back-to-Back Phonemes   Sometimes the phonological environment of a grammatical morpheme makes it impossible to tell whether the learner used the morpheme or not. For example, in

She's swimming

the initial /s/ sound in *swimming* is indistinguishable from the /s/ representing the contractible auxiliary ('s). Thus, in this utterance one cannot tell whether or not a learner omitted the s auxiliary: *She swimming* sounds the same as *She's swimming.* We call this phenomenon "back-to-back phonemes."

5. Readers who are interested in using the SAI in a similar manner are invited to contact Marina Burt or Heidi Dulay at Burt & Dulay, Inc., San Francisco, California, USA.

TABLE 10-4 Computing the SAI[6]

Characteristic of Response	Subtract from DFV	Example		Scores CRV DFV	

Missing Words or Parts of Words

1. Missing word — value of word or part of word

$$\underset{\underset{\text{it}}{\wedge}}{\text{1. give}} \overset{-1}{\quad} \text{to them} \quad = 4$$

1 1 1 2 = 5

2. Missing part of word

$$\underset{\underset{\text{ing}}{\wedge}}{\text{2. she's jump}} \overset{-1}{\quad} \text{now} \quad = 6$$

2 2 1 1 1 = 7

Extra Words or Words in Wrong Order

3. Extra word — 1 point from total DFV regardless of how many extra or wrong-ordered words

$$\text{3. they have } \overset{-1}{\text{(for)}} \text{ to eat} \quad = 4$$

2 1 1 1 = 5

4. Word in the wrong order

$$\text{4. } \overset{-1}{\text{(it)}} \text{ the dog ate} \underset{\underset{\text{it}}{\wedge}}{} \quad = 5$$

1 1 2 1 = 5

Misformed Words or Parts of Words

5. Misformed word — one-half the value of the word, part of word, or wrong language

$$\text{5. the dog } \overset{-1}{\underset{\text{ate}}{\text{(eat)}}} \text{ the food} \quad = 5$$

1 1 2 1 1 = 6

6. Misformed part of word

$$\underset{\underset{\text{ing}}{\wedge}}{\text{6. she's jump(s)}} \overset{-.5}{\quad} \quad = 5.5$$

2 2 1 1 = 6

7. Wrong language

$$\underset{\underset{\text{because}}{\wedge}}{\text{7. (porque)}} \overset{-.5}{\quad} \text{he's fat} \quad = 5.5$$

1 2 2 1 = 6

| | | Totals | 34 | 40 |

SAI Computation

$$SAI = \frac{CRV}{DFV} \times 100 = \frac{34}{40} \times 100 = 85$$

6. M. Burt, H. Dulay and E. Hernández-Chávez. Reproduced by permission from the *Bilingual Syntax Measure Technical Handbook*. Copyright © 1976 by Harcourt Brace Jovanovich, Inc., New York. All rights reserved.

TABLE 10-5   Percent of Subjects Having Acquired Certain English Structures at Three SAI Levels, Ages 5–8*

ENGLISH	Word order	Pronoun case	Progressive -ing	Copula singular	Short plural	Auxiliary singular	Article	Copula plural	Auxiliary plural	Past regular	Present indicative	Possessive -s	Long plural	Conditional auxiliary	Past Irregular	Perfect auxiliary	Past participle
(SAI = 95-100)	100	100	100	98	99	97	98	94	98	95	94	91	76	75	71	21	10
(SAI = 85-94)	98	97	95	92	91	88	86	85	82	74	63	53	51	34	30	3	2
(SAI = 45-84)	97	96	74	57	68	60	73	59	—	47	28	12	16	12	7	1	1

*Burt, Dulay & Hernández-Chávez, 1976

Utterances contain back-to-back phonemes whenever the phonological character of a morpheme is indistinguishable from an immediately adjoining sound. Back-to-back s's affect five English grammatical morphemes:

Contractible auxiliary: She's smiling.
Contractible copula: He's so cute.
Plural: The boys sing well.
Possessive: Ana's shoes are shiny.
Third singular: He eats so much all the time.

Back-to-back stops also occur frequently and often go unnoticed: Researchers have offered utterances such as *She drop(ped) the flower* as examples of the correct or incorrect use of the past marker (*ed*). In fact, unless the speaker exaggerated the *-ed* sound, it would have been impossible to hear whether the *-ed* was provided.

Back-to-back phonemes should be omitted from consideration altogether when attempting to determine the degree of control a speaker has over the structures in question.

Memorized Wholes   Another potential source of data distortion is the failure to distinguish creative language from items which may have been memorized as whole pieces. Since we discussed such constructions (routines and patterns) at length in Chapter 9, this section serves only to remind researchers to analyze routines and patterns separately, or omit them from analyses that focus on describing the acquisition of productive rules.

If a structure appears in only one context it should be suspect. For example, when children use the *wh*-question structure correctly only in *What's that?*, we cannot assume that they have acquired the *wh*-question structure. In fact, they may produce *Why he here* and other *wh*-transitional constructions at the same time.

Similarly, if the only example of a correctly used possessive is *Grandma's* as in *We're going to Grandma's*, it is likely that the possessive *'s* is part of a memorized pattern rather than a productive rule. Words that are never used in their singular form are also candidates for memorized wholes. It is best to analyze words like *scissors*, *glasses* (eyeglasses) and *slacks* separately from other nouns that are used both in the singular and in the plural.

Back-to-back phonemes and memorized wholes are items in speech data that we have found seriously affect researchers' findings, yet are often overlooked. Perhaps future research will routinely take them into account.

SUMMARY

It has not been easy to compare results from one study to the next because of the variety of techniques and procedures used by L₂ researchers. This chapter describes commonly used techniques and procedures that are basic to almost any L₂ research study, and describes their advantages and disadvantages.

There are two basic types of design in L₂ research: **longitudinal** and **cross-sectional.** In a **longitudinal** design, a few subjects supply many speech samples which are taken at varying intervals over a long period of time. Sample size, criteria for selection of subjects, frequency of data collection, length of elicitation sessions and overall length of study are decisions left to the researcher, and are more often than not contingent upon the researcher's resources.

Although a **longitudinal design** may be very useful in observing the development of language acquisition, its reliance on a small sample size may produce atypical results. Nonetheless, results from longitudinal studies, taken together with results from other longitudinal or cross-sectional studies, may be useful in formulating principles of language learning.

Cross-sectional studies, on the other hand, rely on language data collected from many subjects at one point in time. The subjects should be at different points of development, and thus the language sample is assumed to reflect the characteristics of language systems developing over a period of time.

Elicitation techniques refer to the manner in which language is drawn from subjects by the researcher. The *task mode,* the way in which language is tapped, may take the form of writing, speech, reading or comprehension. The *task focus* may be on natural communication where little, if any, conscious focus is given to linguistic form; or linguistic manipulation, where the focus is entirely on the forms of the language.

Natural communication tasks are of two kinds: structured and unstructured. *Structured tasks* elicit a specified range of structures. Because they are particularly useful when time is limited, they are often used in cross-sectional studies. *Unstructured tasks* are used more frequently in longitudinal studies, where time may not be as crucial a factor, and the researcher wants to obtain unplanned conversation.

Because natural communication tasks and *linguistic manipulation tasks* are unrelated, they produce different results. *Natural communication tasks* provide insights into the acquisition of communicative skills while *linguistic manipulation tasks* provide information about a learner's metalinguistic awarenness.

As of yet, there is no consensus on an overall index to determine stages of L₂ development. Methods in use include: mean sentence length, number of errors, quantity of speech, number of T-units, number of descriptors, degree of grammatical correctness, use of certain transitional constructions and acquisition of certain structures. Researchers, in using these methods, have discovered a number of drawbacks; for example, that quantity of language produced often fails to predict level of development. The *"Syntax Acquisition Index,"* or SAI, which computes the degree of grammatical correctness of a subject's total speech corpus, does not suffer from these defects.

Other problem areas in methodology include the scoring of **back-to-back phonemes** and **memorized routines and patterns.** Back-to-back phonemes appear in utterances such as *she's swimming.* Because the auxiliary -s is "back-to-back" with the -s in swimming, it is difficult to determine its use, or lack of use, in speech. A similar problem exists with memorized routines of patterns. When a subject says *"What's that?",* we cannot assume s/he knows how to formulate *wh*-questions; it is possible that this may just be an example of a memorized routine.

It is hoped that our discussion of existing methodologies and their problems will not only help avoid repetition of past mistakes, but will enhance the quality and encourage further development of research techniques.

STUDY QUESTIONS

1. If you had access to all the students in Grades 1–12 in a school district for 6 months, what kind of L₂ research design would you pick: longitudinal or cross-sectional? Why?

2. If, using a longitudinal design, you obtained results that had impor-

tant and unexpected implications, what should your next research step be?

3. If you wanted to investigate the learning complexity of certain grammatical structures in order to make a statement about the acquisition of communicative skills, what kind of elicitation task would you use? Give an example of the task and provide a rationale for your choice.

4.a. What criteria would you use to determine the overall level of English development for the person who produced the following speech:

"Yesterday we go to a tea. Many womans from Peru was there. They all good friend for many years. They bringed many good things new for us for eat. We talk about reforma educativa in Panama. Our friends say they take us home."

b. Justify your choice of criteria.

c. What is the overall level of the person?

11

From Research to Reality: Implications for the Teacher

The previous chapters of this book presented the research findings available to date and extracted from them a comprehensive picture of second language learning. This chapter goes the next step: to the implied teaching guidelines. We do not prescribe a single teaching method, but guidelines which may be personalized in different ways. For example, one teacher might incorporate a silent phase into the curriculum by having students write responses. Another teacher might have students act out responses or even respond in their first language. All of these activities follow one guideline: not requiring students to speak in the target language before they are ready.

The guidelines are based on "basic" rather than "applied" research studies. Basic studies focus on how learning takes place rather than on the evaluation of teaching techniques. They describe how learners behave, react and think in various learning situations.

Following are the major characteristics of second language learning that form the basis for the teaching suggestions to be presented.

1. There appear to be *innate learning processors* which guide L_2 acquisition. We have called these the Filter, the Organizer, and the Monitor. (See Figure 11-A below and Chapter 3.) The Filter and the Organizer work subconsciously, while the Monitor takes care of conscious processing.

2. Exposure to *natural communication* in the target language is necessary for the subconscious processors to work well. The richer

the learner's exposure to the target language, the more rapid and comprehensive learning is likely to be. (See Chapter 2.)

3. The learner needs to *comprehend the content* of natural communication in the new language. Talk about "here-and-now" topics, for example, characterizes natural communication with child language learners; who usually acquire native-like fluency in a short time. (See Chapter 2.)

4. A *silent phase* at the beginning of language learning (when the student is not *required* to produce the new language) has proven useful for most students in cutting down on interlingual errors and enhancing pronunciation. The optimum length of the phase ranges from several weeks to several months. (See Chapter 2.)

5. The learner's motives, emotions, and attitudes screen what is presented in the language classroom, or outside it. This *affective screening* is highly individual and results in different learning rates and results. (See Chapter 3.)

6. The influence of the *learner's first language* is negligible in grammar. It is significant, however, in pronunciation. Adults are more prone to fall back on their first language; young children rarely do. (See Chapter 5.)

7. Second language learners subconsciously organize the new words and phrases they hear in systematic ways. The principles of organization they use have their source in the structure of the human brain. The result of this human characteristic is the *uniformity and predictability* of basic error types and the order in which certain structures are learned. (See Chapters 6, 7, and 8.)

8. *Conscious learning* and application of grammatical rules have a place in second language learning, but their purpose is different from the subconscious learning which produces native-like fluency. (See Chapter 3.)

9. *Relaxed and self-confident* learners learn faster. (See Chapters 3 and 4.)

10. Learners who start learning a second language *before puberty* tend to achieve greater proficiency in the language than those who start after puberty. (See Chapter 4.)

11. *Differences between children and adults* may affect language acquisition. Adults are more self-conscious than children, thus tend to be less venturesome in using the new language. Adults are better able than children to consciously learn linguistic rules and extract linguistic patterns. Sometimes this ability works to their benefit; other times to their detriment. (See Chapter 4.)

12. Learners learn most from their peers and from *people with whom they identify.* (See Chapters 2 and 3.)

FIGURE 11-A   Working Model for Creative Construction in L_2 Acquisition*

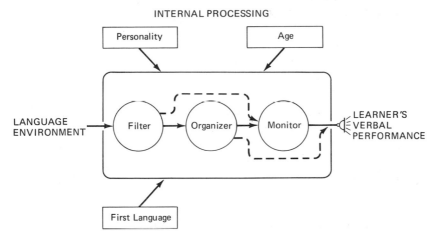

INTERNAL PROCESSING

Personality

Age

LANGUAGE
ENVIRONMENT

Filter → Organizer → Monitor

LEARNER'S
VERBAL
PERFORMANCE

First Language

*An updated version of the chart on page 100, in *Viewpoints on English as a Second Language*, edited by Marina Burt, Heidi Dulay and Mary Finocchiaro. New York: Regents Publishing Co. Inc., 1977. Reprinted by permission.

13. *Correction* of grammatical errors does *not* help students avoid them. (See Chapter 2.)

14. Certain structures are acquired only when learners are mentally ready for them. Exposing a learner to a structure does not guarantee learning. If a learner hears a structure very frequently, the structure may be memorized as an unanalyzed whole instead of being graduallly incorporated into a productive system of rules. (See Chapters 2 and 9.)

These fourteen major conclusions from second language acquisition research suggest the following teaching guidelines.

TEACHING GUIDELINES

1. Maximize the Student's Exposure to Natural Communication   Natural communication means the learner is focused on the message being conveyed, not on the linguistic form of that message. This enhances the creative construction process and the operation of the Organizer.

Classroom Techniques

• Ask real questions—those which you might ask any native-speaking child or adult. For example:

> Are you hungry?
> Do you want some milk or juice?
> Why don't you have your coat on?

Artificial questions are those whose answers are of no interest to either the one who asks it or the one who has to answer it, either because the answer is already known or no one really cares. For example, *What color is my blouse?* Or (holding a pencil) *Is this a pencil?* Or, right after having said *His name is John,* asking *What's his name?*

• Do not require more of a learner than of a proficient native speaker. If a complete sentence is not grammatically required in response to a question, do not require the learner to provide one. One-word answers are sufficient for certain questions. For example:

> Teacher: Is that your pencil? Student: Yes.
>   Or,
> Teacher: What's his name? Student: John.

Insistence on complete sentences when one-word answers would be used in normal conversation may result in students' English sounding stilted and unnatural.

• If you want students to practice using complete sentences, construct questions that will naturally require them. For example:

> Why are you late?
> What happened to your finger?

Neither of these is typically answered with one word by a native speaker. A subject and verb are required.

• Respond to content when communicating with students, not to form. Do not correct pronunciation or grammar when students are communicating with you or each other. For example:

> Teacher: Why are you late?
> Student: I miss bus.
> Teacher: Why did you miss the bus?

Do not say *No, say "I missed the bus,"* which will destroy the spontaneity of the communication. If you wish, you might say *Oh, you missed the bus* without drawing further attention to it. Correction should be limited to exercises where the focus is on the form of the language.

- During communication, accept nonverbal responses as well as responses in the student's native language at first. (You should *not* respond in that language too, however. Respond in the target language.) If students nod their heads or gesture responses correctly, accept them and continue. This tells you the student has understood you, but is not yet ready to communicate verbally in the new language.
- Encourage and create situations where your students can interact with native speakers of the target language. If students are learning English in the U.S., make sure they interact with native English-speaking students. If your students are learning French or some other foreign language in the U.S., encourage trips to communities or countries where the target language is spoken natively.
- Do not do grammar lessons during communication activities.

2. Incorporate a Silent Phase at the Beginning of Your Instructional Program   As mentioned earlier, the silent phase is a time during which learners listen and watch, and perhaps respond in their native language or through physical activities. They are not forced to speak in the target language yet.

Classroom Techniques

- Do not force students to produce the target language during the initial weeks of instruction. Instead, accept nonverbal responses, written responses, or responses in the native language. If students volunteer to speak in the new language, however, accept their responses.
- Techniques used in programs that have incorporated the silent phase:
    * Adult students wrote their responses for some weeks, after which they began to respond verbally (Postovsky, 1975, in a Defense Language Institute program).
    * Students (child and adult) acted out their responses during the initial weeks, after which they began to speak the target language (Asher, 1965, 1969; and Asher, Kusudo, and de la Torre, 1974). These findings have now been integrated into a text which

provides many ideas and lessons for the silent phase of an English curriculum (Romijn and Seely, 1979).
* Students (child and adult) were allowed to respond in their native language initially. After several weeks, students began to respond in the target language (Terrell, 1977).

3. Use Concrete Referents to Make the New Language Understandable to Beginning Students

A concrete referent is anything or any activity which can be seen, heard, felt or smelled as it is being verbally described.

Classroom Techniques

• Use demonstrable objects and activities as lesson topics. Most teachers already use visual aids such as hand puppets and toys, or they use activities such as growing plants, cooking, games, etc. when teaching children. For older students, use science experiments, arts and crafts and other interesting and demonstrable activities.

4. Devise Specific Techniques to Relax Students and Protect Their Egos

Relaxed students learn more easily. This is especially true for adults, most of whom are anxious and nervous about making errors in front of their peers. People who are in authoritative positions in their jobs are especially sensitive to making mistakes or sounding strange.

Classroom Techniques

• Have students invent new identities. They could pick a new name in the new language and take on an identity (e.g. a favorite actor, a gypsy, a policeman etc.) No real identities are known until the end of the program. This reduces the students' fear of looking silly when trying to speak the new language. (This technique has worked extremely well in natural language classes for adults given by The Natural Language Institute in Berkeley, California, for example.)
• Play baroque music softly during the lesson. (Great success has been reported by Lozanov and his colleagues who used this technique to facilitate foreign language and other kinds of learning.)
• Use comfortable chairs (Lozanov).
• Do breathing and stretching exercises before lessons.
• Do not focus on students' language errors, but on the content of what they say in the target language.

5. Include Some Time for Formal Grammar Lessons for Adults Many adults need to learn some formal grammar in order to feel that they are indeed learning a new language. Some adults can also consciously apply simple grammatical rules to produce sentences in the new language.

Classroom Techniques

• Include a regular time or a phase in your curriculum for formal grammar lessons. The amount of time allotted should be small in relation to the rest of the curriculum.
• During grammar lessons make clear that you are now focusing on the structure of the language rather than on communication.
• Focus on low-level, easy rules, not complex ones, e.g. the *it's/its* distinction is a low-level rule. When to put an apostrophe in *its* can be taught. On the other hand, the definite/indefinite *a/the* distinction seems to resist explicit instruction. The rules governing the use of *a* and *the* are so complex, they are not adequately stated in many grammar books. This distinction will be acquired subconsciously, if it is acquired at all.

6. Learn the Motivations of Your Students and Incorporate This Knowledge Into Your Lessons Knowing why your students are in your class, and knowing with whom they want to associate and like whom they want to sound will help explain their different success rates and the domain of the target language they learn.

Classroom Techniques

• Observe the peers with whom your students associate, and note the language variety they use.
• Accept speech that is different from what you have taught if the learner's peers use it too. (It is a waste of time to do anything else. The peer pressure is much stronger than that of the teacher or parent.)
• In order to teach students another "dialect" than the one they are learning from their peers (if it is different from that you are teaching), describe to the students the social situations in which each dialect is used. Avoid value judgments. For example, if the standard dialect which you are teaching is used to interview for a job, say so. Students can then practice interviewing for a job, using the standard dialect. If a nonstandard dialect is used among friends, say so. They can use it during those situations. If students know

when to use each "dialect," there will be a purpose for them to learn each.

7. Create an Atmosphere Where Students Are Not Embarrassed by Their Errors

Classroom Techniques

- Expect errors (See Chapter 7).
- Do not focus on student errors during communication.
- Do not show impatience with student errors.
- Respond to the content of student speech, not the language form they use.
- Use role playing activities to minimize students' feelings of personal failure when they make errors.

8. If You Teach Dialogues, Include Current and Socially Useful Phrases
It has been observed that second language learners pick up socially useful phrases almost from the first day. With these phrases, they can get around a foreign country and participate in social activities.

Classroom Techniques

- Observe and note the most common social interactions in which the students are interested, e.g. games, introductions, working together, shopping, asking directions.
- List the stock phrases that are always a part of these situations. For example, for games: *It's my turn; We won.* For introductions: *Good Morning . . . How are you?* For working together: *What's that? Do you want X?* For socializing: *Would you like to dance? Sure.*
- Build dialogues around such exchanges.

9. Certain Structures Tend to Be Learned Before Others. Do Not Expect Students to Learn "Late Structures" Early

Classroom Techniques

- Become familiar with the general learning order observed for structures researched and presented here (Chapter 8).
- Avoid teaching late structures early but feel free to use them in your speech at any point in the instructional program.
- You need not teach to the learning order. Familiarity with it will help explain student learning patterns and give you an accurate

sense of what to expect from them in so far as the learning of basic English structures is concerned.

10. Do Not Refer to a Student's L_1 When Teaching the L_2 The second language is a new and independent language system. Since successful second language learners keep their languages distinct, teachers should, too. No reference need be made to the student's first language unless the student requests it.

Classroom Techniques

• Avoid contrasting the L_1 and L_2 when explaining grammatical structure.
• Avoid translation tasks as a major technique. Use only where necessary to clarify meaning.

There are undoubtedly many more guidelines and techniques that, like these, work in concert with learners' natural tendencies to construct the new language creatively and systematically. If language teaching builds upon these tendencies, both teacher and learner should find the second language experience exciting and productive.

Appendix A
Computing Rank
Order Correlation

SPEARMAN RANK ORDER CORRELATION

A very common statistical test used to determine the degree of similarity between two sets of ranks is the **Spearman rank correlation coefficent,** sometimes called *rho*. We will show how the Spearman rank order correlation can be applied, as well as misapplied.

TABLE AA   Use of the Rank Order Correlation (*rho*)

Subjects:	(1): 22 adult ESL students[a]			(2): One adolescent ESL acquirer[b]		
	Score	*Raw Score*	*Rank*	*Score*	*Raw Score*	*Rank*
copula	.87	(259/298)	1	1.00	(42/42)	1
progressive	.84	(23.5/28)	2	.60	(6/10)	4
plural (-s)	.71	(192/271)	3	.87	(130/150)	2
article	.69	(283/409)	4	.84	(156/184)	3
past irregular	.67	(62/92)	5	.16	(12/74)	7
past regular	.64	(35/55)	6	.33	(6/18)	5.5
auxiliary	.56	(46.5/83)	7	.33	(8/24)	5.5
3rd person (-s)	.36	(23.5/66)	8	.00	(0/32)	8

[a] Krashen, Houck, Giunchi, Bode, Birnbaum, and Strei, 1977.
[b] Jorge, from Rosansky, 1976.
Only morphemes appearing in at least ten obligatory occasions are included.[1]

Table AA presents the difficulty order for grammatical morphemes from two studies previously described. Krashen et al. (1977),
who used free speech data from a group of adult ESL students, and
a single cross-section of one subject, Jorge, from Rosansky (1976).
The table also gives each structure's percentage correct in obligatory
occasions.

The computation of the rank order correlation is quite simple.
After setting up the two sets of items to be compared in a manner
similar to Table BB, rank orders are designated. In the case of a tie
(as in column 2, past regular and auxiliary), each item receives the
average of the ranks that would have been assigned had no tie occurred. For example, the rank assigned to the past regular and auxiliary for the adolescent ESL learner is 5.5 (6 + 5 = 11; 11/2 = 5.5).

The second step in computing *rho* is to subtract the ranks of Column 2 from the ranks of Column 1 (or vice-versa; numbers in Column 1 can be subtracted from those in Column 2; it makes no difference). The resulting difference scores are then squared. The
squares are summed (Σd_2) and multiplied by six, as illustrated below.

TABLE BB   Computing the Rank Order Correlation

Rank Order (1)	Rank Order (2)	Difference between Rank (d)	d^2	
1	1	0	0	
2	4	2	4	
3	2	1	1	
4	3	1	1	
5	7	2	4	
6	5.5	.5	.25	
7	5.5	1.5	2.25	
8	8	0	0	
			12.5	× 6 = 75

Finally, the rest of the formula for *rho* is applied.

$$rho = 1 - \frac{6\Sigma d^2}{N^3 - N}$$

In our example, we have already computed $6\Sigma d$ (= 75). N stands for
the number of pairs to be related (8 in the example). Thus the formula is computed for our example as follows:

$$rho = 1 - \frac{75}{8^3 - 8} = 1 - \frac{75}{504} = .85^1$$

Rho indicates the degree of agreement in ranks between the two sets of items. Perfect agreement is 1.0, while a perfectly inverse relationship (a high rank in one set corresponding to a low rank in another) would be −1.0. No relationship at all would result in a rank order correlation of .00.

Researchers rely both on the absolute value of the correlation as well as its "significance level." The significance level of a correlation refers to the probability that the obtained correlation was simply a chance result. For the correlation of .85 obtained in the example, the odds of obtaining a correlation this high by chance are less than one in 20 (written $p > .05$). In general, for this kind of research, this probability value is low enough for the researcher to assume that such a correlation was not due to chance but was instead due to the fact that there is good agreement between the rank orders of the items. (For further discussion, see any one of several statistics texts, e.g. Marascuilo and McSweeney, 1977; Ferguson, 1971; Blalock, 1960; Siegel, 1956.)

The rank order correlation provides a useful, yet rough, estimate of the agreement between two sets of ordered items. Its insensitivity to absolute differences between items, however, can be problematic. Thus, this statistic should be used with caution.

Because of this problem, this statistic can suggest differences in acquisition order when in reality there are none. For example, there is nothing to prevent the researcher from performing a rank order correlation using items such as these:

progressive	.95
plural (-s)	.93
article	.94
copula	.98
auxiliary	.98
possessive	1.00
past irregular	.80
past regular	.50
3rd person (-s)	.11

From Rosansky, 1976; Cross-section of her subject, *Jorge*.

---

1. Technically, the presence of tied ranks calls for a special calculation that has the effect of reducing the correlation slightly. This procedure is described in detail in Siegel, 1956, pp. 206–210. To demonstrate the effect of this additional calculation, if it were applied to the example given in the table, the new correlation would be .8502, as compared with the original .8512.

Rank order correlation methods allow their application (or mis-application) to closely bunched data of this sort. Conversely, when scores are far apart between two items, ranking obscures that fact. Scores of .98, .97, and .54, for example, are simply ranked 1, 2, and 3.

Another problem is the fragility of the rank order correlation. When the number of items to be compared is ten or less, a shift in rank order of one item may change the correlation considerably. For example, if Jorge had missed only four more progressive endings, giving him .20 (2/10), the agreement between the two sets would drop to .56. This problem is alleviated somewhat by involving greater numbers of items, and by insisting on a minimum number of occasions for each item.

THE KENDALL COEFFICIENT OF CONCORDANCE

The **Kendall coefficient of concordance** (the "Kendall W") is very similar to the rank order correlation. It is simply a method of deter-mining rank order correlations on more than two sets of ranks at the same time. The advantages and disadvantages of the Kendall W are similar to those discussed in relation to the rank order correla-tion.

Table CC gives some data that is eligible for analysis using the Kendall W. Bound morphemes from six studies are listed with their ranks. N refers to the number of items ranked (five in this case), and K refers to the number of studies (six). The next step is to sum the observed difference ranks for each structure obtained in each study (e.g. the first calculation is $1+1+2+2+2+2=10$. Note that if the studies agreed perfectly, this number would be 6, and each subsequent number would be larger). These sums are then added together, and divided by N to obtain a mean (average) sum of ranks. We are now in a position to obtain s, which is the numerator of the fraction in the formula for W. s is the sum of squares of the ob-served deviations from the mean of the ranks. In other words, we subtract each sum from the mean sum of ranks (in this example, 16), and square each number, and add them together. This gives s. We then plug values of s, k, and N into the formula to obtain W (see Table CC).

The interpretation of W is similar to the interpretation of *rho*. A perfect agreement means $W = 1.0$; while $W = -1.0$ indicates an in-verse relationship. $W = .00$ indicates no relationship at all. In the example, $W = .8611$, indicating very good agreement among the

studies for the order of acquisition or difficulty of bound morphemes.

As in the case of the rank order correlation, slight changes in rank
can seriously alter the value of W when N's are small. It is, like the
rank order correlation, a valuable tool for obtaining a rough idea of
agreement between studies, but it is not as sensitive as language
acquisition data seem to require. The fact that large differences between scores are treated the same as small differences seriously
limits the value of this technique for describing language acquisition data.

TABLE CC   Use of the Kendall Coefficient of Concordance (W)

Study	Plural (−s)	Progressive	Past Irregular	Possessive	3rd Person (−s)
de Villiers and de Villiers (1973)	1	2	3	4	5
Dulay & Burt (1973)	1	2	3	5	4
Dulay & Burt (1974)	2	1	3	5	4
Bailey et al. (1974)	2	1	3	5	4
Larsen-Freeman (1975)[a]	2	1	5	3	4
Larsen-Freeman (1975)[b]	2	1	4	3	5
	10	8	21	24	27

N = number of morphemes ranked = 5

k = number of studies = 6

Steps in Determining the Kendall Coefficient of Concordance

1. Sum the observed ranks in each column.
2. Add together the summed ranks and divide by N, obtaining the mean rank:
   $10 + 8 + 21 + 24 + 27 = 90$
   $90/5 = 16$
3. Subtract each sum from the mean rank:
   $10 - 16 = 6$ (ignore the sign)
   $8 - 16 = 8$
   $21 - 16 = 5$
   $24 - 16 = 8$
   $27 - 16 = 11$
4. Square each result, and sum the squares:
   $36 + 64 + 25 + 64 + 121 = 310 = s$
5. Use the formula
$$W = \frac{s}{1/12 \ k^2(N^3 - N)}$$
$$= \frac{310}{1/12 \ (36) \ (120)} = .8611$$

[a,b] Larsen-Freeman administered the BSM to the same group of subjects two months apart.

Glossary

acquisition hierarchy The order in which groups of items of grammar, discourse, or phonology are acquired, where a group consists of one or more items.

acquisition order The order in which items or groups of items of grammar, discourse, or phonology are acquired; discovered directly by longitudinal studies (done over time), or indirectly by cross-sectional studies (done at one point in time). The term *acquisition order* may refer to acquisition hierarchies or sequences.

acquisition sequence The order of acquisition of single items of grammar, discourse, or phonology.

addition error *See* "error: addition."

adult language learner A learner who begins to learn a language after puberty.

affect The learner's motives, needs, attitudes, and emotional states.

alternation *See* "error: alternation."

ambiguous *See* "error: ambiguous."

archiform *See* "error: archiform."

back-to-back phonemes A situation in which the sound of a required grammatical item is very similar to the sound adjacent to it, making it virtually impossible to tell whether the item was supplied. E.g. *She's swimming; He dropped the flower.*

bilingual (simultaneous) acquisition The acquisition of two languages simultaneously from infancy.

borrowing The use of linguistic material from one language when speaking or writing another.

child language learner   A learner who begins to learn a language before puberty.

code alternation   A construction that includes lexical and syntactic items from more than one language. A code alternation may be the result of borrowing or code switching.

code switching   Rapid shifting from one language to another by bilinguals.

communication   An exchange or transmittal of message(s) between two or more parties.

   one-way communication   A communication situation in which the learner listens to or reads the target language but does not respond in any way.

   restricted two-way communication   An exchange in which messages directed to the learner are in the target language, but the learner responds in his or her first language or with gestures.

   full two-way communication   A verbal exchange in which the learner listens to someone speaking the target language and responds in the target language.

   natural communication   A communication situation in which people focus on the ideas being discussed rather than on their grammatical structure.

communication effect taxonomy   *See* "taxonomy: communicative effect."

comparative taxonomy   *See* "taxonomy: comparative."

complexity   Difficulty or amount of knowledge in a linguistic structure.

   learning complexity   The degree of difficulty a learner experiences in acquiring a language structure.

   linguistic complexity   The amount of linguistic knowledge in a structure.

concrete referent   Anything that can be seen, heard, felt, smelled, or touched by the learner that clarifies the meaning of what is said to the learner.

contrastive analysis (C.A.)   The comparison of the linguistic structures of two or more languages, to determine their similarities and differences.

   C.A. hypothesis   A research hypothesis stating that where structures in L_1 differ from those in L_2, errors that reflect the structure of L_1 will be produced, and where structures in L_1 and L_2 are the same, no errors will be made.

   C.A. position   The belief of some applied linguists that a learner's first language "interferes" with his or her acquisition of a second language and therefore comprises the major obstacle to successful mastery of the new language.

creative construction   The subconscious process by which language learners gradually organize the language they hear, according to rules that they construct to understand and generate sentences.

delayed oral practice A language teaching technique in which students are not asked to produce the new language orally during the initial phase of instruction.

developmental error *See* "error: developmental."

double marking *See* "error: double marking."

elicitation task The manner in which spoken or written performance is drawn from the language learner by a teacher, tester, researcher, or speech clinician.

empathy An individual's capacity for participation in another's feelings or ideas.

error A part of a conversation or a composition that deviates from some selected norm of mature language performance.

    addition error The presence of an item that must not appear in a well-formed utterance. May be a regularization, double marking, or simple addition error.

    alternation The use of members of one grammatical class for each other (e.g. plural for singular). Also called "alternating form."

    ambiguous error One that can be classified equally well as developmental or interlingual.

    archiform The use of one member of a class of forms to represent others in the class (e.g. *Them going to town; I know them*).

    developmental error One that is similar to those made by children learning the target language as their first language.

    double marking An error in which a concept is expressed twice when the language requires its expression only once, e.g. double negation: we *hardly never* go.

    global error One that affects overall sentence organization.

    interlingual error One that reflects the learner's first language structure.

    local error One that affects single elements (constituents) in a sentence.

    misformation Use of the wrong form of a morpheme.

    misordering error The incorrect placement of a morpheme.

    omission The absence of an item that must appear in a well-formed utterance.

    regularization The application of a regular rule to an item which requires a special rule, e.g. *eated, sheeps*. Also called "overgeneralization."

error analysis Listing and classification of the errors contained in a sample of learner's speech or writing.

expansion The systematic modeling of either the correct or more complete version of a learner's utterance without calling the learner's attention to the activity.

feedback The response given to specific aspects of learner speech during a verbal interaction.

filter   That part of the internal processing system that subconsciously screens incoming language based on motives, needs, attitudes, or emotions.

foreign language   A language not used by residents of the country or community in which that language is being learned. E.g. French learned in New York.

foreign language environment   *See* "language environment: foreign."

formal language environment   *See* "language environment: formal."

formal operations   Piaget's term for when a thinker acquires new concepts primarily from verbal rather than from concrete experience.

full two-way communication   *See* "communication: full two-way."

global error   *See* "error: global."

grammatical morpheme   A grammatical item which does not contribute much to the meaning of sentences, including noun and verb inflections, articles, auxiliaries, copulas, and prepositions.

host language   The language used by residents of the country or community in which that language is being learned, e.g. English learned in England.

host language environment   *See* "language environment: host."

immersion program   A second language teaching program in which the language the students are learning is a minority language and is used as the medium of instruction for most of the academic subjects in the students' school curriculum.

instrumental motivation   *See* "motivation: instrumental."

integrative motivation   *See* "motivation: integrative."

interference:

   psychological interference   The influence of old language habits on new language behavior.

   sociolinguistic interference   The use of items from another language when speaking, e.g. the use of Yiddish diminutives when speaking English. Sociolinguistic interference occurs when countries or communities that speak different languages are in contact.

interlanguage   A term used to refer to the speech or writing of second language learners in the second language.

interlingual error   *See* "error: interlingual."

$L_1, L_2 \ldots$ First language; second language, etc.

language environment   Everything learners hear or see in the language they are learning.

   natural language environment   One where the focus of the speakers is primarily on the content of the communication.

   formal language environment   One where the focus of the speakers is primarily on the form of the language.

foreign language environment One where the language being learned is *not* the language of the country or community in which it is being learned.

host language environment One where the language being learned is primarily spoken by residents of the country or community in which it is being learned.

lateralization Specialization of function by each side of the brain; e.g. the left side is responsible for analysis, while the right side is responsible for spatial perception. Also called "cerebral dominance" or "cerebral asymmetry."

linguistic category taxonomy *See* "taxonomy: linguistic category."

linguistic manipulation task An elicitation task that focuses learners' attention on the form of the language they produce, rather than on its meaning.

local error *See* "error: local."

macro-environmental factors Broad, over-all characteristics of the language environment.

micro-environmental factors Characteristics of certain structures of the language the learner hears (e.g. salience, feedback, frequency).

misformation *See* "error: misformation."

misordering *See* "error: misordering."

monitor That part of the learner's internal system that consciously inspects and, from time to time, alters the form of the learner's production.

motivation The incentive, the need, or the desire that the learner feels to learn the second language.

    instrumental motivation The desire to achieve proficiency in a new language for utilitarian reasons (e.g. getting a job).

    integrative motivation The desire to achieve proficiency in a new language in order to participate in the life of the community that speaks the language.

    social group identification motive The desire to learn a language or dialect spoken by a social group with which the learner identifies.

natural communication *See* "communication: natural."

natural communication task A task that focuses the student's attention on the idea or opinion being expressed rather than on the language forms used. A natural communication task may be structured or not.

    structured communication task A natural communication task guided by a set of questions designed to elicit particular structures.

    unstructured communication task A natural communication task in which there is no attempt to elicit specific structures.

natural language environment *See* "language environment: natural."

negative transfer *See* "transfer, defined by behaviorist psychologists: negative."

obligatory occasion A configuration of one or more linguistic items that requires the use of certain other items.

occurrence study *See* "study: occurrence."

omission error *See* "error: omission."

one-way communication *See* "communication: one-way."

organizer The part of the internal processing system that is responsible for the learner's gradual and subconscious organization of the new language system.

pattern A memorized phrase or sentence with an open slot; *e.g.*, "That's a _____." or "I want _____."

personality An aggregate of traits characteristic of a particular individual.

positive transfer *See* "transfer, defined by behaviorist psychologists: positive."

proportion study *See* "study: proportion."

quasi-proportion study *See* "study: quasi-proportion."

regularization *See* "error: regularization."

research design The structure of a research study.

  longitudinal design The structure of a study of a few learners over an extended period of time.

  cross-sectional design The structure of a study of a large group of learners at one point in time.

restricted two-way communication *See* "communication: restricted two-way."

routines Whole phrases or sentences memorized and used as single items; *e.g.*, "How do you do?"

salience The ease with which a structure is heard or seen.

second language A language learned after the basics of the first have been acquired. A second language may be a "foreign" or a "host" language.

second language acquisition The process of learning another language after the basics of the first have been acquired, starting at about age five. Also called "sequential language acquisition."

silent period The initial phase of the language learning process during which the learner simply listens to the new language and is not made to produce it.

social group identification motive *See* "motivation: social group identification."

structured communication task *See* "natural communication task: structured."

structured conversation A structured communication task in which responses are oral.

study:

  occurrence study A study in which the occurrence of error types is reported but no attempt is made to count them or to determine their proportion.

proportion study A study in which all the errors in a speech or writing sample are classified and counted to determine the proportion of each error type.

quasi-proportion study A study in which all errors in a speech or writing sample are classified but not counted, permitting only subjective estimates of the proportion of each error type.

surface strategy taxonomy *See* "taxonomy: surface strategy."

syntax acquisition index (SAI) A measure that reflects the degree of grammatical correctness of a sample of language produced by a learner.

target language The language being learned or taught.

task focus The kind of focus required of the learner when performing an elicitation task. Task focus may be on content or on linguistic forms or rules.

task mode The language mode (understanding, speaking, reading, or writing) tapped by an elicitation task.

taxonomy Classification:

linguistic category taxonomy Classification of errors according to their linguistic category.

surface strategy taxonomy Classification of errors according to the ways the surface structure of the language is altered.

comparative taxonomy Classification of errors based on the comparison between the structure of the L_2 error and that of other constructions, such as L_1 errors.

communicative effect taxonomy Classification of errors according to their effect on the listener or reader.

transfer, defined by behaviorist psychologists The automatic, uncontrolled, and subconscious use of previously learned behaviors in the attempt to produce new responses, *e.g.*, use of L_1 behavior when producing the L_2.

negative transfer Transfer resulting in errors, due to differences between previously learned responses and new responses to be learned.

positive transfer Transfer resulting in correct performance, due to the similarity between the new behavior and the old.

transfer, defined by educational psychologists The use of past knowledge in new situations.

transitional construction The interim language forms that learners use while they are still learning the grammar of a language. Also called "developmental sequences."

unstructured communication task *See* "natural communication task: unstructured."

Bibliography

AGUIRRE, A. 1975. Judgments of grammaticality in code-alternation by Chicano university students. Unpublished manuscript, Stanford University. Department of Sociology, Stanford, Ca.

ALAJOUANINE, T. 1956. Verbal realization and aphasia. *Brain* 79:95–133.

ALBERT, M. L., and OBLER, L. K. *The Bilingual Brain.* New York: Academic Press, 1978.

ALLWRIGHT, R. L. 1975. Problems in the study of the language teacher's treatment of learner error. In M. Burt and H. Dulay (eds.), 1975, *New Directions in Second Language Learning, Teaching, and Bilingual Education.* Washington, D.C.: TESOL, 96–109.

ANDERSEN, R. March 1976. A functor acquisition hierarchy study in Puerto Rico. Paper presented at the 10th Annual TESOL Convention, New York.

ANDERSON, J. 1978. Order of difficulty in adult second language acquisition. In W. Ritchie (ed.), *Second Language Acquisition Research: Issues and Implications.* London: Academic Press, 91–108.

d'ANGLEJAN, A., and TUCKER, G. R. 1975. The acquisition of complex English structures by adult learners. *Language Learning* 25:281–96.

ANISFELD, M., and TUCKER, G. R. 1967. English pluralization rules of six-year-old children. *Child Development* 38:1201–17.

ASHER, J. 1965. The strategy of the total physical response: an application to learning Russian. *International Journal of Applied Linguistics* 3:291–300.

———. 1966. The learning strategy of the total physical response: a review. *Modern Language Journal* 50:79–84.

———. 1969. The total physical response technique of learning. *Journal of Special Education* 3:53–262.

———. 1969a. The total physical response approach to second language learning. *Modern Language Journal* 53:1.3–7.

————. 1972. Children's first language as a model for second language learning. *Modern Language Journal* 56:133–39.

ASHER, J., and GARCIA, R. 1969. The optimal age to learn a foreign language. *Modern Language Journal* 53:334–41.

ASHER, J.; KUSUDO, J.; and de la TORRE, R. 1974. Learning a second language through commands: the second field test. *Modern Language Journal* 58:24–32.

AUSUBEL, D. 1962. Implications of preadolescent and early adolescent cognitive development for secondary-school teaching. *The High School Journal* XLV:268–75.

AUSUBEL, D., and AUSUBEL, P. 1971. Cognitive development in adolescence. In H. Thornburg (ed.), 1971, *Contemporary Adolescence: Readings*. Belmont, Cal.: Brooks/Cole, 42–49.

BAILEY, N.; MADDEN, C.; and KRASHEN, S. D. 1974. Is there a "natural sequence" in adult second language learning? *Language Learning* 24:235–43.

BANANTHY, B.; TRAGER, E. C.; and WADDLE, C. D. 1966. The use of contrastive data in foreign language course development. In A. Valdman (ed.), *Trends in Language Teaching*. New York: McGraw-Hill.

BART, W. M., and KRUS, D. J. 1973. An ordering-theoretic method to determine hierarchies among items. *Educational and Psychological Measurement* 33:291–300.

BENITEZ, C. 1970. A study of some non-standard English features in the speech of seventh-grade Mexican Americans enrolled in a remedial reading in an urban community of South Texas. M.A. thesis, Texas A and I University. Kingsville, Texas.

BENTON, R. 1964. Research into the English language difficulties of Maori school children, 1963–1964. Wellington, New Zealand: Maori Education Foundation.

BERKO, J. 1958. The child's learning of English morphology. *Word* 14:159–77.

BERLIN, C.; HUGHES, L.; LOWE-BELL, S.; and BERLIN, H. 1973. Dichotic right ear advantage in children 5 to 13. *Cortex* 9:393–402.

BERTKAU, J. 1974. An analysis of English learner speech. *Language Learning* 24:2.279–86.

BEVER, T. 1970. The cognitive basis for linguistic structures. In J. R. Hayes (ed.), *Cognition and the Development of Language*. New York: John Wiley & Sons, 279–352.

Bilingual Inventory of Natural Language. Los Angeles: Checkpoint Systems, 1976.

Bilingual Syntax Measure I (Gr.K-2), 1975, English, Spanish, and Pilipino editions. Including: English *Manual* for administration, scoring, and use of English edition; Spanish *Manual* for administration, scoring, and use of Spanish edition; *Child Response Booklets; Respuestas del Niño; Munting Aklat para sa Sagot; Class Record Sheet;* and *Picture Booklet*. New York: Harcourt Brace Jovanovich.

Bilingual Syntax Measure II (Gr.3–12), 1978, English and Spanish editions.

Including: English *Manual* for administration, scoring, and use of English edition; Spanish *Manual* for administration, scoring, and use of Spanish edition; *Child Response Booklet; Respuestas del Niño; Class Record Sheet;* and *Picture Booklet.* New York: The Psychological Corp.

BIRNBAUM, R.; BUTLER, J.; and KRASHEN, S. February 1977. The use of the monitor in free and edited ESL compositions. Paper presented at the Los Angeles Second Language Research Forum, UCLA.

BLALOCK, H. 1960. *Social Statistics.* New York: McGraw-Hill.

BLOUNT, B. G. 1969. Acquisition of language by Luo children. Unpublished Ph.D. dissertation. University of California, Berkeley.

BOGEN, J. 1969. The other side of the brain I: Dysgraphia and dyscopia following cerebral commissurotomy. *Bulletin of the Los Angeles Neurological Society* 34:73–105.

————. 1969a. The other side of the brain II: an appositional mind. *Bulletin of the Los Angeles Neurological Society* 34:135–62.

BOYD, P. A. 1975. The development of grammar categories in Spanish by Anglo children learning a second language. *Language Learning* 25:125-36.

BROWN, H. D. 1973. Affective variables in second language acquisition. *Language and Learning* 23:231–44.

————. 1977. Cognitive and affective characteristics of good language learners. In C. Henning (ed.), *Proceedings of the Los Angeles Second Language Research Forum, UCLA,* 349–54.

BROWN, J., and JAFFE, J. 1975. Hypothesis on cerebral dominance. *Neuropsychologia* 13:107–10.

BROWN, R., and BELLUGI, U. 1964. Three processes in the child's acquisition of syntax. *Harvard Educational Review* 34:133–51.

BROWN, R. 1973. *A First Language.* Cambridge, Ma.: Harvard University Press.

BROWN, R., and HANLON, C. 1970. Derivational complexity and order of acquisition in child speech. In J. R. Hayes (ed.), *Cognition and the Development of Language.* New York: John Wiley & Sons, 155–207.

BRUCK, M.; LAMBERT, W.; and TUCKER, G. R. 1974. Bilingual schooling through the elementary grades: the St. Lambert project at grade seven. *Language Learning* 24:183–204.

————. 1975. Assessing functional bilingualism within a bilingual program: the St. Lambert project at grade eight. Paper presented at TESOL Convention, Los Angeles.

BUDZYNSKI, T. 1977. Tuning in on the twilight zone. *Psychology Today* 8:39–44.

BURLING, R. 1959. Language development of a Garo and English speaking child. *WORD* 15:45–68.

BURT, M. K. 1975. Error analysis in the adult EFL classroom. *TESOL Quarterly* 9:53–63.

BURT, M., and DULAY, H. 1978. Some guidelines for the assessment of oral language proficiency and dominance. *TESOL Quarterly* 12:2.177–91.

BURT, M.; DULAY, H.; and HERNÁNDEZ-CHÁVEZ, E. 1975. *Bilingual Syntax Measure I.* New York: Harcourt Brace Jovanovich.

————. 1976. *Technical Handbook: Bilingual Syntax Measure*. New York: Harcourt Brace Jovanovich.

————. 1978. *Bilingual Syntax Measure II*. New York: The Psychological Corp.

BURT, M.; DULAY. H.; HERNÁNDEZ-CHÁVEZ, E.; and TALEPOROS, E. 1980. *Bilingual Syntax Measure II Technical Handbook*. New York: The Psychological Corp.

BURT, M.; DULAY, H.; and MCKEON, D. 1980. *The English Second Language Development of Pueblo Indian Children*. Report prepared for the Division of Learning and Teaching, National Institute of Education, Washington, D.C.

BURT, M., and KIPARSKY, C. 1972. *The Gooficon: A Repair Manual for English*. Rowley, Ma.: Newbury House.

BUTTERWORTH, G., and HATCH, E. 1978. A Spanish-speaking adolescent's acquisition of English syntax. In E. Hatch (ed.), *Second Language Acquisition*. Rowley, Ma.: Newbury House, 231–45.

CANCINO, H. E.; ROSANSKY, E. J.; and SCHUMANN, J. 1974. Testing hypotheses about second language acquisition: the copula and negative in three subjects. *Working Papers on Bilingualism* 3:80–96.

————. 1975. The acquisition of the English auxiliary by native Spanish speakers. *TESOL Quarterly* 9:421–30.

CANDLIN, C. N. 1973. Preface. In J. Richards (ed.), *Error Analysis: Perspectives on Second Language Acquisition*. London: Longman.

CARROLL, J. 1963. The prediction of success in intensive foreign language training. In R. Glazer (ed.), *Training, Research, and Education*. Pittsburgh: University of Pittsburgh Press.

————. 1967. Foreign language proficiency levels attained by language majors near graduation from college. *Foreign Language Annals* 1:131–51.

————. 1973. Implications of aptitude test research and psycholinguistic theory for foreign language teaching. *Linguistics* 112:5–13.

CATHCART, R., and OLSON, J. 1976. Teachers' and students' preference for correction of classroom conversation errors. In J. Fanselow and R. Crymes (eds.), *On TESOL '76*. Washington, D.C.: TESOL, 41–53.

CAZDEN, C. B. 1965. Environmental assistance to the child's acquisition of grammar. Ph.D. dissertation, Harvard University, Cambridge, Ma.

————. 1972. *Child Language and Education*. New York: Holt, Rinehart & Winston.

CAZDEN, C. B.; CANCINO, H.; ROSANSKY, E.; and SCHUMANN, J. 1975. *Second Language Acquisition Sequences in Children, Adolescents and Adults*. Final Report submitted to the National Institute of Education.

CERASCO, J. 1968. Specific interference in retroactive inhibition. *Journal of Psychology* 58:65–77.

CHASTAIN, K. 1975. Affective and ability factors in second language learning. *Language Learning* 25:153–61.

CHAUDRON, C. 1977. A descriptive model of discourse in the corrective treatment of learners' errors. *Language Learning* 27:1.29–46.

CHIHARA, T., and OLLER, J. 1978. Attitudes and attained proficiency in EFL: A sociolinguistic study of adult Japanese speakers. *Language Learning* 28:55–68.

CHOMSKY, C. 1969. *The Acquisition of Syntax in Children Age 5 to 10*. Cambridge, Ma.: M.I.T. Press.

CHOMSKY, N. 1957. *Syntactic Structures*. The Hague: Mouton.

———. 1959. A review of B. F. Skinner's verbal behavior. In J. A. Fodor and J. J. Katz (eds.), 1968, *The Structure of Language*. Englewood Cliffs, N.J.: Prentice-Hall.

———. 1965. *Aspects of the Theory of Syntax*. Cambridge, Ma.: M.I.T. Press.

CHOMSKY, N., and HALLE, M. 1968. *The Sound Pattern of English*. New York: Harper & Row.

CHRISTISON, M. A. 1979. Natural sequencing in adult second language acquisition. *TESOL Quarterly* 13:1, 122.

CLARK, R. 1974. Performing without competence. *Journal of Child Language* 1:1–10.

CLARK, H., and CLARK, E. 1977. *Psychology and Language*. New York: Harcourt Brace Jovanovich.

COHEN, A. D., and ROBBINS, M. 1976. Toward assessing inter-language performance: the relationship between selected errors, learners' characteristics and learners' explanations. *Language Learning* 26:54–66.

CONTREERAS, H., and SAPORTA, S. 1971. Phonological development in the speech of a bilingual child. In J. Akin et al. (eds.), *Language Behavior: A Book of Readings in Communication*. The Hague: Mouton, 280–94.

COOK-GUMPERZ, J., and GUMPERZ, J. 1976. Context in children's speech. Papers on Language and Context. Working Papers #46. Language Behavior Research Laboratory, University of California, Berkeley.

CORDER, S. P. 1967. The significance of learners' errors. *International Review of Applied Linguistics* 5:161–70.

———. 1972. The elicitation of interlanguage. Unpublished manuscript, University of Edinburgh.

———. 1974. Approximate systems and error analysis: review of current issues and research. Presentation at the ACTFL Annual Meeting, Denver, Colorado.

CROSS, T. 1977. Mother's speech adjustments: The contribution of selected child listener variables. In C. Snow and C. Ferguson (eds.), *Talking to Children*. New York: Cambridge University Press, pp. 151–88.

CURRAN, C. 1961. Counseling skills adapted to the learning of foreign languages. *Bulletin of the Menninger Clinic* 25:78–93.

DALE, P. S. 1976. *Language Development: Structure and Function*. New York: Holt, Rinehart & Winston.

DE SILVA, Z. S. 1963. *Beginning Spanish*. 2d ed. New York: Harper & Row.

DORE, J. 1974. A pragmatic description of early language development. *Journal of Psycholinguistic Research* 4:423–30.

DORMAN, M., and GEFFNER, D. 1973. Hemispheric specialization for speech perception in six-year-old black and white children from low and middle socioeconomic classes. *Cortex* 10:171–76.

DULAY, H., and BURT, M. 1972. Goofing: an indicator of children's second language learning strategies. *Language Learning* 22:235–52.

———. 1973.   Should we teach children syntax? *Language Learning* 24:245–58.

———. 1974.   You can't learn without goofing: an analysis of children's second language errors. In J. Richards (ed.), 1974, *Error Analysis*. London: Longman, 95–123.

———. 1974a.   Errors and strategies in child second language acquisition. *TESOL Quarterly* 8:129–36.

———. 1974b.   Natural sequences in child second language acquisition. *Language Learning* 24:37–53.

———. 1974c.   A new perspective on the creative construction process in child second language acquisition. *Language Learning* 24:253–78.

———. 1975.   A new approach to discovering universals of child second language acquisition. In D. Dato (ed.), 1975, *Developmental Psycholinguistics* (Monograph Series on Languages and Linguistics). Washington, D.C.: Georgetown University Press, 209–33.

———. 1975a.   Creative construction in second language learning and teaching. In M. Burt and H. C. Dulay (eds.), *New Directions in Second Language Learning, Teaching, and Bilingual Education*. Washington, D.C.: TESOL, 21–32.

———. 1977.   Remarks on creativity in second language acquisition. In M. Burt; H. Dulay; and M. Finocchiaro (eds.), 1977, *Viewpoints on English as a Second Language*. New York: Regents, 95–126.

———. August 1977a.   Learning and teaching research in bilingual education. Paper commissioned by DHEW/National Institute of Education, Office of the Director, 1977.

———. From research to method in bilingual education. In J. Alatis (ed.), 1978, *International Dimensions of Bilingual Education*, Washington, D.C.: Georgetown University Press, 551–75.

DULAY, H.; HERNÁNDEZ-CHÁVEZ, E.; and BURT, M. 1978.   The process of becoming bilingual. In S. Singh & J. Lynch (eds.), *Diagnostic Procedures in Hearing, Speech and Language*. Baltimore: University Park Press, 251–303.

DUSKOVA, L. 1969.   On sources of error in foreign language learning. *International Review of Applied Linguistics* 4:11–36.

ELKIND, D. 1970.   *Children and Adolescents: Interpretative Essays on Jean Piaget*. New York: Oxford University Press.

ERVIN-TRIPP, S. 1973.   Some strategies for the first two years. In A. Dil (ed.), *Language Acquisition and Communicative Choice*. Stanford, Cal.: Stanford University Press.

———. 1974.   Is second language learning like the first? *TESOL Quarterly* 8:111–27.

ESPINOSA, A. 1917.   Speech mixture in New Mexico: the influence of the

English language on New Mexican Spanish. In H. M. Stephens and H. E. Bolton (eds.), *The Pacific Ocean in History*. Published by the authors, 408–28. Reprinted in E. Hernández-Chávez, E. Cohen, and A. Beltramo (eds.), 1975. *El Lenguaje de los Chicanos: Regional and Social Characteristics of Language Used by Mexican Americans*. Arlington, Va.: Center for Applied Linguistics, 99–114.

FANSELOW, J. 1977. The treatment of error in oral work. *Foreign Language Annals* 10:583–93.

FATHMAN, A. 1975. Language background, age and the order of acquisition of English structures. In M. Burt and H. Dulay (eds.), 1975, *New Directions in Second Language Learning, Teaching, and Bilingual Education*. Washington, D.C., TESOL, 33–43.

FELDMAN, C. 1971. The effects of various types of adult responses in the syntactic acquisition of 2–3 year olds. Unpublished paper. University of Chicago.

FELIX, S. 1976. Wh-pronouns in first and second language acquisition. *Linguistische Berichte* 44:52–64.

———. 1977. Entwicklungsprozesse im naturlichen und gesteuerten Zweitsprachenerwerb. *Anglistik und Englischunterricht* 1:39–60.

———. 1978a. *Linguistische Untersuchungen zum naturlichen Zweitsprachenerwerb*. Munich: W. Fink.

———. 1978b. Some differences between first and second language acquisition. In Snow, C., and Waterson, N. (eds.), *The Development of Communication*. London: John Wiley & Sons, 469–79.

———. 1979. Zur Relation zwischen naturlichem und gesteuertem Zweitsprachenerwerb. In R. Kloepfer (ed.), *Bildung und Ausbildung in der Romania*, Munich: W. Fink, 355–70.

———. 1980a. *Zweitsprachenerwerb als kreativer Prozess*. Tubingen: Gunter Narr.

———. 1980b. Interference, interlanguage, and related issues. In S. Felix (ed.), *Second Language Development: Trends and Issues*. Tubingen: Gunter Narr, 93–108.

———. 1980c. The effect of formal instruction on second language learning. Paper presented at the Third Second Language Research Forum, February 1980, UCLA.

FELIX, S. 1981. Competing cognitive structures in second language acquisition. Presented at the First European/North American Workshop on Second Language Acquisition, Los Angeles.

FERGUSON, C. A. 1975. Sound patterns in language acquisition. In D. P. Dato (ed.), *Georgetown University Round Table on Languages and Linguistics 1975*. Washington, D.C.: Georgetown University Press, 1–16.

FERGUSON, G. 1971. *Statistical Analyses in Psychology and Education*. 3d ed. New York: McGraw-Hill.

FILLMORE, L. 1976. The second time around: cognitive and social strategies in second language acquisition. Ph.D. dissertation, Stanford University.

FODOR, J.; BEVER, T.; and GARRETT, M. 1974. *The Psychology of Language*. New York: McGraw-Hill.

FODOR, J., and GARRETT, M. 1966. Some reflections on competence and performance. In J. Lyons and R. Wales (eds.), *Psycholinguistics Papers: The Proceedings of the 1966 Edinburgh Conference*, 135–62.

FRIES, C. 1945. *Teaching and Learning English as a Foreign Language*. Ann Arbor: University of Michigan Press.

———. 1957. Foreword. In R. Lado, *Linguistics Across Cultures: Applied Linguistics for Language Teachers*. Ann Arbor: University of Michigan Press.

FULLER, J. K. 1978. An investigation of natural and monitored difficulty orders by non-native adult students of English. Doctoral dissertation, Florida State University.

GAIES, S. 1977. The nature of linguistic input in normal second language learning: linguistic and communicative strategies in ESL teachers' classroom language. In H. D. Brown, C. Yorio, and R. Crymes (eds.), *Teaching and Learning English as a Second Language: Trends in Research and Practice*. Washington, D.C.: TESOL, 204–12.

GARDINER, M.; SCHULMAN, C.; and WALTER, D. 1973. Facultative EEG asymmetries in babies and adults. Brain Information Service Conference Report No. 34. University of California at Los Angeles. Los Angeles, California.

GARDNER, R. 1960. Motivational variables in second language learning. In R. Gardner and W. Lambert (eds.), 1972. *Attitudes and Motivation in Second-Language Learning*. Rowley, Ma.: Newbury House.

GARDNER, R., and LAMBERT, W. 1959. Motivational variables in second language acquisition. *Canadian Journal of Psychology* 13:266–72.

———. (Eds.) 1972. *Attitudes and Motivation in Second-Language Learning*. Rowley, Ma.: Newbury House.

GARDNER, R.; SMYTHE, P.; CLEMENT, R.; and GLIKSMAN, L. 1976. Second language learning: A social-psychological perspective. *Canadian Modern Language Review* 32:198–213.

GARY, J. O. 1975. Delayed oral practice in initial stages of second language learning. In M. Burt and H. Dulay (eds.), 1975, *New Directions in Second Language Learning, Teaching, and Bilingual Education*. Washington, D.C.: TESOL, 89–95.

GENESEE, F. 1977. Is there an optimal age for starting second language instruction? *McGill Journal of Education* 13:145–54.

GEORGE, H. V. 1972. *Common Errors in Language Learning*. Rowley, Ma.: Newbury House.

GILLIS, M., and WEBER, R. 1976. The emergence of sentence modalities in the English of Japanese-speaking children. *Language Learning* 26:77–94.

GLEASON, H. 1951. *Introduction to Descriptive Linguistics*. New York: Holt, Rinehart & Winston.

GONZALEZ, P. C., and ELIJAH, D. V. 1979. Error patterns of bilingual readers. *NABE Journal* 3:3.15–25.

GOODGLASS, H. 1973. Developmental comparison of vowels and consonants in dichotic listening. *Journal of Speech and Hearing Research* 16:744–52.

GRAUBERG, W. 1971. An error analysis in German of first-year university students. In G. Perren and J. Trim (eds.), *Applications of Linguistics.* Cambridge, England: Cambridge University Press, 257–63.

GREENBERG, J. H. 1961. Some universals of grammar with particular reference to the order of meaningful elements. In J. H. Greenberg (ed.), *Universals of Language.* Cambridge, Ma.: M.I.T. Press.

GUIORA, A.; BEIT-HALLAHMI, B.; BRANNON, R.; DULL, C.; and SCOVEL, T. 1972. The effects of experimentally induced changes in ego states on pronunciation ability in a second language: An exploratory study. *Comprehensive Psychiatry* 13:421–28.

GUIORA, A.; BRANNON, R.; and DULL, C. 1972a. Empathy and second language learning. *Language Learning* 22:111–30.

GUIORA, A.; PALUSZNY, M.; BEIT-HALLAHMI, B.; CATFORD, J.; COOLEY, R.; and DULL, C. 1975. Language and person: studies in language behavior. *Language Learning* 25:43–61.

GUMPERZ, J., and HERNÁNDEZ-CHÁVEZ, E. 1971. Cognitive aspects of bilingual communication. In W. H. Whitely (ed.), *Language Use and Social Changes.* London: Oxford University Press, 111–25.

———. 1972. Bilingualism, bidialectalism and classroom interaction. In C. B. Cazden, V. P. John, and D. Hymes (eds.), *Functions of Language in the Classroom.* New York: Teachers College.

HAKUTA, K. 1974. Prefabricated patterns and the emergence of structure in second language acquisition. *Language Learning* 24:287–98.

———. 1975. Becoming bilingual at age 5: the story of Uguisu. Unpublished Senior Honors Thesis, Harvard University.

———. 1976. A case study of a Japanese child learning English as a second language. *Language Learning* 26:2.321–51.

HANANIA, E. A. B., and GRADMAN, H. L. 1977. Acquisition of English structures: A case study of an adult native speaker of Arabic in an English-speaking environment. *Language Learning* 27:75–92.

HANSEN-BEDE, L. 1975. A child's creation of a second language. *Working Papers in Bilingualism*, No. 6:103–23.

HART, J. T. 1967. Memory and the memory-monitoring process. *Journal of Verbal Learning and Verbal Behavior* 6:685–91.

HATCH, E. 1971. The young child's comprehension of time connectives. *Child Development* 42:2111–13.

———. 1972. Studies in second language acquisition. Paper presented at the Third International Congress of Applied Linguistics, Copenhagen.

———. 1976. Comments on the monitor model. Presentation to the UCLA-USC Second Language Acquisition Forum, May 25, 1976, UCLA.

———. (Ed.) 1978. *Second Language Acquisition.* Rowley, Ma.: Newbury House.

———. 1978a. Discourse analysis and second language acquisition. In E.

Hatch (ed.), *Second Language Acquisition*. Rowley, Ma.: Newbury House.

————. 1978b. Introduction. In E. Hatch (ed.), *Second Language Acquisition*. Rowley, Ma.: Newbury House, 1–18.

HAUGEN, E. 1953. *The Norwegian Language in America*. Philadelphia: University of Pennsylvania Press.

————. 1956. *Bilingualism in the Americas: A Bibliography and Research Guide*. American Dialect Society, 26. University of Alabama: University Press.

————. 1978. Comments from the audience. Georgetown University Round Table on Languages and Linguistics. In J. Alatis (ed.), *International Dimensions of Bilingual Education*. Washington, D.C.: Georgetown University Press.

HEILER, B. 1966. An investigation of the causes of primary stress mislocation in the English speech of bilingual Mexican-American students. M.A. thesis. University of Texas, El Paso.

HENDRICKSON, J. M. 1976. The effects of error correction treatments upon adequate and accurate communication in the written compositions of adult learners of English as a Second Language. Doctoral dissertation, Ohio State University, Columbus.

————. 1977. Goof analysis for ESL teachers. Unpublished paper. Ohio State University.

HENDRICKSON, J. 1978. Error corrections in foreign language teaching: recent theory, research and practice. *Modern Language Journal*, 381–92.

HERNÁNDEZ-CHÁVEZ, E. 1972. Early code separation in the second language speech of Spanish-speaking children. Paper presented at the Stanford Child Language Research Forum, Stanford University, Stanford, Ca.

————. 1977. The development of semantic relations in child second language acquisition. In M. Burt, H. Dulay, and M. Finocchiaro (eds.), *Viewpoints on English as a Second Language*. New York: Regents.

————. 1977a. The acquisition of grammatical structures by a Mexican American child learning English. Doctoral dissertation. University of California, Berkeley.

HERNÁNDEZ-CHÁVEZ, E.; COHEN, E.; and BELTRAMO, A. (Eds.) 1975. *El Lenguaje de los Chicanos: Regional and Social Characteristics of Language Used by Mexican Americans*. Arlington, Va.: Center for Applied Linguistics.

HERNÁNDEZ-CHÁVEZ, E.; VOGEL, I.; and CLUMECK, H. 1975. Rules, constraints, and the simplicity criterion: an analysis based on the acquisition of nasals in Chicano Spanish. In A. Ferguson, L. Hyman, and J. Ohala (eds.), *Nasalfest: Papers from a Symposium on Nasals and Nasalization Language Universals Project*. Stanford University, Stanford, Cal.

HEYDE, A. 1977. The relationship between self-esteem and the oral production of a second language. In H. D. Brown, C. Yorio, and R. Crymes (eds.), *Teaching and Learning English as a Second Language: Trends in Research and Practice*. Washington, D.C.: TESOL, 226–40.

HOLLEY, F., and KING, J. 1971. Imitation and correction in foreign language learning. *Modern Language Journal* 55:8.

HOUCK, N.; ROBERTSON, J.; and KRASHEN, S. 1978. On the domain of the conscious grammar: morpheme orders for corrected and uncorrected ESL student transcripts. *TESOL Quarterly* 12:335–39.

HUANG, J. 1970. A Chinese child's acquisition of English syntax. Unpublished M.A. thesis. University of California at Los Angeles.

HUANG, J., and HATCH, E., 1978. A Chinese child's acquisition of English. In E. Hatch (ed.), *Second Language Acquisition*. Rowley, Ma.: Newbury House.

HUNT, K. Syntactic maturity in school children and adults. *Monographs of the Society for Research in Child Development*, 1970, 35:1 (Serial #134).

Illyin Oral Interview 1973. Rowley, Ma.: Newbury House.

INHELDER, B., and PIAGET, J. 1958. *The Growth of Logical Thinking from Childhood to Adolescence*. New York: Basic Books.

INHELDER, B.; SINCLAIR, H.; and BOVET, M. 1974. *Learning and the Development of Cognition*. Cambridge, Ma.: Harvard University Press.

IOUP, G., and KRUSE, A. 1977. Interference versus structural complexity in second language acquisition: language universals as a basis for natural sequencing. Paper presented at the Eleventh Annual Convention of Teachers of English to Speakers of Other Languages. Miami, Florida.

JACOBOVITS, L. 1970. *Foreign Language Learning: A Psycholinguistic Analysis*. Rowley, Ma.: Newbury House.

JACOBS, R., and ROSENBAUM, P. 1968. *English Transformational Grammar*. Waltham, Ma.: Blaisdell.

JOHANSSON, S. 1975. The uses of error analysis and contrastive analysis. *English Language Teaching* 29:330–36.

JAIN, M. 1974. Error analysis: source, cause and significance. In J. C. Richards (ed.), *Error Analysis*. London: Longman, 189–215.

KAHANE, H.; KAHANE, R.; and SAPORTA, S. 1971. Development of verbal categories in child language. In A. Bar-Adon and W. Leopold (eds.), *Child Language: A Book of Readings*. Englewood Cliffs, N.J.: Prentice-Hall.

KEENAN, E. 1975. *Papers and Reports on Child Language Development No. 10*, Department of Linguistics, Stanford University.

KESSLER, D., and IDAR, I. 1977. The acquisition of English syntactic structures by a Vietnamese child. Paper presented at the National Association of Bilingual Education Annual Convention. New Orleans, La.

KERNAN, K. 1969. The acquisition of language by Samoan children. Unpublished Ph.D. dissertation. University of California, Berkeley.

KINSBOURNE, M. 1975. The ontogeny of cerebral dominance. In D. Aaronson and R. Rieber (eds.), *Developmental Psycholinguistics and Communication Disorders*. New York: New York Academy of Sciences, 244–50.

KLEINMAN, H. 1978. The strategy of avoidance in adult second language acquisition. In W. C. Ritchie (ed.), *Second Language Acquisition Research: Issues and Implications*. New York: Academic Press, 157–74.

KLIMA, E. 1968. Negation in English. In J. A. Fodor and J. J. Katz (eds.), *The Structure of Language*. Englewood Cliffs, N.J.: Prentice-Hall, 246–323.

KLIMA, E., and BELLUGI, U. 1966. Syntactic regularities in the speech of children. In J. Lyons and R. J. Wales (eds.), *Psycholinguistic Papers*. Edinburgh: Edinburgh University Press, 183–219.

KRASHEN, S. 1973. Lateralization, language learning, and the critical period: some new evidence. *Language Learning* 23:63–74.

———. 1973a. Mental abilities underlying linguistic and non-linguistic functions. *Linguistic* 115:39–55.

———. 1975. The development of cerebral dominance and language learning: more new evidence. In D. Dato (ed.), *Developmental Psycholinguistics: Theory and Applications*. Washington, D.C.: Georgetown University Press, 209–33.

———. 1975a. The critical period for language acquisition and its possible bases. In D. Aaronson and R. Rieber (eds.), 1975, *Developmental Psycholinguistics and Communication Disorders*. New York: New York Academy of Sciences, 211–24.

———. 1976. Formal and informal linguistic environments in language acquisition and language learning. *TESOL Quarterly* 10:157–68.

———. 1976a. Cerebral asymmetry. In H. Whitaker and A. Whitaker (eds.), *Studies in Neurolinguistics* 2:157–91.

———. 1977. The monitor model of adult second language performance. In M. Burt, H. Dulay, and M. Finocchiaro (eds.), *Viewpoints on English as a Second Language*. New York: Regents, 152–61.

———. 1977a. Some issues relating to the monitor model. In H. D. Brown, C. Yorio, and R. Crymes (eds.), *Teaching and Learning English as a Second Language: Trends in Research and Practice*. Washington, D.C.: TESOL, 144–48.

———. 1978. Individual variation in the use of the monitor. In W. Ritchie (ed.), *Second Language Acquisition Research: Issues and Implications*. New York: Academic Press, 175–83.

KRASHEN, S.; BUTLER, J.; BIRNBAUM, R.; and ROBERTSON, J. 1978. Two studies in language acquisition and language learning. *ITL: Review of Applied Linguistics* 39–40:73–92.

KRASHEN, S., and HARSHMAN, R. 1972. Lateralization and the critical period. *Working Papers in Phonetics (UCLA)* 23:13–21.

KRASHEN, S.; HOUCK, N.; GIUNCHI, P.; BODE, S.; BIRNBAUM, R.; and STREI, G. 1977. Difficulty order for grammatical morphemes for adult second language performances using free speech. *TESOL Quarterly* 11:338–41.

KRASHEN, S.; LONG, M.; and SCARCELLA, R. 1979. Age, rate, and eventual attainment in second language acquisition. *TESOL Quarterly* 13:573–82.

KRASHEN, S.; MADDEN, C.; and BAILEY, N. 1975. Theoretical aspects of grammatical sequencing. In M. Burt and H. Dulay (eds.), *Second Language Learning, Teaching, and Bilingual Education*. Washington, D.C.: TESOL, 44–54.

KRASHEN, S., and PON, P. 1975. An error analysis of an advanced ESL learner. *Working Papers on Bilingualism* 7:125–29.

KRASHEN, S.; ROBERTSON, J.; LOOP, T.; and RIETMANN, K. 1977. The basis for grammaticality judgements in adult L_2 performance. Paper presented at the Los Angeles Second Language Acquisition Research Forum, UCLA.

KRASHEN, S., and SELIGER, H. 1975.   The essential characteristics of formal instruction. *TESOL Quarterly* 9:173–83.

————. 1975a.   Maturational constraints in the acquisition of a second language and second dialect. *Language Sciences* 38:28–29.

KRASHEN, S.; SFERLAZZA, V.; FELDMAN, L.; and FATHMAN, A. 1976.   Adult performance on the SLOPE test: More evidence for a natural sequence in adult second language acquisition. *Language Learning* 26:145–51.

KUNO, S. 1974.   The position of relative clauses and conjunctions. *Linguistic Inquiry* 5:1.

LABOV, W. 1966.   The effects of social mobility on linguistic behavior. *Sociological Enquiry* 36:186–203.

————. 1972.   *Sociolinguistic Patterns*. Philadelphia: University of Pennsylvania Press.

LADO, R. 1957.   *Linguistics Across Cultures*. Ann Arbor: University of Michigan Press.

————. April 1978.   Language and thought: effect of translation versus interpretation. Paper presented at the Annual TESOL Convention. Mexico City.

LAMBERT, W., and TUCKER, G. R. 1972.   *Bilingual Education of Children*. Rowley, Ma.: Newbury House.

LANCE, D 1975.   Spanish-English code switching. In E. Hernández-Chávez, E. Cohen, and A. Beltramo (eds.), *El Lenguaje de los Chicanos: Regional and Social Characteristics of Language Used by Mexican Americans*. Arlington, Va.: Center for Applied Linguistics, 138–53.

LANE, H. 1962.   Some differences between first and second language learning. *Language Learning* 12:1.

LANGE, D. 1979.   Negation im natürlichen englisch-deutschen Zweitsprachenerwerb: Eine Fallstudie. *International Review of Applied Linguistics* 17:331–48.

LARSEN, D., and SMALLEY, W. 1972.   *Becoming Bilingual: A Guide to Language Learning*. New Canaan, Conn.: Practical Anthropology.

LARSEN-FREEMAN, D. 1975.   The acquisition of grammatical morphemes by adult learners of English as a Second Language. Doctoral dissertation. University of Michigan.

————. 1976.   An explanation for the morpheme acquisition order of second language learners. *Language Learning* 26:125–34.

————. An ESL index of development. *TESOL Quarterly*, December 1978, 12:4.439–48.

LENNEBERG, E. 1962.   Understanding language without ability to speak: a case report. *Journal of Abnormal and Social Psychology* 65:419–25. Reprinted in A. Bar-Adon and W. Leopold (eds.), 1971, *Child Language: A Book of Readings*. Englewood Cliffs, N.J.: Prentice-Hall, 227–34.

————. 1967. *Biological Foundations of Language.* New York: John Wiley & Sons.

LIGHT, R., and MARGOLIN. Analysis of variance for categorical data. *Journal of American Statistical Association,* 1971, 66:534–44.

LINDHOLM, K., and PADILLA, A. 1978. Language mixing in bilingual children. *Journal of Child Language* 5:2.327–35.

LOCOCO, V. 1975. An analysis of Spanish and German learners' errors. *Working Papers on Bilingualism* 7:96–124.

————. 1976. A comparison of three methods for the collection of L_2 data: free composition, translation and picture description. *Working Papers on Bilingualism* 8:59–86.

LONG, M. 1977. Teacher feedback on learner error: mapping cognitions. In H. D. Brown, C. Yorio, and R. Crymes (eds.), *Teaching and Learning English as a Second Language: Trends in Research and Practice.* Washington, D.C.: TESOL, 278–94.

LONG, R. 1961. *The Sentence and Its Parts: Grammar of Contemporary English.* Chicago: University of Chicago Press.

LUKMANI, Y. 1972. Motivation to learn and language proficiency. *Language Learning* 22:261–73.

MADDEN, C.; BAILEY, N.; EISENSTEIN, M.; and ANDERSON, L. 1978. Beyond statistics in second language acquisition research. In W. C. Ritchie (ed.), *Second Language Acquisition Research: Issues and Implications.* New York: Academic Press, 109–25.

MAJOR, R. C. 1976. One gramatica or duas? phonological differentiation of a bilingual child. Paper presented at the LSA Summer Meeting, Oswego, New York.

MAKINO, T. 1979. English morpheme acquisition order of Japanese secondary school students. Unpublished doctoral dissertation. University of New Mexico.

MARASCUILO, L., and MCSWEENEY, M. 1977. *Nonparametric and Distribution-Free Methods for the Social Sciences.* Monterey, Cal.: Brooks Cole.

MAZEIKA, E. J. 1971. A comparison of the phonologic development of a monolingual and a bilingual (Spanish-English) child. Paper presented at the biennial meeting of the Society for Research in Child Development, Minneapolis.

MEELGREN, L., and WALKER, M. 1973. *New Horizons in English, Book II.* Menlo Park: Addison-Wesley, Unit II, 11–18.

MEISEL, J. 1980. Linguistic simplification. In S. Felix (ed.), *Second Language Development: Trends and Issues.* Tubingen: Gunter Marr.

MERCHESE, M. 1970. English patterns difficult for native Spanish-speaking students. Mimeo. Hartford: Connecticut Board of Education.

MELTON, A. W. 1961. Comments on Professor Postman's paper. In C. N. Cofer and B. Musgrave (eds.), *Verbal Learning and Verbal Behavior.* New York: McGraw-Hill.

————. 1967. Repetition and retrieval from memory. *Science* 158:532.

MILON, J. P. 1974. The development of negation in English by a second language learner. *TESOL Quarterly* 8:137–43.

––––––. 1975. Dialect in the TESOL program: If you never you better. In M. Burt and H. Dulay (eds.), *New Directions in Second Language Learning, Teaching, and Bilingual Education*. Washington, D.C.: TESOL, 159–67.

MOLFESE, D. 1972. Cerebral asymmetry in infants, children, adults: auditory evoked responses to speech and music stimuli. Ph.D. dissertation. Pennsylvania State University, University Park, Pa.

Moreno Oral English Proficiency Test. San Diego: Moreno Educational Company, 1973.

MOSKOWITZ, A. I. 1970. The two-year-old stage in English phonology. *Language* 46:426–41.

NAIMAN, N. 1974. The uses of elicited imitation in second language acquisition research. *Working Papers on Bilingualism* 2:1–37.

NAIMAN, N.; FROHLICH, M.; STERN, D.; and TODESCO, A. 1978. *The Good Language Learner*. Toronto: Ontario Institute for Studies in Education. Any references to Naiman et al. refer to this work.

NATALICIO, D., and NATALICIO, L. 1971. A comparative study of English pluralization by native and non-native English speakers. *Child Development* 42:1302.

NELSON, J. 1980. Language systems in adult informal second language learners. Doctoral dissertation. McGill University.

NELSON, K. 1975. The nominal shift in semantic-syntactic development. *Cognitive Psychology* 7:461–79.

NELSON, K. E.; CARSKADDON, G.; and BONVILLIAN, J. D. 1973. Syntax acquisition: impact of experimental variation in adult verbal interaction with the child. *Child Development* 44:497–504.

NEMSER, W. 1971. Approximate systems of foreign language learners. *International Review of Applied Linguistics* 9:115–23.

NEWMARK, L. 1966. How not to interfere with language learning. *International Review of American Linguistics* 40:77–83.

NEWPORT, E.; GLEITMAN, H.; and GLEITMAN, L. 1977. Mother, I'd rather do it myself: some effect and non-effects of maternal speech style. In C. Snow and C. Ferguson (eds.), *Talking to Children*. New York: Cambridge University Press, 100–149.

NICKEL, G., and WAGNER, K. H. 1968. Contrastive linguistics and language teaching. *IRAL* 6:233–55.

OLLER, J. 1973. Cloze tests of second language proficiency and what they measure. *Language Learning* 23:105–18.

––––––. 1977. Attitude variables in second language learning. In M. Burt, H. Dulay, and M. Finocchiaro (eds.), *Viewpoints on English as a Second Language*. New York: Regents, 172–84.

OLLER, J.; BACA, L.; and VIGIL, A. 1977. Attitudes and attained proficiency in ESL: a sociolinguistic study of Mexican-Americans in the Southwest. *TESOL Quarterly* 11:173–83.

OLLER, J.; HUDSON, P.; and LIU, P. 1977. Attitudes and attained proficiency in ESL: a sociolinguistic study of native speakers of Chinese in the U.S. *Language Learning* 27.

OLSSON, M. 1974. *A Study of Errors, Frequencies, Origin and Effects*. Goteborg, Sweden: Pedagogiska Institutionen.

OYAMA, S. 1973. A sensitive period for the acquisition of a second language. Ph.D. dissertation. Harvard University, Cambridge, Ma.

————. 1976. A sensitive period for the acquisition of a non-native phonological system. *Journal of Psycholinguistic Research* 5:261–85.

PADILLA, A. M., and LINDHOLM, K. 1976. Acquisition of bilingualism: an analysis of linguistic structure of Spanish/English speaking children. In G. Keller, R. Teschner, and S. Viera (eds.), *Bilingualism in the Bicentennial and Beyond*. New York: Bilingual Press.

PARK, T. 1979. Some facts on negation: Wode's four-stage developmental theory of negation revisited. *Journal of Child Language* 6:147–51.

PATKOWSKI, M. 1980. The sensitive period for the acquisition of syntax in a second language. *Language Learning* 30:449–72.

PAULSTON, C. B. 1972. Structural pattern drills: a classification. *Foreign Language Annals* 4:187–93.

PETERS, A. 1977. Language learning strategies: does the whole equal the sum of the parts? *Language* 53:560–73.

PIENEMANN, M. 1980. The second language acquisition of immigrant children. In S. Felix (ed.), *Second Language Development*. Tubingen: Gunter Marr, 41–56.

PIMSLEUR, P. 1966. Testing foreign language learning. In A. Valdman (ed.), *Trends in Language Teaching*. New York: McGraw-Hill, 175–214.

PIMSLEUR, P.; MOSBERG, L.; and MORRISON, A. 1962. Student factors in foreign language learning. *Modern Language Journal* 46:160–70.

PLANN, S. 1977. Acquiring a second language in an immersion classroom. In H. D. Brown, C. A. Yorio, and R. Crymes (eds.), *Teaching and Learning English as a Second Language: Trends in Research and Practice*. Washington, D.C.: TESOL, 213–25.

POLITZER, R. 1968. An experiment in the presentation of parallel and contrasting structures. *Language Learning* 18:35–53.

POLITZER, R., and RAMIREZ, A. 1973. An error analysis of the spoken English of Mexican-American pupils in a bilingual school and a monolingual school. *Language Learning* 23:1.

POSTMAN, L., and STARK, K. 1969. Role of response availability in transfer and interference. *Journal of Experimental Psychology* 79:68–77.

POSTMAN, L.; STARK, K.; and FRASER, J. 1968. Temporal change in interference. *Journal of Verbal Learning and Verbal Behavior* 1:672–94.

POSTOVSKY, V. 1974. Effects of delay in oral practice at the beginning of second language learning. *Modern Language Journal* 58:5–6.

————. 1977. Why not start speaking later? In M. Burt, H. Dulay, and M. Finocchiaro (eds.), *Viewpoints on English as a Second Language*. New York: Regents, 17–26.

PRESTON, M.; YENI-KOMSHIAN, G.; and STARK, R. 1967. Voicing in initial stop consonants produced by children in the prelinguistic period from different language communities. In *Annual Report*. Neurocommunication Laboratory, The John Hopkins University School of Medicine, 307–23.

PRICE, E. 1968. Early bilingualism. In D. Dodson, E. Price, and L. Williams (eds.), *Towards Bilingualism*. Cardiff: University of Wales Press.

PRITCHARD, D. 1952. An investigation into the relationship between personality traits and ability in modern languages. *British Journal of Educational Psychology* 12:147–48.

Psychology Today. 1971. *Developmental Psychology Today*. Del Mar, California: CRM Books.

RAVEM, R. 1968. Language acquisition in a second language environment. *International Review of Applied Linguistics* 6:175–85.

———. 1974. The development of wh-questions in first and second language learners. In J. C. Richards (ed.), *Error Analysis: Perspectives on Second Language Learning*. London: Longman.

REBER, A. 1976. Implicit learning of synthetic languages: the role of instructional set. *Journal of Experimental Psychology: Human Memory and Learning* 2:88–95.

RICHARDS, J. 1971. Error analysis and second language strategies. *Language Sciences* 17:12–22.

———. 1971a. A non-contrastive approach to error analysis. *English Language Teaching* 25.

———. 1974. *Error Analysis: Perspectives on Second Language Learning*. London: Longman.

———. 1974a. Social factors, interlanguage and language learning. In J. Richards (ed.), *Error Analysis: Perspectives on Second Language Learning*. London: Longman, 64–91.

———. 1975. The context for error analysis. In M. Burt and H. Dulay (eds.), *New Directions in Second Language Learning, Teaching, and Bilingual Education*. Washington, D.C.: TESOL, 70–79.

RITCHIE, W. 1978. The right root constraint in an adult-acquired language. In W. Ritchie (ed.), *Second Language Acquisition Research: Issues and Implications*. New York: Academic Press, 33–62.

———. 1978a. *Second Language Acquisition Research: Issues and Implications*. New York: Academic Press.

ROMIJN, E., and SEELY, C. 1979. *Live Action English for Foreign Students*. San Francisco: Alemany Press.

ROSANSKY, E. 1975. The critical period for the acquisition of language; some cognitive developmental considerations. *Working Papers in Bilingualism* 6:92–102.

———. 1976. Methods and morphemes in second language acquisition. *Language Learning* 26:409–25.

RUTHERFORD, W. 1975. *Modern English*, vol. 1 (Second Edition). New York: Harcourt Brace Jovanovich.

SAEGERT, J.; SCOTT, M.; PERKINS, J.; and TUCKER, G. 1974. A note on the relationship between English proficiency, years of language study and medium of instruction. *Language Learning* 24:99–104.

SAWYER, J. 1957. A dialect study of San Antonio, Texas: a bilingual community. Unpublished Ph.D. dissertation. University of Texas. Microfilm Publication No. 25, 178.

———. 1959. Aloofness from Spanish influence in Texas English. *Word XV*. 2:270–81.

———. 1975. Spanish-English bilingualism in San Antonio, Texas. In E. Hernández-Chávez, E. Cohen, and A. Beltramo (eds.), *El Lenguaje de los Chicanos: Regional and Social Characteristics of Language Used by Mexican Americans*. Arlington, Va.: Center for Applied Linguistics, 77–98.

SCARCELLA, R., and HIGA, C. Input and age differences in second language acquisition. In S. Krashen; R. Scarcella; and M. Long (eds.), *Child-Adult Differences in Second Language Acquisition*. Rowley, Ma.: Newbury House. In press.

SCHACHTER, J. 1974. An error in error analysis. *Language Learning* 24:205–14.

SCHACHTER, J., and CELCE-MURCIA, M. 1977. Some reservations concerning error analysis. *TESOL Quarterly* 11.4:441–51.

SCHACHTER, J.; TYSON, A.; and DIFFLEY, F. 1976. Learner intuitions of grammaticality. *Language Learning* 26:67–76.

SCHLUE, K. 1976. An inside view of interlanguage. M.A. thesis. University of Los Angeles, English as a Second Language Department.

SCHNEIDER, W., and SHIFFRIN, R. M. 1977. Controlled and Automatic Human Information Processing. I. "Detection, Search and Attention." *Psychology Review* 84.1, pp. 1–66.

SCHUMANN, J. 1974. Implications of pidginization and creolization for the study of adult second language acquisition. In J. Schumann and N. Stenson (eds.), *New Frontiers in Second Language Learning*. Rowley, Ma.: Newbury House, 137–52.

———. 1975. Affective factors and the problem of age in second language acquisition. *Language Learning* 25:209–35.

——— 1976. Social distance as a factor in second language acquisition. *Language Learning* 26:135–43.

SCHUMANN, J.; HOLROYD, J.; CAMPBELL, R.; and WARD, F. 1978. Improvement of foreign language pronunciation under hypnosis: a preliminary study. *Language Learning* 28:143–48.

SCOTT, M., and TUCKER, G. 1974. Error analysis and English language strategies of Arab students. *Language Learning* 24:69–98.

SCOVEL, T. 1969. Foreign accents, language acquisition, and cerebral dominance. *Language Learning* 19:245–54.

———. 1977. The ontogeny of the ability to recognize foreign accents. Paper presented at the Los Angeles Second Language Acquisition Research Forum, UCLA.

SELIGER, H. 1977. Implications of a multiple critical periods hypothesis for second language learning. In W. Ritchie (ed.), 1978, *Second Language Acquisition Research: Issues and Implications*. New York: Academic Press, 11–19.

SELIGER, H.; KRASHEN, S.; and LADEFOGED, P. 1975. Maturational constraints in the acquisition of a native-like accent in second language learning. *Language Sciences* 36:20–22.

SELINKER, L. 1972. Interlanguage. *International Review of Applied Linguistics* 10:209–31.

SELINKER, L.; SWAIN, M.; and DUMAS, G. 1975. The interlanguage hypotheses extended to children. *Language Learning* 25:139–55.

SERAFATINIDES, E., and FALCONER, M. 1963. Speech disturbances in temporal lobe seizures: a study of one hundred epileptic patients submitted to anterior temporal lobectomy. *Brain* 86:333–46.

SHEARER, B. 1978. Suggestive language. *TESOL Newsletter* 12, 4, 1978. Reprinted from the *London Sunday Times*, November 19, 1972.

SHELDON, A. 1973. The role of parallel function in the acquisition of relative clauses in English. Mimeo. Indiana Univerity Linguistics Club.

SHIFFRIN, R. M., and SCHNEIDER, W. Controlled and Automatic Human Information Processing. II. "Perceptual Learning, Automatic Attending and a General Theory." *Psychology Review* 84.2, pp. 127–90.

Short Test of Linguistic Skills. 1976. Chicago: Chicago Board of Education.

SIEGEL, S. 1956. *Non-parametric Statistics*. New York: McGraw-Hill.

SILVERBERG, R., and GORDON, H. In press. Differential aphasia in two bilinguals. *Neurology*.

SLAMECKA, N. J. 1968. An examination of trace storage in free recall. *Journal of Experimental Psychology* 76:504–13.

SLOBIN, D. 1968. Antonymic phonetic symbolism in three natural languages. *Journal of Personality and Social Psychology* 10:301–5.

SLOBIN, D. I. 1971. *Psycholinguistics*. Glenview, Ill.: Scott, Foresman.

————. 1973. Cognitive prerequisitives for the development of grammar. In C. Ferguson and D. Slobin (eds.), *Studies of Child Language Development*. Holt, Rinehart & Winston, 175–208.

SMITH, A. 1966. Speech and other functions after left "dominant" hemispherectomy. *Journal of Neurology, Neurosurgery and Psychiatry* 29:467–71.

SNOW, C., and FERGUSON, C. 1977. *Talking to Children*. New York: Cambridge University Press.

SNOW, C., and HOEFNAGEL-HOHLE, M. 1978. Age difference in second language acquisition. In E. Hatch (ed.), *Second Language Acquisition*. Rowley, Ma.: Newbury House, 333–44.

SNOW, C., and WATERSON, N. 1978. *The Development of Communication*. London: John Wiley & Sons.

SORENSON, A. 1967. Multilingualism in the Northwest Amazon. *American Anthropologist* 69:674–84.

SPOLSKY, B. 1969. Attitudinal aspects of second language learning. *Language Learning* 19:272–83. Reprinted in H. B. Allen and R. N. Campbell (eds.), 1969, *Teaching English as a Second Language: A Book of Readings*. New York: McGraw-Hill, 403–14.

SPOLSKY, B.; SIGUARD, B.; SAKO, M.; WALKER, E.; and ARTURBURN, C. 1968. Preliminary studies in the development of techniques for testing overall second language proficiency. *Language Learning*, Special Issue, No. 3, 79–98.

STAFFORD, C., and COVITT, G. 1978. Monitor use in adult second language production. *ITL: Review of Applied Linguistics* 39–40:103–25.

STAGNER, R. 1974. *Psychology of Personality*, revised fourth edition. New York: McGraw-Hill.

STEVICK, E. 1976. *Memory, Meaning and Method*. Rowley, Ma.: Newbury House.

STEWART, W. A. 1964. Nonstandard speech and the teaching methods in quasi-foreign situations. In W. A. Stewart (ed.), *Nonstandard Speech and the Teaching of English*. Washington, D.C.: Center for Applied Linguistics. 1–15.

STOCKWELL, R. P., and BOWEN, J. D. 1965. *The Sounds of English and Spanish*. Chicago: The University of Chicago Press.

SWAFFER, J., and WOODRUFF, M. 1978. Language for comprehension; focus on reading. *Modern Language Journal* 61:27–32.

SWAIN, M. 1972. Bilingualism as a first language. Unpublished Ph.D. dissertation. University of California at Irvine.

———. 1978a. Bilingual education for the English-Canadian. In J. Alatis (ed.), *International Dimensions of Bilingual Education*. Washington, D.C.: Georgetown University Press, 141–54.

———. 1978b. French immersion, early, partial, or late? *The Canadian Modern Language Review* 34:577–85.

TAYLOR, B. 1974. Toward a theory of language acquisition. *Language Learning* 24:23–35.

———. 1975. The use of overgeneralization and transfer learning strategies by elementary and intermediate university students learning ESL. In M. Burt and H. Dulay (eds.), *New Directions in Second Language Learning, Teaching, and Bilingual Education*. Washington, D.C.: TESOL.

TERRELL, T. 1977. A natural approach to second language acquisition and learning. *Modern Language Journal* 61:325–37.

TESZNER, D.; TSARARAS, A.; GRUNER, J.; and HECAEN, H. 1972. Asymétrie Brodite-Gauche de planum temporale. *Revue Neurologique* 125:444–49.

TORRANCE, E. P. 1966a. *Torrance Tests of Creative Thinking: Norms— Technical Manual*. Princeton, N.J.: Personnel Press.

———. 1966b. *Torrance Tests of Creative Thinking: Directions Manual and Scoring Guide; Verbal Test and Figural Test (Research Edition)*. Princeton, N.J.: Personnel Press.

TUCKER, G. R.; HAMAYAN, E.; and GENESEE, F. 1976. Affective, cognitive and social factors in second language acquisition. *Canadian Modern Language Review* 23:214–26.

TULVING, E., and MADIGAN, S. A. 1970. Memory and verbal learning. *Annual Review of Psychology* 21:437–84.

UPSHUR, J. A. 1962. Language proficiency testing and the contrastive analysis dilemma. *Language Learning* 12:123–27.

VALDMAN, A. 1974. Error analysis and pedagogical ordering. Reproduced by Linguistic Agency University at Trier, D-55 Trier, West Germany.

————. 1975. Error analysis and pedagogical ordering. In S. P. Corder and E. Roulet (eds.), *Some Implications of Linguistic Theory for Applied Linguistics*. Paris: Didier; Brussels: Aimav.

VAN LANCKER, D. 1975. Heterogeneity in language and speech. *UCLA Working Papers in Phonetics* 29.

VENABLE, G. P. 1974. *A Study of Second Language Learning in Children.* 641 M.Sc.(Appl) II Project, McGill University.

VILDOMEC, V. 1963. *Multilingualism.* Leyden, Netherlands: A. W. Sythoff.

de VILLIERS, J., and de VILLIERS, P. 1973. A cross-sectional study of the acquisition of grammatical morphemes in child speech. *Journal of Psycholinguistic Research* 2:267–78.

VOGEL, I. 1975. One system or two: an analysis of a two-year-old Romanian-English bilingual's phonology. In *Papers and Reports on Child Language Development* No. 9, 43–62. Linguistics, Stanford University.

WADA, J.; CLARKE, R.; and HAMM, A. 1975. Cerebral hemispheric asymmetry in humans. *Archives of Neurology* 32:239–46.

WAGNER-GOUGH, J. 1975. Comparative studies in second language learning. M.A. thesis. University of California at Los Angeles.

WAGNER-GOUGH, J., and HATCH, E. 1975. The importance of input data in second language acquisition studies. *Language Learning* 25:297–308.

WEINREICH, U. 1953. *Languages in Contact: Findings and Problems.* The Hague: Mouton.

WESCHE, M. 1977. Learning behaviors of successful adult students on intensive language training. In C. Henning (ed.), *Proceedings of the Los Angeles Second Language Research Forum*, UCLA, 355–70.

WHITAKER, H. A. 1971. Neurolinguistics. In W. O. Dingwall (ed.), 1971, *A Survey of Linguistic Science.* College Park: University of Maryland Press.

WHITE, L. 1977. Error analysis and error correction in adult learners of English as a second language. *Working Papers in Bilingualism* 13:42–58.

WILLIAMS, G. 1972. Some errors in English by Spanish-speaking Puerto Rican children. In *Language Research Report.* Cambridge, Ma.: Language Research Foundation, 6:85–102.

WITELSON, S., and PALLIE, W. 1973. Left hemisphere specialization for language in the newborn. *Brain* 96:621–46.

WITKIN, H. A., and GOODENOUGH, D. R. 1976. Field dependence and interpersonal behavior. *Research Bulletin.* Princeton, N.J.: Educational Testing Service.

WITKIN, H. A.; MOORE, C. A.; GOODENOUGH, D. R.; and COX, P.

W.   In press. Field dependent and field independent cognitive styles and their educational implications. *Review of Educational Research.*

WITTROCK, M.; BEATTY, J.; BOGEN, J.; GAZZANIGA, M.; JERISON, H.; KRASHEN, S.; NEBES, R.; and TAYLOR, T. 1977.   *The Human Brain.* Englewood Cliffs, N.J.: Prentice-Hall.

WODE, H. 1976.   Developmental sequences in naturalistic L$_2$ acquisition. In E. Hatch (ed.), 1978, *Second Language Acquisition.* Rowley, Ma.: Newbury House, 101–17.

————. 1976a.   The acquisition of L$_2$ /r/. *Englisches Seminar der Universität Kiel Arbeitspapiere zun Spracherwerb,* Nr.11, 1–41.

————. 1980a.   *Learning a second language.* Tubingen: Gunter Marr.

WODE, H.; BAHNS, J.; BEDEY, H.; and FRANK, W. 1978.   Developmental sequence: an alternative approach to morpheme order. *Language Learning* 28:1.175–85.

WOLFRAM, W. 1972.   Overlapping influence and linguistic assimilation in second-generation Puerto Rican English (PRE). In D. M. Smith and R. V. Shuy (eds.), *Sociolinguistics in Cross-cultural Analysis.* Washington, D.C.: Georgetown University Press.

YAMADA, J.; TAKATSUKA, S.; KOTAKE, N.; and KURUSU, J. 1980.   On the optimum age for teaching foreign vocabulary to children. *International Review of Applied Linguistics* 28: 245–47.

Index

Subjects